Praise for *Poison Candy*

"Like a real-life story by James M. Cain, *Poison Candy* has a beautiful dame who's full of venom and a trusting mug who's too blinded by her charms to know she's taking him for all he's worth—or that she's planning to kill him. Told from the perspective of tough-talking woman prosecutor Elizabeth Parker and veteran crime writer Mark Ebner, this tale of greed and manipulation in Palm Beach County is impossible to put down. What's most fascinating about Dalia Dippolito, the story's would-be murderer, is her steadfast denial of reality, even as she appears on reality TV. Add to this the fame-hungry Florida cops who filmed their investigation for the TV show *Cops*—in a video that went viral, of course—and you have a perfect crime for our time."

>   —Nancy Jo Sales, *Vanity Fair*, author of *The Bling Ring*

"Start with a South Florida trifecta of cash, cocaine, and call girls. Throw in Nancy Grace, street gangs, and even a cop reality show. Then top it off with an absorbing courtroom drama starring the beautiful aspiring black widow. A great read—and it's all true."

>   —Roy Black, senior partner at Black, Srebnick,
>   Kornspan & Stumpf, P.A. and legal commentator

"*Poison Candy* gives us a comprehensive look inside the investigation into Dalia Dippolito's plot to kill her husband, peppered with insights that can only be told by an insider. Elizabeth Parker presented a compelling case at trial and now gives us all the juicy tidbits banned from the courtroom. *Poison Candy* proves the adage that truth is stranger than fiction. This is a must-read for true-crime aficionados."

>   —Beth Karas, legal analyst and former correspondent for
>   Court TV's *In Session*

POISON CANDY

The Murderous Madam: Inside Dalia Dippolito's Plot to Kill

By **ELIZABETH PARKER**
and **MARK EBNER**

BenBella Books, Inc.
Dallas, TX

BenBella Books, Inc.
10300 N. Central Expressway
Suite #530
Dallas, TX 75231
www.benbellabooks.com

Send feedback to feedback@benbellabooks.com

Printed in the United States of America
10 9 8 7 6 5 4 3 2 1

Library of Congress Cataloging-in-Publication Data:

Parker, Elizabeth, 1972–
    Poison candy : the murderous Madam: inside Dalia Dippolito's plot to kill / by Elizabeth Parker and Mark Ebner.
        pages cm
    Includes bibliographical references and index.
    ISBN 978-1-939529-02-2 (hardback)—ISBN 978-1-939529-03-9 (electronic)
  1. Murder—Florida. 2. Murderers—Florida. 3. Dippolito, Dalia. 4. Wives—Florida.
  5. Conspiracy—Florida. 6. Marital conflic—Florida. I. Ebner, Mark C. II. Title.
    HV6533.F6P37 2014
    364.152′3092—dc23

                                                                        2013036896

Editing by Erin Kelley   Cover design by Rob Johnson
Copyediting by Annie Gottlieb   Text design and composition by Publishers'
Proofreading by Rainbow Graphics   Design and Production Services, Inc.
    and Michael Fedison   Printed by Bang Printing

Distributed by Perseus Distribution
www.perseusdistribution.com

To place orders through Perseus Distribution:
Tel: 800-343-4499
Fax: 800-351-5073
E-mail: orderentry@perseusbooks.com

Significant discounts for bulk sales are available. Please contact Glenn Yeffeth at glenn@benbellabooks.com or 817-750-3628.

To my parents, Edwin and Donna Parker,
for their unconditional love and never-ending support.

Contents

Foreword

· ·

T rial lawyers often write books about the high-profile cases they have handled in court, especially those which captivated the press and the public. Most but not all of such books are about cases that the author won. Unfortunately, editors who want a book to flow smoothly and read easily have a say in its ultimate structure, which usually causes many of the nuts and bolts of preparing and trying a case to be eliminated.

Elizabeth Parker served in the Palm Beach County State Attorney's Office as a prosecutor for thirteen years. Like many of those who can legitimately call themselves "trial lawyers," she gained and honed her skills on the battlefront; there are no graduate schools that truly produce capable courtroom warriors. To achieve that status, one has to ". . . grow, like Topsy . . ." Ms. Parker has plainly proven herself to be such a warrior. Indeed, careful scrutiny of her new offering, *Poison Candy*, about the sordid and bewildering journey of a sociopathic sexual acrobat named Dalia Dippolito, illuminates a lawyer who apparently fought off any demands for shortcuts or editorial expediency, thus delivering an excellent account of the investigation, pretrial preparation, and courtroom trial of the culprit.

Ms. Parker, painfully aware of the flights of fancy offered by the plethora of immensely popular TV crime detection shows, attempts to lead her readers away from the valley of the shadow of fiction (like getting DNA test results in minutes) and into the green pastures of what really happens when an attempted assassination is afoot and the cops and prosecutors are alert enough to grab control of the caper while it is still in the "attempted" phase. The detail set forth in the police work done and the subsequent preparation and prosecution of the case is meticulous. These are rare qualities in books of this genre, and much to be admired by those who would like the public to have a better understanding of what *really* goes on in a serious criminal case.

This is not to suggest that this book is dull or in any way mired down in detail. It has more than its share of bizarre twists and machinations. Mike Dippolito, an ex-convict serving out twenty-eight years of probation for some "confidence-man" crimes, considers himself to be a bit of a clever fellow. He is actually driven more by gullibility than guile. The mastermind in this sorry play is a twenty-eight-year-old woman of Peruvian-Egyptian descent, Dalia, who began her sex-for-money career as an "escort" at nineteen, and apparently honed her skills in sexual dexterity to a highly effective level. It is fascinating to see her victim, Mike, tumble for her various acts over and over again, forcing himself to digest lie after lie without vomiting.

If I were teaching law on more than a single-lecture basis, I would require that my students read this book. Not just those who were aspiring to become litigators, but law students generally. The truth is, by the time trial lawyers get to take over a case, it is often fouled beyond recognition by lawyers who got the case originally, knew little or nothing about the realities of litigation, blew one opportunity after another to gather or preserve critical evidence, and have thus inflicted mortal wounds on the viability of the case. They remain steadfastly ignorant as to what should be done in the legal emergency room when a case is new, because they plan on negotiating a settlement of some sort and thus avoiding the division of fees with a certified courtroom gunslinger.

Elizabeth Parker is a gunslinger, and it is fortunate for "fair trial" considerations that the "hired gun" for the defense is a trial lawyer of high skill and long experience, Mike Salnick. He is a resourceful and formidable adversary for any prosecutor, and almost opens a crack in the door that leads to the chamber of reasonable doubt. Unfortunately, his client has soiled every escape route with her conduct, emails, text messages, and legally taped statements to police. Parker is offering no quarter, and Salnick must take the case to the wire. He cannot put Dalia on the witness stand, where she would have been shredded by Parker. Parker's case preparation was pervasively well managed. Her skills at cross-examination are well documented by transcript segments of the defense case where she dismantles a number of witnesses.

I regularly enjoy courtroom fiction masterfully orchestrated by the likes of Scott Turow, John Grisham, David Baldacci, and other authors of well-deserved stature. But for a hard-scrabble look at the way criminal cases really work, this book gets high marks. Read it.

F. Lee Bailey

*F. Lee Bailey is one of the nation's foremost defense lawyers,
as well as a successful businessman, author, and lecturer. His
phenomenally successful career as a trial lawyer has been
highlighted by such well-known cases as that of Dr. Samuel Sheppard,
The Boston Strangler, OJ Simpson, and the heiress Patricia Hearst.*

Prologue

· ·

There's a reason they call it Florida.

Discovered in 1513 by the Spanish explorer Juan Ponce de León, the patron saint of perpetual youth, who allegedly came there seeking its fabled rejuvenating waters, it was christened "La Florida" or "Flowery Land" for its exotic vegetation and boundless verdure. Today, though, it represents a narrow corridor between the people of North America, drawn to its warmth and facile money—the newly wed and the nearly dead—and the people of Central and South America, coveting unlimited opportunity or safe harbor—seeds and spores blown in on a wild wind. The cultural collision that occurs along this unintended isthmus produces a strain of humanity that can best be described as florid—an exotic mélange of hothouse flowers and preening psychopaths and gold-plated warriors and vulgarians of every stripe, channeled into a giant cocktail shaker and agitated to a high froth. Criminals and visionaries who appear interchangeable. Beauty for the harvesting. Human orchids.

Those who set out to tell its tales are often accused of hyperbole, of gilding the lily to marshal its perfumes and colors and violent sensations for dramatic effect. But really, we're stenographers at best. No one could improve on the rich cast of characters routinely on public display—especially in the crime blotters and the tabloid record.

That's certainly the case in the sinuous public saga of Dalia Dippolito, a dusky immigrant beauty whose Egyptian Muslim father and Peruvian Catholic mother settled in the mecca of South Florida to provide their children with the best chance at a bright future. Dalia took that chance and gambled it as high as the table stakes would go: becoming an escort by at least age nineteen, parlaying those skills into work as a part-time madam, and sharpening her talons for the first easy score she could sink them into.

That score came along in 2009, when she was twenty-eight, in the form of Mike Dippolito, a good-natured, hapless ex-con with a war chest of cash and a nagging weakness for cocaine and call girls, both of which had been a problem for him in the past. In a six-month span, Dalia moved in with him, convinced him to divorce his wife, married him, got her name on the deed to his townhouse, embezzled his money (again and again and again, in breathtaking ways), worked overtime with a small army of abettors to get his probation revoked, gaslighted him into believing that hoods and gangsters were out to get him, messed with his mind, announced herself pregnant with his child—and when all of that couldn't get him locked up and out of her life, she paid someone to have him killed.

I was the lead prosecutor in that case, and I ultimately secured a conviction in the two-week trial in West Palm Beach—one week on, one week off while the judge attended to other business, and another week to complete testimony. In the nearly two years beforehand, I was in a privileged position to observe all of the players in sometimes painful detail. Together, they were the envy of any pulp novel.

There was the Husband, designated victim and my lead witness, a South Philly hustler and would-be bruiser with a soft creamy center, like Rocky Balboa with tribal tattoos, able to attend what would have been his funeral, like Tom Sawyer, due to the unlikely intervention of a shady character with criminal connections.

The Good Samaritan Boyfriend, a West Bank–born gun-toting baller and professional card counter with a would-be check-cashing/convenience store empire—not a terrorist, but he played one on TV—who only intervened when he finally realized his sex-for-barter good-time girl was just crazy enough to dispatch her husband and leave him the designated fall guy.

Her *Other* Other Boyfriend (OOB), a bicoastal mall contractor living in New York and a clueless patsy who enabled Dalia's endless scams in order to hasten their own promised life together. Somehow, he didn't get the memo on women who kill, and the men who volunteer as their victims.

The Stonecold Killer (ScoldK) from the notorious local Buck Wild Gang who saw this tiny spitfire as a loose cannon and liability and severed his business relations with her, only to be convicted on gun charges in a racketeering trial in the next courtroom over.

The calls-'em-as-he-sees-'em Brooklyn-born Career Cop (CC), who criticized his superiors' decision to put trial evidence on the Internet and allow a *COPS* crew to tag along, whose run-ins with Internal Affairs provided a pretext for the inevitable appeal.

The respected defense counsel who failed to recognize the crucial distinction between a lion tamer and lunch.

And that's before we even get to the fake Haitian hit man.

I had a full plate to deal with.

*   *   *

Although I was born in Boston in 1972 and lived in Rochester, New York, until I was six, I grew up in Miami. I attended Westminster, a private Christian high school, and I witnessed firsthand how *Miami Vice* managed to capture South Florida's nascent cocaine culture, in turn giving the city its brand and identity for the eighties and beyond. Watching *Charlie's Angels* as a young girl had instilled in me a deep longing to become a cop, even if its name and premise—a disembodied male voice exercises undue influence over beautiful starlets, who inexplicably do his bidding—was probably closer to the Manson girls than to *Matlock*.

I attended college in Auburn, Alabama, where I received a Bachelor of Arts degree in psychology with a minor in criminology, with the idea of becoming a counselor of abused children, since I hated predators of any kind. But I didn't really like the subjectivity of psychology, where both the diagnosis and treatment often depended on the interpretation of the clinician; I favored the hard boundaries of the legal system over the loose protocols of trial and error. While in college, I interned in the Child Support Enforcement Unit of the Lee County District Attorney's office in Opelika, Alabama, and spent every free hour watching courtroom trials. By the time I was gearing up for a master's in social work, jurisprudence was burning in my blood, and I attended law school at Loyola University in New Orleans instead. I interned as a law clerk under longtime hard-nosed District Attorney Harry Connick, Sr., whom I looked up to and considered a mentor. I assisted homicide unit prosecutors in trial, often sitting beside them at the attorney's table. In the summers, I interned in the juvenile division of the State Attorney's office in Miami-Dade County. When I graduated law school, even though Miami-Dade seemed a shoo-in, I applied for a job at the Palm Beach County State Attorney's Office on the advice of Jeb Bush, who had taken an interest in my career, and who considered that office the best in the state. That's where I stayed for the next thirteen years.

Palm Beach County is a study in extremes: It houses a large population of seasonal migrant workers, many of them from Mexico, Guatemala, or Haiti, which is among the poorest populations in Florida, if not in the nation. Yet just forty miles to the east is Palm Beach proper, where some of the wealthiest (and most notorious) people in the world live or have had houses: Donald Trump, Rush Limbaugh, Bernie Madoff, Conrad Black, Bill Koch, John Lennon, and the Kennedys, to name a few. (The Kennedy estate was the site of the infamous William Kennedy Smith rape case in 1991, in which he was ultimately acquitted.)

I started out in the Misdemeanor Division, where I spent two years (a few months of that in the Domestic Violence Unit); graduated to the Felony Division; then to the Traffic Homicide Unit; and finally up the chain to administrate and oversee the Misdemeanor Division and the Domestic Violence Unit as a Chief Assistant State Attorney reporting directly to the elected State Attorney, Michael McAuliffe. As far back as New Orleans, the homicide prosecutors I worked with had called me Little Dog because I was so tenacious as a law clerk and intern. Once I graduated, passed the Florida Bar, and began trying cases of my own in Palm Beach County, I was known as a pit bull—someone who latched onto the jugular, set my jaw, and never let go. I could process a lot of information quickly and retain it, and I became known as someone who could dismantle an expert witness brutally and succinctly in cross-examination. Things like DUI Manslaughter had blood and forensic toxicology issues, or accident reconstruction that employed complicated math and physics, each of which came with its own expert opinion, and I quickly became the first line of defense against their often cryptic conclusions. I went on to train new prosecutors in how to try DUI cases all over the state of Florida.

When you pass the Florida Bar and are sworn in as an Assistant State Attorney, you also receive a badge in a black case to signify that you are a law enforcement officer. I learned early on the importance of working closely with cops, and spent much time in the field with them—visiting crime scenes, intuiting defense arguments and counterarguments, and following any loose thread wherever it seemed to lead. I took pride in seeing myself as an investigative prosecutor, and although I enjoy the pitched battle of litigation, my favorite part is immersing myself in the infinite detail of the investigation. It was not uncommon for me as a rookie prosecutor to call officers on the midnight shift and meet them to prepare for trial or visit some key location in the case. I also did police ride-alongs, participating in countywide enforcement operations. By the time I became a Chief Assistant Attorney, one of three under the State Attorney, I was routinely assigned any case with high visibility or that was being tried in the media—from cops charged with DUI, Stalking, or Domestic Battery to those that caught the attention of the cable news scourges.

I first took notice of Dalia Dippolito while watching the *Nancy Grace* show. I was at home when the crime-scene video exploded on-screen, showing a police officer dramatically revealing the details of a contract murder; the distraught widow collapsing in grief, as if on cue; her insistent demands to see the body; her disoriented concern not for her husband, or even her valuables, but for her two dogs still inside. Not only did this seem an apparent breach of protocol—video evidence leaked to a news outlet, obviously by someone inside the department—but the video itself seemed off: no one seemed to be behaving normally. Or rather, everyone seemed to behave exactly the way they thought they should if they were watching themselves on television.

Because of the nature of the crime—a wife hiring a hit man to kill her husband—the case came to the Domestic Violence Unit I supervised, and because of its high-profile nature, elected State Attorney Michael McAuliffe and I agreed that I would handle it. And as we soon learned, almost nothing we saw in that first video was as it seemed. The murder had, in fact, been staged. The police were actually the perpetrators, having created a fake crime scene to prolong the illusion that a crime had been committed. The bereaved widow was really the criminal mastermind, and she had swept the house of valuables before vacating the premises. Her appearance in the video—at this exact time and place—was designed to be her alibi, and her performance had been perfected to convince anyone watching (the cops, prosecutors, an unsuspecting world) of her innocence. And the video had been shot not by TV news crews, but by the Boynton Beach Police Department itself, which meant that the cameras *in the video* had been staged as well. And they were—by the TV show *COPS*. Before I ever saw it, in fact before it ever made it to TV, the video had gone viral online, garnering over 300,000 views by the time of the trial.

Perhaps it puts South Florida in some kind of context to note that, until that moment, this seemed like just another case. Granted, it was crazy, but we see so much crazy stuff down here, especially in domestic violence cases, that eventually nothing seems shocking. I've seen cases come through the office in which an abusive boyfriend with a history of killing animals, whose father went to prison for murder, smashed his girlfriend in the face with a steam iron and then forced her into a bathtub full of water, threatening to electrocute her with a hair dryer. Another guy pushed his pregnant girlfriend into the Intracoastal Waterway, knowing she couldn't swim, and then dived in after her and tried to drown her. A jealous boyfriend beat a woman with an electrical cord, doused her with kerosene, tried to set her on fire, and finally raped her on a bed where their four-year-old child lay sleeping next to them. It sounds like worst-case scenarios selected for TV crime dramas, and yet it was relentless. Attempted murder-for-hire may be exotic, but in a large state prosecutor's office, it's certainly not the worst thing we'd see on any given day.

Dalia Dippolito, however, is another story.

You would have to search long and hard for someone as cunning, calculating, determined, devious, infinitely cynical, and unremittingly apathetic toward the moral consequences of her actions and the suffering of her victims as Dalia Dippolito. The term *sociopath* is overused, but having spent some time observing humanity at its worst and most desperate, I think if there's a textbook candidate out there, it's her. There are many people who, at the lowest moment of their life—driven by some spasm of emotion they're powerless to stop, having sunk to behavior they'd never have thought themselves capable of—will do reprehensible, vicious things. But many of them, the day after, will regret it. As far as I can tell, Dalia was incapable of that kind of empathy. Kindness equaled weakness, and weakness was meant to be exploited.

Dalia manipulated many of those around her by claiming she was the victim of domestic abuse. If anything, she was the abuser. This wasn't your typical domestic violence situation where you see verbal abuse escalating to physical violence, followed by the batterer's promises to never do it again. One of the things that's so chilling about this case is that Mike Dippolito thought he had the perfect marriage. Oftentimes a batterer will systematically use threats, intimidation, isolation, and physical violence as a way to control and dominate their intimate partner. With Dalia her abuse was more subtle. There was no overt intimidation or physical violence, but she used sex to dominate Mike. She emotionally abused him by constantly playing mind games to dissolve the foundation of their shared reality. Her actions created true fear to the point he could no longer carry on with his daily routine. She controlled him through isolation. Mike had no outside relationships, and she made certain that his life revolved around her. She lied about virtually everything and controlled decisions big and small, allowing her to minimize or deny her deceit and shift the blame onto others. She faked a pregnancy, and used it to justify her behavior and keep Mike from discovering her true intentions. These behaviors are some of the most apparent forms associated with domestic violence. Her genius was that she managed to keep the abuse a secret even from its intended target. The victim never knew he was a victim.

It's said that if you're a hammer, then everything looks like a nail. That describes a lot of the men I've known in my life—professionally and personally. But a softer version of that applies to women: If you're a key, then everything looks like a lock. If your gift is that you can open doors that remain closed for a reason, then it's just a matter of finding the perfect door. For Dalia, Mike was the perfect door. And once she was inside, she found nothing but spoils ripe for the taking.

*   *   *

Dalia Dippolito was saucy, sexy, and desirable, but she also knew how to comfort and control men. She wasn't like their other girlfriends; she was never difficult or self-obsessed, she sensed what they needed and gave it to them, starting and ending with sex. She was literally too good to be true, because what she was conducting was not a love affair but a criminal caper. She was poison candy—sweet, delicious, mouthwatering on the outside, but deadly within, and designed to cripple the innocent. She was something only a monster could imagine, or something you'd find in a fairy tale.

The State Attorney and I agreed there would be no plea bargain. She would have to plead guilty and throw herself on the mercy of the court, or else we would prepare for a full-blown trial. And since Dalia didn't strike me as someone who would surrender willingly—not as long as there were still potential victims out there to seduce, cajole, exploit, or leverage—I set out to learn everything I could about her: her origins, her methods, and the extent of her boundless destruction.

CHAPTER 1

. . . .

On the House

Mike Dippolito had had some bumps in life, but he'd done his time and probably other people's, too. At forty, he was looking to work off his failed obligations, burn off some of the bad karma that clung to him like barroom smoke, and enjoy the tidy life he'd managed to carve out for himself, against all odds. He made more than a decent living—having caught the first wave of small-business Internet marketing and search optimization—and he had a wife who loved him and who had stood by him during his almost two years in custody between county jail and Moore Haven Correctional Institute. That may have been country-club time, but it was still no place for a teddy bear like Mike. Despite the tribal tattoos on his sizable guns, battle scars of a drug binge a decade ago, and a still formidable-looking build from the two hours he obsessively spent at the gym every morning, he was no match for the hard-bitten types you meet on the inside. Mike was what the psych counselors called "credulous": his particular pathology was that he always saw the best in people. It's not a bad way to go through life, except for the red bull's-eye it stencils on your forehead.

As far as I can tell, everything he's claimed in his deposition, police statements, multiple interviews with me, and trial testimony has all checked out. He had to go over many parts of his statements three or four times, just so the seasoned detectives and lawyers in the room could keep the facts straight. Mike is one of those guys who seems to be running on salesman's energy. Not like he's a hustler, but just full of this upbeat enthusiasm that's infectious, like he has to keep one foot on the brake just to stop his

1

excitement from getting away from him. He's got a heart murmur—an irregular heartbeat he's had since birth—and ADD and OCD, he thinks, which lends him a jagged momentum that propels him through life. He's done all kinds of jobs, including line cook at Friday's and making pies at his mom's pizza kitchen, but what he's good at is sales. So after he got out of prison, a friend taught him about online marketing and lead management tools (the same leads that everybody's after in *Glengarry Glen Ross*, but multiplied by the digital universe), and the tide of money started breaking over the side by the bucketful. He got married to his girlfriend Maria on 7-7-07, leased a Porsche 997, swore an oath of sobriety, and his luck appeared to be limitless.

Then in October 2008, while Maria was away for three weeks, while they were working late, a colleague showed Mike some escort websites where you could order girls off a menu. Mike stayed away from porn like he stayed away from drugs; with his obsessive nature, they amounted to the same thing. Back in his drug days, he would lock himself in a hotel room with enough drugs for the weekend and order up girls one after another, like he was shopping for shoes. More than one of them got a look at his party favors and wanted to stay with him. After a day or so, the escort service would call asking for their girl back.

But here he was late at night, stuck at the office, nothing waiting for him back home, and so he started snooping around online. He saw a girl on Eros.com—skinny, exotic looking, blurry-faced. She said she was visiting from out of town, and he figured what the hell? It was easy, a simple business equation, and $300 later it would be like nothing had ever happened. So he pulled the trigger.

She picked up on the first ring. She had to call back two or three times to get directions. She was twenty-seven, genuinely attractive, and knew how to work a miniskirt—rarer than you might think in her line of work. And at twenty-seven, she was old enough to know her own heart. She used her real name—Dalia Mohammed—and not Breezy Bordeaux or Heavenly Heidi or all the other bad stripper names that come with the territory. It was awkward at first; she acted nervous, which he actually found endearing, but then they talked a little and they started to connect, which put them both at ease. When she left, she told him she'd be in town for a few more days if he wanted to see her again. The next day, he was still thinking about her, but when he called she was out getting her nails done. The day after that, she came by again.

As she was leaving, he said, "I might be down at the beach tomorrow."

She said, "Well, then I might stop by."

But then, instead of turning to leave, she followed him back inside and they went through the motions all over again—this time, on the house. That weekend, she stopped by at ten on a Saturday morning, and they stayed in bed that whole next day. He describes her as coy, innocent, like a schoolgirl, except the sex was mind-blowing. They connected in a way he hadn't before, and that seemed too spontaneous and real to be transactional. Whirlwind was an understatement. When his wife got back, he told her their marriage was over and that he was leaving.

With that much memorable sex there was plenty of time for pillow talk. Dalia told him she had been living in California with a commercial builder, and she had her real estate license. She also ran a massage parlor out of a fake chiropractic clinic in Orange County, she said. The builder, another Mike—last name Stanley—had to put his name on the building lease because she had no credit. He also set up a corporation for her called Eye, Inc., with which she planned to run her escort business through a website called Eyesnatch.com. She had other girls working for her whom she sent out on assignment, through Craigslist and another site called Sugar Daddy—she was like an air traffic controller working her second cell phone—and occasionally she turned tricks, promising a "GFE," or "Girlfriend Experience": sexual adventure plus value-added affection, part of which entailed not watching the clock. She told Mike she used to run a similar massage parlor in South Florida—her grandmother sometimes would go with her to bring food to the girls.

Dalia had grown up in Boynton Beach, right around the corner from Mike, where her mother and sister still lived. She'd attended a Christian school there, and had tried to run away at seventeen, after learning her parents were getting divorced, by catching the first flight from Miami to New York. Her plans were thwarted when the NYPD met her at JFK airport and sent her back to her parents. She'd had some scrapes along the way, too—she was a hustler, but he liked that. She was enterprising and industrious, just like him, and she was open and direct about it. She didn't do drugs, had rarely more than a glass of wine at dinner, so there didn't seem to be a lot of dirt to gather. Maybe he saw himself in her. All he knew was she had her own money, and by telling him all this up front she gave him no reason to think she was a liar.

Dalia told him she needed to go back to California to tie up some loose ends. When she came back to town two weeks later he picked her up at the airport. By then he had rented a house, so she came over and essentially never left. In short order, he met her mom and sister and brother, and they made him feel like he was a part of their family. He took them all out to an Italian restaurant in Delray Beach for Dalia's birthday at the end of October. "Her mom was part of the sale," he says.

Sometime during that meal, he turned around to see a guy in a suit standing behind Dalia's chair holding flowers. Everyone's eyes got real big, but Dalia quickly took him outside to talk to him. When she came back thirty seconds later, he had disappeared. That was Michael Stanley, the builder from California, apparently still carrying a torch for her. She assured Mike that she had dealt with it, and so he forgot all about it. As far as he could tell, his own relationship with her was perfect.

Dalia had breast enhancement surgery in November, but Mike says that he didn't pay for it. For New Year's Eve 2008, they flew to Las Vegas for an Ultimate Fighting Championship event at the MGM Grand. Mike was restricted from traveling outside the tri-county area as a condition of his probation. He filed a formal request with his probation officer and was granted an exception, but he had to include a business meeting during their vacation.

For the first time, in Vegas, things didn't go well between them. At the hotel, Mike got up early to hit the gym like he always did. When he didn't wait for her, Dalia became petulant and spiteful. The weekend never recovered, and it was his first indication that Dalia's insistent cheerfulness and attentiveness might have their limits. This was territory he knew well, and he didn't want to back into another relationship that looked like all play but soon enough became full-time work. He decided that when they got back he was going to end it. Things had gone too fast, and the momentum had taken them too far. Back in Boynton Beach, though, when he tried to have the talk with her, she was incredulous.

"I've never had someone break up with me!" she screamed at him.

"Yeah, well, I guess I'm your first," he shot back.

She appeared indignant and demanded $2,500 to move into her own apartment. Finally, in exasperation, he gave it to her, considering the cost worth it to get her out of his life. Whatever it was, it was over.

Later on that month, they met for coffee to sift through the ashes. This time, Dalia was contrite, apologetic, and disconsolate. Mike is still not certain how it happened—it seemed like everything came crashing down at once—but he blurted out, "Maybe we should just get married."

It wasn't something he'd thought about; he certainly didn't have a ring. He just needed some clarity and some finality, and for a moment the planets aligned so that this made the most sense. Dalia leaped at the prospect. In retrospect, it seemed like their unofficial honeymoon in Vegas demanded a wedding to shore up the symmetry.

On January 28, 2009, Mike's divorce to Maria became final. They had been married exactly one year. The next day, the 29th, he closed on a townhouse in Boynton Beach, five minutes away from Dalia's mother, for which he paid $238,000 in cash converted to a cashier's check made out in Dalia's name. (He'd bought his own mother a condo with cash the year before.) Dalia brokered the deal through her real estate license and collected the commission. They spent every spare moment shopping for furnishings, with Dalia taking the lead in establishing the décor.

On February 2, 2009, less than one week after his divorce was finalized, Mike and Dalia were married. Dalia's mother had offered to pay for a proper ceremony, but they went down to the courthouse instead. On their way in, Mike ran into the attorney who had represented him in his divorce.

"Hey, Mike, what are you doing here?" the lawyer asked.

"Funny thing," said Mike.

Mike had grown up a working-class Philly boy (just like Rocky Balboa) in the suburbs of Blue Bell and Norristown. His drug-addicted parents were largely missing in action, so he spent time on the streets where he learned his hustle—slinging drugs, and especially any questionable fast-talking sales con, no matter how hinky. There have been some Dippolitos in organized crime—"Joe Dip" and "Charlie Dip" worked under Jack Dragna in Los Angeles in the fifties and sixties—but the closest Mike ever came as a kid was the new Cadillac or Corvette his father came home with every other weekend. That ended when the family friend who owned a car dealership in Florida wound up doing fifteen years. Mike's father ran numbers, was well liked in the neighborhood, and dodged a lot of bullets that hit his friends, until liver and kidney failure finally caught up with him. Mike called his mom "Sis," and his fondest memories were of dancing with her in her room before she went out for the evening. He'd been raised by his grandparents.

Although he was a gearhead in high school, Mike's dreams of becoming an auto mechanic got pawned for drugs like everything else. He developed a Budweiser habit at ten, sold pot from the ninth grade on, and soon graduated to coke and crack. He became a drug dealer in order to be popular, so he set his price point way below the market average. At those prices, it turned out it was impossible not to fall for his own sales pitch, and soon he was alternating between shooting coke and heroin. A couple of boneheaded stunts (a friend pulled a cap gun on another kid while they were all getting high, and the cops showed up) introduced him to the juvenile justice system, and his best friend today is the counselor that first got him into treatment. Between the ages of fifteen and eighteen, Mike went to rehab more times than he can remember. The last time, he stayed sober five and a half years—until a guy in their crew started eating Percocet and they all went down like a chain reaction, the counselor included. Now addicted to heroin, Mike started selling crack between midnight and 8 a.m. on a street corner in the Dominican part of North Philly, where he was known as White Boy Mike. A couple of times he came up short on the count: once he claimed the Philadelphia cops took him down on a bad bust, hoping he would fail to show up in court so they could bring him in on a bench warrant, and another time a pretty girl ripped him off for a dozen dime bags. The guys he was selling for confronted him with baseball bats and demanded that he bash the girl's head in with a brick, but he couldn't do it, so thirty of them administered the beating of his life. As he was just about to lose consciousness, one of the kids whose family laid claim to the corners reached in and dragged him out of there and drove him to the hospital. It taught him that you can be in the worst place in the world and still run into a decent person.

He called a buddy in Boca Raton, Florida, and three days later he was sitting by the pool at a halfway house, because in Florida, even the halfway houses have swimming pools. There were women for the asking, even if women in halfway houses tend toward the incendiary, and a late-night Denny's run for the Grand Slam breakfast effortlessly snagged him a manager-in-training job. Florida was looking more and more like paradise. When the training part looked like it was taking too long, he got a job with Coca-Cola as a service tech, and found he could fix anything. He could have retired there, except that he thought a minor back injury was going to be his ticket to Workman's Comp Heaven. When that plan didn't work out, he met a girl whose day job was spending her nights at raves selling ecstasy to stoner kids. With a background in sales, Mike was a natural. But getting back in the money also meant getting back in the drugs.

Now strung out on a designer high for spoiled teenagers, something his program buddies would have been appalled by if they'd known, he took a boiler-room job selling gold coins in nearby Broward County. He was good at it, but he hated the work, which was repetitive and mind-numbing. Then somebody steered him to a similar operation that traded in foreign currency. All he had to do was get the fish on the line and then turn them over to somebody else to close. After he got the knack of it, it was like shooting them in a barrel.

"Is this Joe? Joe Smith? Hey, Joe, this is Mike from such-and-such trading. This is a courtesy call, not a sales call. Just want to see if you're actively involved in the markets. No? Okay, great. Like I said, this is not a sales call. What we do is broker in the foreign currency sector of the market. You know, basically the dollar versus the Japanese yen. Are you familiar with that? No? Well, no problem, I'm gonna send you out some information. You still at XYZ address? Great. Okay, just a few suitability questions. This isn't for everybody; I want to make sure it suits you. If you see something you like, can you put in five, ten, twenty thousand? A million?"

Mike was a quick study, and he prided himself on learning the business from the ground up. He fancied himself a broker. Problem was, there wasn't any business. That was the whole business model: ask someone for his money, put it in your pocket. Mike called it a greed investment. His wake-up call came when the Feds raided their room, and they just rolled it up and moved across the street under another name. Once he could see through the illusion, his mojo evaporated. That moment might have come sooner if he hadn't been in the throes of what he calls "a vicious drug addiction." He worked three separate rooms in all, where he had a reputation for softening up the cold calls and getting them in a good mood for the handoff. Some of the rooms were tipped up with organized crime: one had ties to the Bonnano family in New York, and another one was affiliated with Sammy "The Bull" Gravano—after he brought down John Gotti and the Gambino family in New York, and right before he went down on ecstasy charges in Arizona. Mike estimates they made between $13 million and $20 million in about a year and a half; his take was a couple hundred thousand. When the third room blew up, he decided to set up his own shop—right when the Commodity Futures Trading Commission started issuing licenses, which of course he ignored. But by then, it was just a matter of time.

He was spending every weekend holed up in a motel room in a dope haze, hoarding all his money in precious metals and seeing his bank accounts seized because his transactions were so suspect, the bank knew he wouldn't challenge it. State authorities finally got him on trying to cash a bad check, but by that point, everyone he knew was in jail. When they came for him, all he really felt was relief. He sat in county for fourteen months, gained twenty pounds, gave up shaving, and was disgusted with himself and with life. His girlfriend, later his wife, sold her car to pay for his lawyer, who settled his case for two years in prison, minus time served, followed by twenty-eight years of probation, plus full restitution to his victims. According to Mike, the lawyer claimed that after five years they could negotiate a settlement of the amount of restitution he owed and be done with it, but that turned out to be all lies. The State considers a plea an enforceable contract and once a person has signed on the dotted line, the opportunity to negotiate is over. Mike pled guilty to "organized fraud, unlicensed telemarketing, and grand theft." His amount of restitution was set at $219,000. When he checked into Moore Haven in Glades County to serve the remaining ten months on his sentence, of which he did about eight and a half, the guards laughed at him for pulling such a ridiculous stretch of probation following his prison time.

He got his GED while he was in prison and came out at age thirty-two—older and presumably wiser.

CHAPTER 2

The Spanish Prisoner

T he way Mike describes it, the honeymoon with Dalia never really ended. The only thing that got in the way is what he calls "the money non-sense." Dalia seemed to magically perceive whatever he needed and made sure he got it. She would pick up dinner or buy him things when they were out shopping, even if it was mostly with his money. And they always had fun: whenever he saw Colombians or Puerto Ricans on the street playing their music or celebrating a national holiday, he would tease her, saying, "Isn't that the Peruvian flag? Aren't those your people?"

They constantly sent gushy notes back and forth, even kept a dry erase board on the refrigerator where they could leave spontaneous messages or cute pictures—"Miss you . . . Thinking of you . . . Love you so much."

One time Mike drew a smiley face, then the next day Dalia added stick-figure legs, then Mike added the hands, and back and forth until finally a penis and testicles had been added—an image he later had to painstakingly explain in court, much to the amusement of the assembled courtroom.

Here is the card Dalia sent him for Valentine's Day in 2009, handwritten in blue pen in a delicate script:

To my husband, love of my life, my soul mate, my best friend, my everything: You make me so incredibly happy. Since I met you I never hesitated and never had any doubts! You are such an amazing husband. Baby, you are my dream. I promise to love you now, always and 4ever. —Dalia.

On the opposite page, a postscript read:

With you everything has always felt right!

And from what he says, the sex was mind-blowing. She was extremely experienced, and she had a kinky, masochistic side that Mike was hesitant about at first. Here's Mike:

We'd have sex all day sometimes. All day, all night. I'd have to go to a meeting, and we'd fuck for a couple of extra hours. A couple of times, she was like, "Choke me." That's not my thing, but I'd start choking her, and she'd be like, "Harder!" One time I was choking her so fucking hard, I was really squeezing the shit out of her, and the funny thing was, she liked it more! And then she said, "Hit me," so I cracked her with an open hand. The funny part was, she loved it, and I still didn't do enough. I'm not nasty like that, but, I'm telling you: I could have gone ten times further.

"If any of that was real," adds Mike, "I had everything I wanted." (Except his freedom, since he was on probation until 2032.)

Before the marriage, Dalia brought a complaint to Mike: that endless probation he'd been saddled with through bad lawyering and epic inattention was going to wreak havoc on their impending marriage. They couldn't travel, they had to hide their money—it was annoying and invasive. She had already seen him go back to his original lawyer to explore the possibility of a settlement, only to be blown off. They drove all the way down to Miami when Mike wasn't even supposed to leave the county, and the guy canceled on them at the last second. A second lawyer took a $500 retainer and burned up six months without accomplishing anything. Why didn't they just fix it? How much would it take to get the government out of his hair for good? Over time, he'd managed to whittle the $219,000 down to $191,000. Dalia told him if he could come up with $100,000, she would put in $91,000, and they could be rid of this problem forever. She had her own money saved from her escort work and the girls she booked. They were going to be married and own a house together (even if he paid for it and added her name to the deed days later). They'd work it out in the long run.

Mike was overwhelmed by her offer. They had initially vowed to keep their finances separate in case things got messy. The fact that she cared enough to take on this shared sacrifice—and that he had spotted this quality in her when others clearly had not—just made him fall in love with her all over again. It restored his faith in people, and cracked his shell a little bit. Probation, and the restitution that enforced it, was the solitary bane of his existence—something he would be shackled to until he was well past retirement age—and suddenly it could all just disappear, shaken off like a bad dream. His mind was flooded with possibilities about almost everything, all those options he hadn't dared to think about for years because they'd tear him apart.

Dalia told Mike to make out checks to her in small amounts—between $6,000 and $8,000—small enough so that it wouldn't attract the attention of the courts or the IRS. In addition to full restitution, there was also a civil lien against him on behalf of the Commodity Futures Trading Commission, and they had already seized a $25,000 IRS refund. Of course, the beneficiaries of the CFTC lien were the same fourteen victims who presumably were to be made whole again through full restitution. Why they should want to hunt him down for money he was trying to pay them back anyway was beyond him. Still, he had managed to squirrel away close to a quarter of a million dollars, which he kept in cash and locked in a safety deposit box, far from the prying eyes of bank examiners or forensic accountants. This was at a time when the financial world was collapsing and banks were failing left and right—especially in Miami, which is perhaps the fast-money capital of the Western Hemisphere. It was enough so that he could have paid the restitution in full, but it also would have cleaned him out. Starting over is not the same thing as starting over with nothing.

Mike never thought to question her motives. She had a job selling real estate, she went out two or three times a week to show properties, and she was about to close on a house. "She seemed successful," he says. "I had no reason to question it. That was part of the attraction." So he wrote Dalia $87,000 in checks over a period of several weeks, adding $13,000 in cash to make it an even hundred grand. She was supposed to deposit it in her bank account and send a wire transfer of the full $191,000 to his Fort Lauderdale lawyer, who would take care of all the further details. He wrote the first check on February 18 for $6,000, and he could feel the dread slowly starting to lift.

As the weeks dragged on, though, it was clear that something wasn't right. The wire transfer should have gone through immediately—that's the whole point, so you don't have to be driving bags of cash around South Florida. Every time he asked her about it—and he asked her a lot—there was some new wrinkle and a new excuse to explain it. She claimed it had been wired through a Cayman Islands account to save on transfer fees, then that the wire had been reversed. She produced an official receipt to prove it. At one point, she even suggested that Mike's Fort Lauderdale attorney, Michael Entin, must have stolen it, and she would call his office every morning to see if the money had arrived. Mike gave Dalia three weeks to sort it out *or else*. He didn't care where the money came from. All he could think about was getting off probation. This should have been done by now, and here he was coming up on yet another meeting with his probation officer.

On the night of March 12, David Banks, Mike's probation officer, made a surprise visit to their townhouse just shy of midnight with half a dozen Boynton Beach police officers in tow. He was apologetic, but he had received an anonymous phone call that Mike was dealing steroids and ecstasy, and he planned to conduct an "administrative search" of the premises. Mike was mystified; he had been on probation for almost six years now without the slightest problem. His house had certainly never been searched in the middle of the night. Despite the fact that the search turned up nothing, Banks continued to stop by unannounced in the afternoons, ostensibly to check up on how Mike was doing.

That weekend, on a whim, Dalia suggested they get away and booked them a room at the Ritz-Carlton in Manalapan. She thought it would do them both good to clear their minds, and she paid over $1,200 for their night there. The next morning, Mike got up early and went down to the gym like he always did. Coming back from his workout, he noticed a group of cops congregated in the lobby, conspicuous at that hour of the morning. When he went down to check out, they were still there, and when the valet brought his truck around, two of them approached him and asked, "Is this your car?" When he told them it was, they said they'd had a report of suspicious drug activity associated with the vehicle, and would he mind if they searched it. He told them it had been in valet since he and his wife arrived, but the officers were free to do what they wanted. While Mike stood there in growing embarrassment, on display for all the high rollers getting into their Bentleys and Jags, the cops conducted a cursory inspection of his SUV. When that turned up nothing, one of them thanked him for his cooperation, and for being such a gentleman about it. Dalia watched this all unfold from the lobby. Afterward, they both thought it was weird. On the drive home, Dalia called Michael Entin in a panic and relayed the story to him. Mike was required to disclose this encounter with law enforcement to his probation officer.

The next day was Mike's weekly AA meeting, where he was responsible for making coffee. On the way there, he and a friend stopped at a convenience store to pick up some sugar, and Mike decided to fill up with gas. When he popped the gas tank, there was a plastic bag containing a handful of pills and a small quantity of white powder taped inside. Rattled, he ripped it out and threw it in the nearest trash can. It was only later that he realized it probably had been there during his impromptu police search the day before. Someone was setting him up.

Eventually, Mike's lawyer told him the cash never showed up, and in his professional opinion, it was never going to. Mike confronted Dalia and accused her of lying, telling her he was moving out of the house because he could no longer trust her. She finally admitted that she'd lost the money. She had tried to make a profit on the wire transfer and she'd been scammed. She promised to make up the loss when she got her commissions on a couple of houses she was selling. Instead of being angry, he felt like they were finally getting somewhere because she had come clean.

On March 29, a Sunday, they'd been out for the afternoon when, two minutes from their house, they decided to continue driving north and have dinner at CityPlace, an Italian-styled open-air promenade with shops and restaurants in nearby West Palm Beach. At the restaurant, a guy at the bar kept looking over at him—it was like the final scene in *The Sopranos*. Mike even commented on it: "What's with this guy?" Returning to the parking garage afterward, they noticed a dozen cops huddled thirty yards from Mike's slate-grey Chevy SUV. Mike joked, "They must be for us." But before they reached the truck, a policeman intercepted him, again asking, "Is this your vehicle?" Mike laughed and said, "Before we go any further, this is the second time this has happened to me in two weeks."

He went into detail on the previous incident, then gave them carte blanche to search his car. This time, they conducted a thorough search—ten or fifteen minutes, refusing to give up even after it failed to produce any results. For her part, Dalia seemed irritated at having to be there.

Finally, they brought in a trained German shepherd drug dog that immediately hit on something behind the spare tire at the rear of the car. Mike didn't even know how to get the spare off, and once they figured it out, they discovered it had been put on backward. Inside the tire well, one of the cops found a cigarette package with a gram and a half of coke in it. Mike was horrified, and some of that shock must have registered with the cops. It wasn't just that he had alerted them to the possibility that there might be drugs planted on his vehicle beforehand; it didn't make any sense. Why would you hide two grams of coke for personal use in such a hard-to-reach spot? In the time it would have taken him to get the spare off and retrieve the contraband, he could have snorted that amount and gone to buy more. When one of the female cops took him aside for a chat, Mike told her he was six years sober, and a drug test could verify it. He started to cry—he couldn't help himself. She confided that an unidentified caller had claimed there would be a kilo of cocaine in the vehicle. In the end, they took his contact info and let him go. (Mike began collecting the police reports of these "random searches" in an envelope in his glove compartment for the next time he was stopped.)

On the way home, with Dalia driving, Mike asked her, "Did you put that shit in my truck?" Instead of looking at him or proclaiming her innocence, Dalia revved the engine and floored it—she got the car up to maybe 100 miles per hour on the interstate. It was the reaction of a child, except one in control of a mortal weapon. He began screaming for her to pull over and quickly dropped the accusation.

And then the next day, miraculously, Dalia came home with a cashier's check in the amount of $191,000. He stopped her when she tried to explain the metaphysical happenstance by which this unlikely outcome had been achieved. He didn't want to hear it. For the first time since she had offered to help him, things were finally moving in the right direction. Then he looked at the check and "rubbed it on his arm" to ensure that it was real.

It was an authentic cashier's check, all right, and in the correct amount. But in place of Dalia's name was a name he had never heard before: Erik Tal.

When he queried her on it, Dalia identified him as the husband of a girlfriend of hers, Kerrian Brown, a pretty Jamaican woman and mother of four whom she had worked with at Beachfront Realty. She told Mike that she'd had to reverse the wire to a third party. Or something. But it was money, and it was accessible, so he let it go.

The next morning, March 30, they drove to Entin's Fort Lauderdale office forty minutes away. But as soon as they were seated at his desk, Dalia became hysterical. Mike had doubted her after the CityPlace incident the day before, their trust was now broken, and she no longer wished to invest $91,000 in his future. She would not turn over the check to him until she had the money in her hand. Entin advised Mike that if she didn't want to turn over the money, there was nothing he could do about it. He added that wire transfers generally take one to two business days, not all month, and told them to come back when they had come to an agreement. For his part, Mike felt like he was standing at the door of the solution to all his problems, only to have someone slam it in his face and bolt it from the other side. He still had roughly $140,000 in his safety deposit box. So, leaving Dalia there, he drove the half hour to Boca Raton and took out $91,000 in cash, put it in a Publix shopping bag, then returned and gave her the cash. She handed him an envelope with the check in it, and he marched back into the lawyer's office and left it with the receptionist. When he came back out, Dalia was gone.

As Mike stood there at the elevator banks contemplating his next move, the lawyer came running out of his office, screaming excitedly. He showed Mike the check. Everything about it was exactly the same as the check they had just been wrangling over, except now it was for $191.

"I told you there was something wrong with this girl," Entin said.

Mike dialed Dalia, who answered on the first ring. She was down at the car, along with her friend Kerrian Brown and her husband, the enigmatic Erik Tal. Late thirties, skinny, Israeli, with a marked receding hairline and hooded eyes that missed nothing, Erik watched Mike like a cobra to determine which way things were going to go. Mike ignored him, demanding his money back from Dalia, who surrendered it willingly. He told her to get in the car. On the long drive home, she insisted Erik had switched checks on them. All he could think of was, who leaves a $191,000 check out in the open, and why wasn't it in her purse?

Back at home, between her intermittent crying jags, Dalia called Erik, who got on the phone with Mike. The first thing he said was, "I told her to tell you what happened." Erik's story—the one he had gotten from Dalia—was that she had lost the money in a dubious wire-transfer fraud. Whatever the mechanics of it, the money was gone, and she was terrified it would hasten the end of their marriage. So at his wife's behest, and against his better judgment, Erik had agreed to loan her the money for Mike's restitution, as a favor, to be repaid out of the money Dalia was expecting on her real estate closings. He was still willing to go forward with that loan. Only now, on account of the aggravation, it was no longer a favor. In exchange for ten points on the entire $191,000 ($19,000), Erik would loan Mike the $50,000 he still needed to pay off his restitution, once he had exhausted all the money he had on hand. (This represented approximately 23 points on his actual loan of $50,000.) At this point, Mike just wanted it over with and agreed to meet Erik the next day at his bank—the Regions Bank in the same building as Entin's office in Fort Lauderdale.

The following day—ominously enough, April 1—Mike met with Erik and turned over the $91,000 he had given to and immediately taken back from Dalia, a cashier's check in the amount of $30,000, and an additional $20,000 in cash. Erik in turn had his bank issue a second cashier's check in the amount of $191,000 made out to Michael Entin. Then, with Dalia in tow, he went upstairs to take the new check to Michael Entin. Entin asked Dalia to step outside, refusing to speak in front of her. Once they were alone, Entin presented Mike with signed documents that a lawyer had just faxed over on behalf of Erik—whom Mike had just left downstairs—to execute a lien on Mike's house as security on the loan. (Mike had already investigated taking equity out of his house for the restitution, but his credit was so bad he couldn't even get money out of a home he owned outright.) Entin stated he wasn't a real estate attorney and had no experience with property law—especially where a $250,000 townhouse was meant to secure a $50,000 mortgage—and he wanted no part of it. He referred Mike to another attorney who could handle the transaction. Mike literally begged him to reconsider, by now blinded to everything but the few precious millimeters separating him from his freedom, but to no avail. Entin was washing his hands of this entire circus.

By now, Mike was out roughly $240,000—his hundred that first went to Dalia, the ninety he put in at the lawyer's office, and the fifty he came up with to get Erik to loan him the rest—not to mention his attorney's fees. He was tapped. Unlike his attorney, Mike didn't have the luxury of washing his hands of this deal. This was his life. He called the new lawyer, Melissa Donoho, and hired her sight unseen, telling her he would meet her when he brought the check. And since he now had a cashier's check made out to someone who refused to take it, he called Erik, who suggested they meet there at the Regions Bank the following day and get a new check issued under the appropriate name.

But first, at seven forty-five the next morning, Mike went out to walk the dogs as he usually did, only to arrive home to discover two Boynton Beach police officers on his front porch. They said they'd had complaints of shouting and loud noises coming from his townhouse. (Mike can't remember, but he thinks he and Dalia may have argued about the money, and the police report by an Officer Naulty says they admitted as much.) Questioned separately from Dalia, Mike soon learned more details: someone had called the police anonymously and reported screaming and yelling coming from the apartment; it had been going on since the previous evening. The male tenant, a suspected drug dealer, had at one point dragged a female, wearing only a bathrobe, back inside by her hair. There was currently banging coming from inside the apartment, and they feared for the occupants' safety. Mike was petrified, since an arrest for domestic battery would automatically return him to prison. But Dalia adamantly denied all of the above, even when she was separated from Mike and encouraged by the police.

Still visibly rattled, Mike met that afternoon with Erik Tal again at his bank. There Erik explained to Mike that the teller informed him that there had been too much suspicious activity on the account involving six-figure amounts, and they were freezing his account. They tried a second account at Washington Mutual and Erik claims he was told that account had been seized for suspected fraudulent activity also. Erik told Mike to call him in a couple of days and they'd get the whole thing resolved, even if he had to hire a lawyer to figure it out. Mike called Erik later, but received no response and he never saw him again.

This, in essence, is a confidence scheme known as the Spanish Prisoner. In its original form, a Spanish nobleman is imprisoned in a castle, unable to access his sizable fortune. Funds are needed to raise a private army and rescind the ways of unrighteousness. The speaker, his private emissary, asks for a contribution to this cause, upon the resolution of which his listener will be rewarded handsomely. There are invariably further complications, and further funds are required. Often, the nobleman's daughter, a dark-skinned beauty, encourages the mark with her private favors as a rarefied form of collateral. The con ends when the mark's money or his patience is exhausted.

Mike wanted to believe Dalia. She was his wife, and for the longest time, he thought that earned her the benefit of the doubt. Virtually everyone he knew, from the friends he no longer saw to the lawyer who was paid to advise him, told him she was bad news, a human tornado that had picked his backyard to touch down in. Whatever this was, whatever she was doing, eventually there would be no place to go with it. All it would take on his part was the patience of Job. It was like waiting for a fever to break.

But then, incredibly, back at home an even bigger bombshell was waiting for him.

Dalia told him she was pregnant.

She had waited to tell him until she was sure, but she was a month along. Any thoughts he had entertained about selling the house and paying off his restitution would have to wait—as would any dark desires he might have harbored about leaving her. Now every moment was spent in preparation for their burgeoning family. She read baby books constantly, and tried to get him to sit and read them with her. She constantly debated possible baby names. She had regular doctor's appointments, some of which he was scheduled to attend with her, except her doctor always seemed to reschedule at the last minute. She started taking special vitamins. Two weekends in a row, they made plans to visit Home Depot and buy supplies to paint a special mural she had designed for the baby's room. Once he came into the living room to find her crying and cutting up her old clothes with a pair of scissors, lamenting how fat she was becoming. It was all they talked about anymore.

They also started seeing a marriage counselor—one actually named Dr. Happy—to work through their trust issues relating to the disappearance of the money, and to put that all behind them. He tried to tell her that before she ever came along, his life was a flat line, a calm and casual existence. There was no high drama, no unexpected police interrogations, no sudden and emphatic reversals of fortune. He also had been through rehab enough times that he knew how therapy worked. They couldn't "move past" the money issue because he needed that money back. Mike even went as far as to seek counsel from Dalia's mother—about the missing money, the weird coincidences, the pregnancy—but all her mother wanted to talk about was getting Dalia a nanny after the baby came.

At the beginning of May, Dalia tells Mike she received a phone call from Detective Hurley at the Boynton Beach Police Department, who claimed that her husband was in some kind of danger. Although the number he was calling from was that of the police station, when Mike called it back he was told there was not a Detective Hurley with the force. Then on May 27, on a morning when Dalia went to the gym with Mike (which she rarely did), they returned to the car to find a note on the windshield. It was addressed to Mike, unsigned, and it read:

Bring $40,000 9:30 AM Back To This Space and Put it under the car Behind you.

Do not Tell Anyone, Especially Your Wife. I Will Tell You all That Has Happen [sic] To You. Is happening to you and what will Happen on Friday.

Tell No One-Come Alone. Someone who will help you.

The note included a phone number with a 305 Miami area code. Dalia called the police, who came and filed a report. Mike was so shaken he couldn't write up an official statement of what happened, so Dalia did it for him. After the police officer left, she dialed the number on the note and spoke with a woman who she told Mike threatened to kill them both if they didn't come up with the money. Dalia and Mike were curious and they even went to the designated drop together at 9:30 a.m., but no one showed up. Later, Dalia seemed so shaken up that they briefly entertained the idea of getting an attack dog.

Since they had been together in the gym when the note was placed on their car, they began racking their brains over who might be behind this increasingly bizarre series of incidents. As a condition of his 2003 probation, Mike had agreed to cooperate and testify against the others that he was arrested with. Although he hadn't implicated anyone directly, some of the companies he'd worked for had pretty obvious ties to organized crime. These were the sorts of people who could easily see a broad, random threat as a low-premium insurance policy.

But even this seemed far-fetched. For a guy who had been around institutional crime, amassed multiple drug habits, and served two years in state prison, he really didn't have any enemies that he knew of. At one point, Dalia even suggested it might be his ex-wife Maria, still bitter about the divorce and having been replaced by another woman.

When Mike called and asked her, she said, "Are you out of your fucking mind?"

The worst part was the paranoia. He searched the house when he got home, searched the car before he went out, and searched his gym bag when he left the gym. It was making him a nervous wreck.

On July 22, Mike had liposuction on his back and was bedridden for much of the next two weeks, in constant pain. He also had what he believed was food poisoning, and was violently ill for much of that time. The day of the lipo, Dalia informed Mike that she had a friend in Miami who was a judge, and he had recommended a lawyer who could help Mike get something called Administrative Probation, whereby he could manage all compliance issues by mail, leaving him free to travel or relocate at will. Moreover, probation would terminate altogether once he had completed full restitution to his victims. She had gone out of pocket for the retainer, and the lawyer would be calling him soon. Mike was skeptical, but figured what did he have to lose? Maybe she was trying to make amends.

The next day, the attorney, Richard, called from a Miami number and relayed a more detailed version of the information Dalia had given. He instructed Mike to write a letter to the judge explaining why he was requesting administrative probation, and to meet him outside the Miami courthouse the following day. He would be tied up in court, but would send his paralegal out to collect the copy of the letter from Mike. Dalia volunteered to write the letter for Mike, and she drove them down to Miami, where they met the paralegal on the courthouse steps and gave him the letter for the judge. Several days later, Richard called again from the courthouse (Dalia insisted they check the number) to say that everything was going according to plan. In spite of himself, Mike was starting to get psyched again. Here was his freedom, so close yet again. On the 30th, Richard called again. This time there was good news and bad news: things were proceeding smoothly, but Mike's house presented a huge red flag for purposes of restitution. Unless he wanted them to seize it automatically, he needed to temporarily get it out of his name. When Mike told Dalia what the lawyer had said, she made an appointment to arrange for transfer of title from Mike's name to her name. The next day, July 31, they drove to Independence Title in Delray Beach, where they had done previous business.

The lawyer, Todd Surber, charged them a hundred dollars to swap out the names, and asked them in passing, "Why are you doing this? You're still married."

When Mike was vague in his answer—"You know, business"—Surber thought perhaps they hadn't understood the question. He explained that in the state of Florida, all marital assets are jointly owned. It doesn't matter whose name you put on the title; ownership doesn't change. In so many words, he told them the only way Dalia could do anything with the house outright was if Mike was dead.

On the morning of August 5, a Wednesday, Dalia announced that she was going to the gym. In the ten months he had known her, this was the first time he could remember her going to work out alone, but it was all he could do just to get out of bed, and he envied her. The gym was the one ritual that could clear his head, and locked up here in the house, he felt physically and spiritually ill. On her way out, she wouldn't stop chattering. Maybe she'd pick them up some Starbucks on the way home. He didn't care what she did, as long as he could get some rest.

He awoke what seemed like two minutes later to someone pounding on the door. *Great*, he thought. *Now what?*

He threw on some shorts and staggered down two flights of stairs to the front door. But instead of Dalia coming back for the gym card or I-pod, or even his probation officer getting a head start on the day, he found a tight scrum of police officers and TV cameras, all ready to explode into the foyer. He assumed he was being arrested and waited for someone to grab him, but everyone seemed to freeze. Finally one cop, a Sergeant Sheridan, said, "Are you Mike Dippolito?" The cameras were right in his face; it felt like he was on *COPS*.

"Yeah," said Mike.

"Your wife is going to have you killed," the cop blurted out. "You got to come with us."

The words he was saying made no sense. It was like the first line of a joke, where you just have to accept the premise on faith. He felt light-headed and sat down on the stairs.

"Okay," said Mike. The cameras kept whirring, like everyone was expecting him to say his line, or at least nobody wanted to be the one to cut him off and miss it.

While this was going on, as Mike was processing this raw encroaching data, he suddenly became aware of another sound—a giant roaring express train coming up his back and across his shoulders that would reach the center of his head in three, two, one. This was the tearing of consciousness, the rend in the fabric through which seeped revelation: all those months of denial and bad logic and the common sense he'd kept locked away in a tinfoil box, all now out in the open and soaking up the morning air like it was starved for oxygen. More than anger or disappointment or despair or even the torn ligaments of love, which still dangled from his chest like live nerves, the overwhelming thing Mike felt in that instant was relief. Of course she was going to kill him. Why wouldn't she?

"Can I put some clothes on?" he asked.

"Yeah, I'll go with you," said the cop. "But we got to hurry. She's on her way back."

CHAPTER 3

Whatcha Gonna Do

(WHEN THEY COME FOR YOU)?

P alm Beach County is a strange, at times incestuous, confluence of Assistant State Attorneys, Law Enforcement (city, town, or municipal officers, sheriff's deputies, and state police officers), and private-practice lawyers setting up shop everywhere from pricey high-rise office suites to a table by the rest room in Starbucks. If L.A. has a surfeit of actors and D.C. is a fly swarm of lobbyists, in South Florida it's the attendant professionals it takes to service the burgeoning criminal class, whose quest for money, power, notoriety, revenge, or some nexus of opaque psychological needs never seems to abate. Hemmed in by the Intracoastal Waterway, they bring to mind the image of sharks swimming in a circle. To those of us in the criminal justice system, a lot of times it seems like a company town.

At a special predawn briefing on Wednesday, August 5, 2009, Sergeant Paul Sheridan cataloged the details of a fast-moving undercover operation that had literally dropped into his lap over the weekend. A Confidential Informant had come forward Friday evening with details of a possible murder-for-hire plot. On Saturday, the CI, wired for sound and secret video, met with the suspect at a Mobil gas station to broker a meeting with a possible hit man. That meeting, with undercover officer Widy Jean in the role of the stone-cold contract killer, took place on Monday in a CVS parking lot. The planned assassination was scheduled to take place that Wednesday morning between 6 and 8 a.m. at the victim's residence while the suspect, his wife of six months, killed time at a nearby gym to establish an alibi. Sergeant Craig Anthony and CSI Technician Rob Eichorst were tasked with setting up a fake crime scene in order to coax an inadvertent confession out of the suspect, or at least put her off her guard.

Ninety minutes after the briefing, police converged on a faux-Venetian residential village of identical, priced-to-move townhouses called Renaissance Commons, whose surrounding moat of chain restaurants—Bonefish Grill, Village Tavern, Slainte's Irish Pub, Dominic's Italian—and lifestyle businesses, like the L.A. Fitness gym where the couple worked out and the Starbucks where they told friends they met, made this the perfect controlled environment for a compartmentalized guy like Mike Dippolito. Just after 6 a.m., lead investigators Detective Alex Moreno and Detective Brian Anderson, with Sheridan leading the charge, showed up at Mike's townhouse at the last possible second and eased him into the new world that was cracking open before him. As quickly as they could, they secured the premises and shuttled him to the precinct where he could be quietly sequestered. After securing the perimeter with yellow police tape, Sergeant Anthony used his Sony Camcorder to film the crime scene, while CSI Tech. Eichorst pretended to dust the open front door for prints. A quick walk-through of the interior served as a makeshift prop inventory and continuity record like for any other location shoot—the *nouveau riche* furnishings, tasteful tans and greys, black lacquer furniture, brushed aluminum appliances, scattered chew toys for the dogs (Dalia's snowball of a Maltese, named Bella, and Mike's English bulldog, named Linguini), fake-fur bedspread, big-screen TVs, NordicTrack machine, and shelf full of MMA action figures doing more to establish character than any spare bit of dialogue or action ever could. Notable by their absence were any photos of the happy couple, save for one small picture of the newlyweds in a gold-filigree, heart-shaped frame consigned to a cubbyhole in the bedroom. Outside, a white van marked "Boynton Beach Police Department" was parked curbside, like a big-ticket product placement in a summer blockbuster, and a police cruiser blocked traffic at one end of the street. Meanwhile, across the median, the tabloid TV professionals from *COPS* rolled their own cameras from a discreet distance. They were there to do ride-a-longs with Boynton Beach's finest when somebody interested them in this fast-moving femme fatale sting. For the old hands at *COPS* it was icing on the cake. When Mike said he felt like he was in an episode of *COPS*, little did he suspect that he was right.

Two detectives, Al Martinez and Midian Diaz, had been separately surveilling Dalia since she left the house around 6 a.m. and knew she was at the nearby gym. Once everyone was in place, Sergeant Frank Ranzie placed a call to Dalia's cell phone at 6:21 a.m. and left a message:

"Hi, this message is for Miss Dippolatti [sic]. This is Sergeant Frank Ranzie, Boynton Beach Police Department, Detective Division. I need you to call me as soon as you can, ma'am . . . It's urgent." Preserved on tape, his thick New York accent is a controlled blend of professionalism and muted pity.

She calls back almost immediately.

"Hi, I had a message on my phone?"

"Is this Miss Dippolatti?" Ranzie asks.

"Dippolito," she says.

"Dippolito." He identifies himself again. "We're at your residence, ma'am. Are you nearby?"

She hesitates. "I—I'm nearby. Is everything okay?"

"Well, ma'am, I need to talk to you when you come home," says Ranzie. "It's very urgent. It involves your husband. There's been an incident. Okay? Can you come right back to your residence, please?"

"Yeah, I'll come right now," she says. "Is he okay?"

"Ma'am, I'll tell you everything you need to know when you get here. Okay? Thank you."

One of the singular aspects of this case is that so much of it shows up on tape, where we can judge every gesture and nuance just like the cops or the jury—including virtually every moment between when Dalia is forced to confront her grisly handiwork and when she asks to see an attorney two hours later, drawing an end to this ruse, and the covert police interrogation that follows.

In a matter of minutes, Dalia's Chevy Tahoe entered the block. This was Mike's car—the same one that drugs were planted on repeatedly—but she often drove it. She parked and was directed toward Ranzie—with his stocky build and cut profile, a reassuring presence in a time of crisis. Sergeant Anthony, in his role as vigilant media sentry, captured the entire encounter on video, augmented by the lapel cam Ranzie was wearing. In the footage, Dalia appears tiny in black form-fitting workout pants, a skimpy turquoise tank top, and a black ball cap over thick dark hair gathered in a ponytail. She makes a beeline for Ranzie over by the van, moving very fast and visibly concerned. Ranzie introduces himself, speaking quietly, and she nods quickly.

"I'm the one that called you," he says. "I'm sorry to call you. Listen, we had a report of a disturbance at your house, and there were shots fired. Is your husband Michael?" She nods.

"Okay, I'm sorry to tell you, ma'am, he's been killed." It's a judgment call whether she begins to wail before he even gets the word out, but maybe there's no good end to come from walking into a setup like that. A foot shorter than he is, she collapses into him, as he steadies her with a hand on each shoulder. Ranzie continues.

"He's been killed, ma'am. Try to calm down. Right now we need to get you to the police station."

She says she wants to see him.

"I can't let you in, ma'am, we have to do our job," says Ranzie. "We have to find his killer. You need to calm down. Does he have enemies? Is there anyone who would want to hurt him?"

Hysterically, she answers, "He's on probation"—an odd response, and not an answer to his question. She continues to cry in a single high-pitched wail that modulates in frequency, like a police siren that can't seem to find the right note. Although Ranzie's lapel cam frames it at an oblique angle, there are no tears visible on Dalia's face, and Ranzie later claimed he thought she was faking her reaction. At one point, Detective Brian McDeavitt, a big Irish bruiser, turns his head away from her to stifle a laugh. Ranzie informs her that witnesses said they saw a black male running from the house. She keeps repeating that she wants to see the body—to obtain closure or verify the kill?—until Ranzie asks Detective Jason Llopis to please walk her back to his Dodge Charger and drive her to the station.

"If you want to help your husband, you need to go to the station with these gentlemen and tell us everything you know about who he knows and who he's connected to," Ranzie says.

She responds that she's worried about her dogs. "They're with animal control for right now," he says. "Everything's under control."

"Get her leg in and close the door," he tells McDeavitt as they ease her into the passenger seat—a calculated move to make her feel like the wife of a murder victim and not like a suspect. Through the open window, Ranzie asks for her keys to secure her vehicle. Sergeant Anthony follows them to the station in the Chevy Tahoe.

A tape recorder is already running inside the car so we have access to her conversation during the five-minute drive to the Boynton Beach police station. Dalia continues her intermittent crying inside the vehicle, but after a minute or so settles into a steady stream of observations and veiled suspicions that serve as a run-through for her coming interview. With her squeaky, little-girl voice and eagerness to please, she appears plucky in the face of adversity. Llopis drives and does most of the talking, and McDeavitt rides in back. From this point forward, although the dawning is slow in coming, she is essentially in custody.

> DALIA: I don't believe it. I just want to grab my stuff, please.
>
> LLOPIS: What stuff are you asking about?
>
> DALIA: I want my bag.
>
> LLOPIS: I'll have people bring it to the station, because you're going to be there for a little bit, okay?

By now Eichorst had already grabbed her purse from the backseat and her Metro PCS burner phone from the Chevy console, and police will soon be poring through both while she answers questions at the station. Her breathing still unsteady, Dalia masters her composure and gets down to the business of surveying the landscape.

> DALIA: Can you please tell me what happened?

LLOPIS: Well, we don't have all the details. We responded to a disturbance call. One of the initial reports said there were shots fired, like the sound of gunshots. And there was a black male. That's all we've got. We're at the preliminary stages of it.

This sets off the first note of alarm in Dalia's speech.

DALIA: What did the black guy look like?

LLOPIS: He was dark. We don't have a lot of description yet.

This presents an opening, and she tries to direct them down the false alley that has just materialized.

DALIA: There have been a lot of black people that have been coming into the neighborhood. And normally he keeps the car cover on his Porsche. He hasn't had one on for, I don't know, the last month or something. And he had someone who was coming around, saying, "You've got a really nice ride."

LLOPIS: You've got to think about all this stuff. All this stuff will help.

Now that the subject has been broached, Dalia starts to ramp up. She cuts him off, launching into what seems like a preconceived narrative, one that lifts the corners up just enough to ask more questions than it answers. If there is one trait that all detectives share, it's probably curiosity.

DALIA: He'd had incidents already. We've had . . . My husband's on probation and he owed, like, a lot of people money. And what happened was that he was trying to get off of probation, and I guess people found out he was trying to get off, and it's just been nothing but problems so far.

LLOPIS: Just try and think of whatever you can. Whatever information you can provide to the detectives . . .

DALIA: Well, I went to the police station because somebody had called my cell phone saying that they worked for your police department, that they were a detective. So I went in and I filled out a report with Detective Rainey. Me and my husband went together. And it turns out he told me there is no Detective Hurley here at the station.

LLOPIS: Hurley?

DALIA: Yeah, it was a detective. I have all the police reports and everything. And it seems like somebody just like spoofed the call. I don't know.

She delivers the "I don't know" with almost a verbal shrug. She repeats the story with the cops at the Ritz-Carlton in Manalapan and how they searched the truck. How the same thing happened at CityPlace a couple of weeks later, only "this time they brought a dog" and found a small quantity of cocaine under the tire. And how on a morning just like this one, when they were coming out of the gym, "we found like an extortion note on the car, asking my husband for forty grand."

LLOPIS: Wow . . .

DALIA: And that's what he owes his business partner is forty grand.

LLOPIS: What type of business is he in?

DALIA: He got in trouble for stock fraud, and now he's doing like an Internet thing, but he's been getting a lot of complaints lately because, just, you know, some things that are wrong with what he's doing.

LLOPIS: All this stuff is good. You give it to them when we get there.

His encouragement flushes out her first show of vulnerability, which automatically brings out his masculine protectiveness.

DALIA: What I tell you, like, I don't get in trouble, or am responsible or anything like that, do I?

LLOPIS: (gently) You're saying your husband is into shady stuff—it's
    not your fault.

This leaves the opening she seems to be looking for, and she starts
crying again. She asks to make a call on her cell phone, and between sobs,
she notes that with everything else, Mike had just had surgery. McDeavitt
calls in their location, noting they'll be at the station inside of two minutes,
and there are another thirty seconds of her sniffling and breathing deeply.
Then something occurs to her.

DALIA: Where did you get my number?

LLOPIS: Off your husband's cell phone.

They ride the last thirty seconds in silence.

In fact, the items that Dalia left in the Chevy Tahoe—according to the
surveillance team, in a public parking lot that was known for its break-ins,
where prominent signs warn, "Do Not Leave Valuables in Your Car"—was
a $3,000 leather Prada bag with a number of interesting items in it, namely
keys to a safety deposit box that Mike didn't know existed; her cell phone, of
course, with its secret life laid out in a latticework of intersecting numbers;
and $33,000 worth of jewelry—a $26,000 diamond engagement ring and
another $7,500 worth of silver David Yurman bracelets, chains, and a silver
topaz ring—which comprised every piece of expensive jewelry she owned.

According to Mike, all that Dalia ever took to the gym was a towel
and her iPod.

When they arrived at the Boynton Beach police station, Dalia was
taken to a small interview room and seated at a table. She was soon joined
by Sergeant Paul Sheridan, the senior officer on duty, who had elected to
conduct the first phase of the interview himself. Present in the room with
him as a witness was Detective Brian Anderson, who along with Detective
Alex Moreno was heading up the case. All three had just returned from
the "crime scene." A video surveillance camera mounted in the corner of
the ceiling captured the entire interview.

Sergeant Sheridan, a thick, sedentary Irish cop with a high-pitched, almost patrician voice, takes the lead in the interrogation, even if it won't reveal itself as such until almost the end. But before they can get started, he has two orders of business. In as offhand a manner as possible, Sheridan begins by covering her Fifth Amendment rights, as required by law, reading directly from the Miranda card he holds in his hand.

SHERIDAN: This is a protocol that we have to do, since you're the wife. We have to advise you of your rights, so you know. If you don't understand any of them, you just tell me, and I'll stop and repeat them. And first of all, let me just tell you, I'm sorry for your loss.

DALIA: (crying) I just want to see my husband, please.

SHERIDAN: I understand.

DALIA: They wouldn't let me see him!

SHERIDAN: You don't want to see him. Believe me, you don't . . .

He runs through the familiar litany, instructing her to respond verbally after every one. At the end, he has her sign and date a statement. Then he produces a second piece of paper.

SHERIDAN: Okay, this is something because we're doing videotape that I need you to sign also. It gives us the right to videotape it. You want to read that?

DALIA: I don't want to be videotaped.

SHERIDAN: Well, you're being videotaped. That's all part of it.

She takes a moment to read through the document. Reluctantly, she signs.

This, in fact, is a camera release for the TV show *COPS*, and it would prove to be very controversial—both during the trial and with the TV show itself. In the lobby afterward, *COPS* producer Jimmy Langley berated

Sheridan for trying to do them a favor, tearing up the waiver in front of him, since it was done under the color of law, making it potentially coercive and of no use to them. According to Langley, they never enlist law enforcement to help them secure waivers for exactly this reason, and cameraman Chris Flores later convinced Dalia to sign a second waiver, promising her they would help her tell her side of the story. That offer seems dubious in retrospect, but Dalia may have figured the media exposure gave her one more random variable to manipulate if it ever came down to it. At least that's how it played out.

Leading in to the interview, Sheridan continues the same gambit his officers had set up in the car: get her theories on the culprits as a means to quell her suspicions and maybe soften her up for a confession when they pull the rug out from under. Taking the bait or staking out her ground, Dalia dives right in:

SHERIDAN: Okay, listen, is there anybody that you know that you think would want to kill your husband?

DALIA: My husband's on probation.

SHERIDAN: For what?

DALIA: For his stock fraud.

SHERIDAN: Stock fraud? How long has he been on probation? Probation or parole? Has he spent any time in prison?

She nods.

SHERIDAN: How much? Do you know?

DALIA: Two years in prison and five years on probation. Five or six years.

SHERIDAN: Oh my God. And what was that for?

DALIA: It was for taking money. Like, he ran a boiler room, kind of, where they would take money from people.

When he asks her how long they've been married, she says, "Not even a year."

> SHERIDAN: This is tragic. Is there anybody you could think of that would want to do this to him?
>
> DALIA: I was just telling the officers we've had problems already.
>
> SHERIDAN: What sort of problems?
>
> DALIA: He's been trying to get off probation, and it's just been nothing but problems the whole time that he's been trying to get off. Um, people weren't happy that he was getting off probation because it's a lot of money he's got to pay back.

This is the first glimmer of an actual culprit who might have been responsible for this terrible misdeed, and the first actual lead that she brings to the table. She's trying out a lot of stuff, looking for anything that will stick.

> SHERIDAN: Well, when you say people, what are you talking about? People that were involved with him before?
>
> DALIA: A little bit of everything. This was supposed to be something when he got off probation, it was supposed to be between us, and he went and he told friends of his, he told certain people, and everyone kind of talks. And he's constantly running into a lot of the guys that he was on probation with—like a couple of days ago, we ran into someone. And that was at Target. I mean, the guy comes up to us, and he's in with organized crime. It seems like a lot of the guys from Boca are starting to move up here, and we're constantly running into them. You know what I mean? And a lot of the guys that he knows and things like that. It was a lot of money—it was $191,000 that he had to pay back. So we were going to go ahead, and he had the money to pay off the probation and everything like that. And then I guess, somehow, when he went away, some guys didn't go away—

SHERIDAN: You mean when he went to prison?

DALIA: Right. They left the country. And then somehow he was dealing with some of those guys because they thought that he owed them and . . . I don't know. Something with that that he was taking care of. So the money that he used to get off his probation, he never did it. He did something else with that money.

Mike is a convicted criminal, and the terms "stock fraud" and "boiler room" means he's still got enemies. She says they've been married "not even a year" when it's actually been a few days past six months. And ever since he got this sweetheart deal (two years served, twenty-eight years of probation), "a lot of the guys from Boca" have been showing up in their orbit. Mobbed-up guys, some of whom had to leave the country, but they're back now, with axes to grind.

SHERIDAN: Now, do you know any of these people, their names or anything like that, or where they may live, so that we may be able to follow it up? We're not going to implicate you.

DALIA: The guys that left, I don't know them.

SHERIDAN: You never met them?

DALIA: No. I mean, I know the guy that we ran into a couple of days ago. I know certain names. You know what I mean? And I know certain families—they were on the news. Like the guys that all just went away?

SHERIDAN: Mm-hmm.

DALIA: I forget what family.

Sheridan tells her they work simple homicides; they're not up on who all is connected. He asks for a name and she conjures up a possible suspect from memory for them to work with.

DALIA: Well, I remember, that group of guys, they all went away. But he's saying one of them, I guess somehow he had a problem—I don't know what problem he had, it was before we met. He ran into one of these guys, and the guy thought he owed him something or something happened, but they went away. I don't know if the one guy that I'm telling you about, Pasquale, if he also went away or if he didn't. But this just happened like a month and a half ago—they all got arrested for the same stock fraud stuff again.

Sheridan starts to turn the conversation to some bookkeeping matters—where her dogs are being held—but no! She's on a roll, and she doesn't want to stop.

DALIA: I want to tell you everything that I know.

SHERIDAN: Please do. I want to know.

DALIA: So that's what happened with that. So he didn't know how to tell everybody what was going on with everything, and so he pretty much told them that I had the money and I took it, and I got involved in a Bernie Madoff kind of scheme. Because he didn't know how to tell his mom and everybody what was going on.

Now the damage control. This should start to explain the wire transfers, the confusion with the Fort Lauderdale attorney, and all the other niggling details that will no doubt start streaming into the investigation in a matter of hours and days.

"You're lucky," says Sheridan.

"What?" she asks.

"You're lucky you went to the gym," he says.

She relays the graphic details of Mike's recent surgery—"he had blood built up in his back, so they drained it"—perhaps to siphon off a little bit of victim's sympathy for herself, but immediately follows that up by declaring him a former crack addict and recovering alcoholic.

"Crack—that'll do it to you," Sheridan observes neutrally.

And an obsessive-compulsive.

DALIA: And so with him, it's very important to be on a schedule and to have a system. He's very organized with everything.

You get the sense from her voice that this was the part that actually drove her up the wall.

For the next part, Sheridan chooses his words carefully, as Anderson chimes in for emphasis.

SHERIDAN: Let's get back to his death. I don't know if you know—he was shot. He was shot twice. I want you to know all this.

ANDERSON: Do you know this?

SHERIDAN: Did they tell you that out there?

DALIA: Not exactly. I mean, they told me he was shot. When I was at the gym I got a phone call. I didn't hear my phone ring, and I called back and they told me just to please come, that something happened at my house.

SHERIDAN: Evidently your husband answered the door, and they took him back upstairs, and in the bedroom—

Now for the first time, we see warning lights go off. Maybe that question about the cell phone on the drive in wasn't just her being paranoid after all.

DALIA: We have cameras, though. Why would he answer the door?

SHERIDAN: I don't know.

DALIA: He doesn't answer for anybody he doesn't know. And, like, his probation officer is the only person who . . .

SHERIDAN: I have no idea.

She's thinking this through. Her voice starts to rise.

DALIA: He would not answer the door. We have cameras at our house.

SHERIDAN: Maybe he knows this person. I didn't know you have cameras. Because when we got there, some of your neighbors heard the commotion.

Sheridan is backpedaling. He's looking for a path out of this that will allow them to split the difference and walk it back to their neutral corners.

DALIA: We have cameras. The front door has cameras and the back door has cameras.

SHERIDAN: That's great.

DALIA: But they don't record. Nobody knows. We told everybody they record, but they don't record.

SHERIDAN: Oh God.

Now it's Dalia who's backpedaling. Cameras mean there's a permanent record, which defeats her purpose.

DALIA: Because he didn't want them to make a hole in the garage for the recorder to be there, because of his car.

SHERIDAN: When the officers got there, your door was wide open. They went in to look. They said there were two dogs in the house in a crate or a cage or something like that. And he was found in the bedroom. He'd been shot twice in the head.

DALIA: He went and opened the door and let somebody he didn't know in the house? We don't open for anybody.

A slight edge of anger has entered her voice. Whatever tacit plan she had with the hit man, this wasn't part of it. In fact, Mike's paranoia would have been one of the pillars of certainty on which she built her strategy. If this toppled, then the rest of it was in danger of giving way as well.

Retracing her steps, Dalia remembers that she put the little dog—her white Maltese purse-dog, Bella—downstairs, while Mike stayed upstairs with "the big dog," his English bulldog, Linguini. Backing out of this cul-de-sac, Sheridan tries to focus on the latter.

SHERIDAN: Will he bite somebody?

DALIA: No. He loves everybody. I mean, he will run off with whoever he sees. The one that's very aggressive and mean is the white one.

SHERIDAN: It's the small ones. Thinks he weighs 200 pounds, right?

But Dalia's still got more stories burning a hole in her outbox.

DALIA: There's a lot that I want to tell you.

Sheridan excuses himself, saying he wants to call the officers at the crime scene to determine if the house had been burglarized. Maybe this will explain the discrepancy. He and Anderson leave the room, and Dalia folds up on the table and starts sobbing. Sheridan will later claim that her tears weren't real, meaning this is exclusively for the benefit of the camera. Anderson returns and asks for her phone, apologetically, and Sheridan retakes his seat.

SHERIDAN: Are there any drugs in your house now? Don't worry about somebody being charged.

DALIA: I don't know what you consider steroids.

SHERIDAN: Steroids? For whom?

DALIA: For him. He takes steroids.

Then Sheridan gets cagey.

SHERIDAN: Are you sure that you don't know anybody that would want to kill your husband? You wouldn't want to kill him, I hope.

She shakes her head no.

SHERIDAN: Not at all.

Dalia interprets the question as a referendum on their relationship.

DALIA: I mean, we were fine. There was nothing.

SHERIDAN: There are no problems between you guys? No financial
problems? I mean with you and him.

DALIA: No, there's nothing. I mean, his business has slowed down,
like anything. He's been having a hard time with his partner.
They use the same accountant, and his partner found out—he was
going to see his partner today. His partner found out how much
the company really made, and so that was a problem.

SHERIDAN: Oh, wow. Oops.

DALIA: And he told his partner not even half of what it was, and I
guess he ended up finding out about certain things that we have.

SHERIDAN: Okay. Hang on a second here. I just thought of something.

Sheridan exits for the second time in five minutes. She asks for a glass of
water on his way out, and he returns with bottled water. But his demeanor
has changed—he's neither cagey nor credulous, but more the stern father
Dalia presumably was missing during her formative years.

SHERIDAN: The game's over with, okay? There are no more games
with you and I. Now we're going to get down to serious business.
I want to know if you know this guy?

He opens the door and a black man in cornrows and a black T-shirt,
handcuffed in front—undercover agent Widy Jean, playing the hapless
assassin—is led in with his head hung low (even though in real life, the
wife of a murder victim would never be placed in the same room as her
husband's killer—even if she were a suspect).

SHERIDAN: You know who this guy is?

DALIA: No.

SHERIDAN: You've never seen him before?

DALIA: I've never seen him before—ever.

Sheridan addresses the man in handcuffs.

SHERIDAN: Do you know her?

He shakes his head no.

SHERIDAN: Put your head up!

DALIA: I've never seen him before.

SHERIDAN: What were you doing coming out of her house?

When he refuses to answer, Sheridan shouts to get him out of there and concentrates the brunt of his attention on Dalia.

SHERIDAN: You're going to jail today for solicitation of murder. You're
    under arrest. That's an undercover police officer. We filmed every-
    thing that you did. Recorded everything that you did. You're going
    to jail for solicitation of first-degree murder of your husband.

And just like that it's over. This circular cat-and-mouse game is stopped
in its tracks. This would be the point in a courtroom drama at which the
culprit would burst into tears, admit her guilt, and submit to the gears of
justice and drama, which would downshift to coast into a finish. But not in
this tape. Dalia merely digs in and spends the next forty minutes—the next
sixteen hours, the next four years—denying what everyone around her has
just seen and heard with their own senses, using every tool at her disposal
and every figure within her seductive reach to reverse reality, in a kind of
brazen miracle of epistemology. One that is still ongoing.

DALIA: I didn't do anything.

SHERIDAN: Did you hear what I just told you?

DALIA: I heard what you said but I didn't—

SHERIDAN: Listen to me. Everything has been recorded. You were photographed in the convertible when you sat in his car in front of CVS. What do you want to do?

Dalia continues to repeat "I didn't do anything," the defense of an obstinate child, with the force of a mantra.

"You're going to jail!" Sheridan thunders, and she starts to cry, but she refuses to crack. And then—

SHERIDAN: As soon as I'm done, they're going to come in here and handcuff you and take you to the Palm Beach County Jail and book you for solicitation of first-degree murder on your husband. Your husband is well and alive!

DALIA: Thank God.

SHERIDAN: Oh, yeah—thank God?

DALIA: Can I see him?

SHERIDAN: No, he doesn't want to see you.

He continues to berate her, quoting from the surveillance tapes to bolster his leverage, but all it does is shut her down; she becomes more sullen and unresponsive, punctuating his questions with, "Can I see my husband, please?" Of everyone she's talked to this morning, Mike is the one she's had the best luck in manipulating, and he looks like her safest play. When Sheridan has had enough of talking in circles, he asks for someone to come in and cuff her. Detective Midian Diaz enters and places her in handcuffs. As they open the door, she sees Mike standing in the hallway.

DALIA: Oh my God!

SHERIDAN: (off camera) He's alive!

DALIA: Come here, please. Come here. Mike, come here. Come here, please, come here.

She sounds like she's commanding a pet.

MIKE: I can't. You can't fix it.

DALIA: (screaming) Why not? I didn't do anything!

MIKE: I heard you.

DALIA: Mike, come here, please! Come here!

The *COPS* cameraman can be seen just inside the door, recording everything for posterity.

" . . . Lies and the nonsense," Mike would say later. "I wonder what would have happened if I had grabbed her. That was my one chance. I probably should have took it. It would have made for some great television."

CHAPTER 4

· ·

Gun Club

A fter Sergeant Sheridan had taken a run at her and belly-flopped in the deep end, Dalia was escorted to a private holding cell where she could cool her heels for the next half hour, and where she claimed to have suffered some sort of panic attack or hyperventilation episode. There was a toilet in the cell, but officers escorted her to a more private restroom when she expressed discomfort with the arrangement. When she returned to the interview room, she had lost her handcuffs, her ball cap, and her ponytail.

The second interview was conducted by Detectives Moreno and Anderson. Anderson had remained largely silent as Sheridan tried to ingratiate himself with Dalia and master her trust, and the effort seemed to have bottled up the spleen he was about to break out on her now. Short black hair, middle-aged, but crisis-hardened, with a solid physique, Anderson looked vaguely like Chris Noth on *Law and Order: Criminal Intent*. Moreno, the lead investigator, was forty, Hispanic, and good-looking (if you squinted, you might mistake him for Benjamin Bratt or Lou Diamond Phillips), and he spent some time as an undercover officer and is still a sniper with the SWAT team. Anyone familiar with police procedurals knows that tag-team interviewers usually identify as Good Cop or Bad Cop, moving methodically to sweep and clear the subject's interior space with alternating bursts of kindness and venom. But since Sheridan had already expended about all the kindness the department was prepared to muster, to diminishing returns, Anderson and Moreno had nothing to lose by trying to break her as quickly as they could. Once the gloves come off, a five-foot-nothing kewpie doll would obviously crumble and fold.

Again a surveillance camera in the corner of the ceiling captured the entire conversation, this one more acrimonious than the previous one. For the first four minutes, Dalia intermittently dabs at her eyes with a tissue, a little girl lost, deep in contemplation. Moreno and Anderson enter. Anderson takes his previous seat at the end of the table, partially obscured by the angle, and Moreno kicks it off. He asks Dalia if she has been read and understood her Miranda rights, and she answers, "I wasn't really paying attention," requiring them to go through them again one by one. Afterward, she asks to go to the bathroom.

When the interview finally gets rolling, ten minutes into a forty-minute tape, Dalia appears far more composed than she did the last time through. Apparently tears aren't going to work on this crowd.

MORENO: You mind if I call you Dalia?

DALIA: Yeah, please.

MORENO: Do you understand what happened today? What's going on here?

DALIA: A little. Now, slowly, I'm understanding a little bit better.

MORENO: What's your understanding?

DALIA: I was told one thing, and now it's like, slowly, like, all these things are, like, I don't, I mean, I don't really know what happened.

They take that as a no.

ANDERSON: Do you know that you are arrested today? You're being arrested.

DALIA: That part I understood.

ANDERSON: Do you know what for?

DALIA: Not really, no.

ANDERSON: You don't know the charge?

DALIA: No, nobody really explained it.

ANDERSON: Okay, go ahead and tell her the charge.

MORENO: You're being arrested for soliciting to commit murder. What that means is, you attempted to hire someone to kill somebody else, meaning your husband. And that's why you're here, and that's what you're getting charged with.

DALIA: No.

MORENO: No, you don't understand?

DALIA: No, I never did that.

ANDERSON: Well, that's what you're being charged with, and we have plenty of evidence to back it up. Okay? So, with your rights in mind, we want to give you an opportunity to do some soul-searching maybe, maybe get a lot off your chest, and tell us the truth. That's what we want to hear.

Dalia's response is that she wants to talk to her husband. Or call her mom. Or she repeats her fallback mantra of "I didn't do anything" half a dozen times. Whenever they press harder, she pushes back—like suggesting there might have been impropriety in the document they coerced her to sign.

DALIA: I'm not—I mean, everyone keeps coming and I'm signing all these things and going over all these things, and I don't really know what they're for. I'm just signing it because everyone's saying, "Well, if you sign this, I'll help you," or we'll this or we'll that.

ANDERSON: I don't know about that, but the only thing we were concerned about was the rights card, and we went over that twice.

DALIA: And then you guys came, and I guess that may have been for the release of the tape earlier, I don't know, because he [Sheridan] never came back. And I signed something and I don't really know what it was. I mean, I was hysterical when I came in here.

When Anderson tries to call her bluff, barking out an insult, it just jolts her onto the transactional level where she seems more comfortable anyway, her pecuniary escort's mind sizing them up for leverage.

ANDERSON: You sound like a fool right now denying this. 'Cause, like my partner just said, everything's on tape. Video *and* audio.

DALIA: I just want to go home.

ANDERSON: I know, but you're not going home. See? You're being arrested, so you're not going home.

DALIA: Then what do I have to do to go home? I'd like to go home.

ANDERSON: I know, but you can't. It's impossible.

Moreno leaves the room and returns with a handheld tape recorder, on which plays the surveillance audio of her negotiating with a "hit man," during which she says she's "five thousand percent sure" she wants to go through with it. He notes they have footage of her exchanging money with the hit man.

DALIA: I didn't exchange money with anybody.

MORENO: Well, like I said, we've been working on this case—

DALIA: So then you know. I didn't exchange money with anyone.

If all they've got is the conversation with the hit man, she knows she never discussed any details and she never handed over any money. Everything else is up for interpretation. She softens this bare assertion with what, in less loaded circumstances, might qualify as flirting.

DALIA: I don't want to give you guys a hard time. I don't. You guys have been really nice to me, and I know you didn't have to take special considerations or things like that, and I appreciate it. I really do.

MORENO: But what you need to understand, it's not like you're giving us a hard time or anything. At the end of the day, we go home.

DALIA: I know.

MORENO: And guess what? You're not going home.

DALIA: I know.

They seem to be going in circles. Anderson decides to up the stakes a notch.

ANDERSON: So I'm gonna ask you a question right now. Okay? Ready?

DALIA: No.

ANDERSON: Can I ask you a question?

No answer.

ANDERSON: I'm going to ask you a question, and I want to know the honest answer. Why did you want to have your husband killed?

Dalia gives a single shake of her head.

ANDERSON: You don't know why?

DALIA: No. Why?

ANDERSON: Why did you want Michael killed?

DALIA: I never said I wanted him killed.

ANDERSON: You did—it's on tape.

DALIA: I didn't.

ANDERSON: Yeah, you did. It's on tape—a lot.

DALIA: (deep sigh) I didn't say that I wanted him killed. I didn't.

MORENO: Well, what did you want done?

DALIA: I didn't say that I wanted him killed.

ANDERSON: Okay, what did you want? You wanted something—you met with an undercover cop. Why?

More silence.

ANDERSON: Yeah, it hurts. I know. You can't say it. You don't know what to say.

DALIA: No.

ANDERSON: I want to know the truth, though.

DALIA: I want to talk to you guys. Like, I want to talk to you, and I want to tell you, but it's just, like—is it going to change the outcome of everything? Like, am I gonna get to go home? You know? Because if I'm not, then I'd rather just talk to someone else who can help me.

After two sessions and forty minutes on the hot seat, she demands to speak to someone in charge, like she's just gotten some lip from the girl at the makeup counter at Bloomingdale's.

ANDERSON: You showed no remorse on these tapes about it, and at one point you say, "I want him dead and I'm five hundred percent—"

MORENO: Five thousand.

ANDERSON: Five thousand percent.

DALIA: I never said that I wanted him dead . . .

Anderson's hit his limit.

ANDERSON: (Yelling) You want us to play it for you?

DALIA: Please.

ANDERSON: (Disgusted) Go ahead.

MORENO: That's what you just listened to a minute ago. Do you agree that this is your voice on this video? On this audio?

DALIA: Can you just replay it, please?

MORENO: Let me ask you before I even replay it, because I'm not going to sit here and play games.

DALIA: I don't want to play games.

MORENO: Let me ask you: Do you agree that what you just heard, that that's your voice?

Now she starts to sulk.

DALIA: Don't play it then.

MORENO: Was that your voice or not?

DALIA: I just wanted to hear it. Don't play it then if you don't want to.

MORENO: Well, no. I'm just asking you a simple question, Dalia. Was that your voice?

DALIA: You guys are treating me like a criminal and I'm not. I'm not. Like, I'm not that kind of person. I'm just not. And I know you're hearing what you're hearing, and I know you're saying all these things, and it's fine, but I'm not. I–I–I have no criminal history, I have no criminal record, I have no nothing. I've never even done drugs, period. Nothing of nothing is nothing.

MORENO: Exactly. And that's why it surprises me . . .

DALIA: (Raises her voice) Nothing. Nothing!

She punctuates this by appearing to tear up again.

DALIA: You guys have your minds made up. Both of you have your minds made up about everything I say. I appreciate both of you being nice to me. I really do.

ANDERSON: Is that your voice on the tape? Yes or no?

Silence.

ANDERSON: Go ahead, play it again.

Moreno plays the section again.

DALIA: There's nothing there that says dead or anything about dead. Period . . . I never wanted anybody dead.

ANDERSON: Then why did you—why were you meeting with this black guy? We'll break it down like that. Why did you meet with this guy? Do you know why?

DALIA: Whatever I say to you, with what I say, like, do I go home, is what I'm asking you. Or am I not going home either way?

This tears it, and Anderson hits his tipping point.

ANDERSON: Okay. From this time on, do not ask me if you're going home, because you're not going home. Okay? You're not going home. You're going to jail. So to get back to my question, why did you meet with this black guy?

As he's excoriating her, Moreno lays out color 8″ × 10″ surveillance photos of Dalia and the hit man in the front seat of his car. Dalia leans in to get a better look. When she speaks again, she's lost whatever little-girl quality was shielding her from their harder edge. For the first time in her life, her feminine wiles are not buying her the benefit of the doubt.

DALIA: What is it that you need from me? I don't understand.

ANDERSON: Okay. I'm asking you a question. Why did you meet with this guy?

DALIA: You have your minds made up. You have all the stuff you just showed me. I don't understand why I'm sitting here.

ANDERSON: I want to hear the truth from you—that's why you're here. I want to hear *the* truth.

DALIA: If I'm not going home, then I'd like to speak with an attorney, please.

There is a knock on the door—even before she finishes the sentence—and Sergeant Sheridan enters the room.

ANDERSON: Thank you. There you go.

Finally.

MORENO: Based on that statement, this is going to end our interview, okay? Understand?

Sheridan tells her she can make her phone calls when they get to the Sheriff's Office. "No cooperation?" he asks the detectives.

"No," says Anderson, wishing he had the thirty minutes back.

Outside the station, maybe ten reporters with microphones and video cameras wait for her to make the short perp walk from the building to a waiting vehicle.

"I didn't," she says in response to some inaudible accusation.

"How does it make you feel that he's still alive?" someone asks.

"How you feeling, Dalia? Any regrets?"

"Did you know this morning you were going to jail?"

"I didn't do anything and I didn't plot anything," Dalia declares once she's safely inside the vehicle, framed in close-up as the camera jockeys for position.

"What was that?" a female voice asks, apparently caught off guard.

Dalia repeats what she said, her face scrunching into a sob at the very end.

The Palm Beach County Sheriff's Headquarters Complex is about a twenty-minute drive from the Boynton Beach Police Department, thirteen miles up I-95 just south of the Palm Beach Airport. It's in a single unit with the jail, a large multistory structure with flying wings pasted on at 45-degree angles. Located on Gun Club Road, it is popularly referred to as simply Gun Club. After she was processed, Dalia was finally allowed to make a series of phone calls over the course of several hours. The first was to her mother, Randa Mohammed. The second and third were also to her mother, but dealt exclusively with hiring a lawyer; defense attorney Michael Salnick got on the line during the third call, and I was prohibited from listening to it because of attorney-client privilege. Her fourth and final call was to Mike.

After they woke him up at home at 6 a.m. that morning, Mike rode to the station with Sheridan and Moreno, who were jazzed about having rescued him from such a close scrape. (Mike was still having trouble absorbing the first part—how such a star-crossed love affair could have revealed itself as a flaming meteor as it crashed to earth—and he hadn't quite processed his miraculous survival yet.) He watched Sheridan's interview with Dalia on closed-circuit TV, and then right after he briefly exchanged words with her in the hallway, he was debriefed by Detectives Moreno and Anderson in that same room while Dalia was booked and placed in the holding cell. In his interview, Mike seemed shell-shocked but not all that surprised. He noted that everyone he knew had been predicting some kind of fallout where Dalia was concerned, even if not quite this dramatic, and he'd lost his two best friends over it. Now at least it made sense. When asked how he and Dalia met, he came clean and admitted to soliciting her as an escort, even though it meant possibly violating his probation. Both cops were sympathetic to his plight, and didn't dwell on his prior difficulties.

As Mike explained later, "I'm waiting the whole time for the cops to get nasty with me. They were just really good about it. I'm thinking, 'When am I gonna get in trouble here? It just has to happen.'"

When he left the station and returned home, Mike made the decision to contact Dalia's mother. Dalia's family had always treated him well, and he thought he owed it to them. So by the time Dalia called from jail, her mother was already up to speed on what had happened. On the tape, Randa speaks with a thick Latin American accent, and appears reasonably calm, given the circumstances. Dalia, on the other hand, sounds hysterical.

DALIA: Mom! I'm in jail!

RANDA: I know, Dalia, I find out already.

DALIA: Mom, I need you to call Mike in New York, please!

She repeats this several times.

RANDA: I call already and I call Dad. Everybody knows. What is it you want me to do? Where are you exactly?

DALIA: I'm in the county jail. What did Mike say? Is he coming?

RANDA: Everybody is coming, Dalia, but we're going to get you a lawyer. Don't worry.

DALIA: Mike did this to me. But I didn't do anything!

There is much cross talk. She confirms that she's at Gun Club.

DALIA: I heard Mike is at the house. I want him out of my house!

RANDA: Okay, well right now we're going to need to have a lawyer first.

DALIA: It's my house! The title's in my name!

RANDA: Okay, don't worry about that right now. Right now we need to find out what is going on. Where did it happen?

DALIA: Where did what happen? *This morning*, Mom!

You can hear the petulant teenager coming through in her voice. She runs through the events of the morning in a kind of self-justifying selflessness.

DALIA: There was tape everywhere, the door was open, and they told me that Mike was dead! . . . I wanted to call you, I wanted to call his mom, I wanted to call everybody and they told me no . . . And then I left with the officers to help them try to see who did it!

RANDA: How many times did I told you to leave that guy? How many times did I told you that?

By the time she placed the call to Mike Dippolito two hours later, after the seriousness of her situation must have sunk in, she had calmed down considerably. At times, she sounds positively casual.

MIKE: Hello?

DALIA: Hey. It's me.

Mike laughs nervously, not sure what to make of this.

MIKE: Yeah . . . What's up?

DALIA: Nothing. Mike, can you please come here?

MIKE: What?! Listen: I don't want to fight with you—honestly. *I can't help you.*

DALIA: Mike . . .

MIKE: Don't you understand what just happened?

DALIA: What they're saying is not true.

MIKE: How is that possible?

She keeps him on the phone for another eleven minutes, and the result is like the old vaudeville sketch where a wife catches her husband in bed with another woman and he continues to deny it, right up until the other woman gets dressed and leaves. Except that here, the words she's saying are merely killing time until she can get her hooks back into him, reel him in, exercise that control over him she has tirelessly cultivated over the past ten months—that susceptibility she probably spotted in him the moment she showed up at his apartment on an outcall. If he says he heard the tape, she insists he misunderstood. When he asks her to explain what he saw in the pictures and video at the police station, she splits hairs or says she can only discuss it with him in person. She wants him to get her an attorney, help her mother, try to imagine how this is all making *her* feel. She reminds him of all she does for him, berates his efforts as never enough, tells him how much she has suffered and continues to suffer. It's a tour de force, a breathtaking display of narcissism that runs the gamut of callousness and manipulation. He tries to avoid confronting her on it, until finally, the light streams in and he snaps.

> MIKE: Listen—I don't know how you're gonna actually have the nerve to sit here and lie to me now. I don't understand. I fucking heard you say it, Dalia. I saw your fucking mouth do it. 'Kay? I can't help you, even if I wanted to. Do you get it?
>
> DALIA: Why don't you want to?
>
> MIKE: It's out of my fucking hands!
>
> DALIA: You're not even trying. It's different if you're trying. You're not even trying.
>
> MIKE: What could I possibly do for you? I don't get it. What could I do?
>
> DALIA: You're not even trying.
>
> MIKE: Trying *what*? I'm fucking sitting here like a dumbass.
>
> DALIA: Hmm. Okay, they're getting ready to take me again.
>
> MIKE: Dalia. Listen. I'm gonna give you some advice, and you need to listen. You're gonna be ran around in there for a little while—a couple days. You need to just try and fucking relax, and fucking just go with it. And keep to yourself, and don't say a lot.
>
> DALIA: (sobbing) Mike, I love you. Don't do this to me. Everybody has treated me awful and I didn't do anything to you. You *know* me.

MIKE: I can't help you. There's nothing I can do to help you, you know?

An uncomfortable silence.

DALIA: Hello?

MIKE: You know what I'll do? You know what I'll do for you? Seriously?

DALIA: What?

MIKE: You sign my house back over to me, I'll help your mom. Immensely. Give me my house back. That's it.

DALIA: That's it what?

MIKE: I'll help ya. So I don't have to go through the fucking legal fucking bullshit I have to go through already.

DALIA: What does that mean?

MIKE: It means, sign my property back to me—that you stole, basically.

DALIA: That's what you're thinking? And I didn't steal anything.

MIKE: All right, so listen: I'll have the papers sent over to you somehow, you'll sign them over to me, and then I will help your mother. Okay?

DALIA: I'm not signing anything.

MIKE: I knew you wouldn't sign anything. I knew that wasn't gonna happen. So, I can't help you.

DALIA: That's what you're worried about? I'm sitting here rotting, and you're thinking about the house?

MIKE: Dalia—you tried to have me killed!

DALIA: That's not true.

MIKE: You're a liar. You're a fucking liar.

DALIA: What does your mom say?

MIKE: She's not saying shit. She's sitting there. The fuck my mom's saying? Check it out: My mom, your mom, fucking everybody else's mom? They're all out of it. You know where you're sitting right now? That's the reality. I can't fix it. I just offered to help you, and you had the balls to say no to me. Okay. But I can't help.

DALIA: How do I believe you're gonna help me if I do that?

Still negotiating, pressing her advantage. And Mike hits the wall.

MIKE: 'Cause you know why? 'Cause I'm the one person on the phone that's ever done what they said they were gonna do. Okay? Me!

DALIA: How do I believe that?

MIKE: Don't say shit. I just said I'd help you, okay? And you just basically said fuck you to me, which is hilarious considering your situation, and considering what the fuck just happened today. Have your mom call me, I'll talk to her about it, and I told you what I'd do. I'll fix it. I'll help you.

DALIA: How?

MIKE: You got to fucking do the right thing.

DALIA: I have to go. I'm getting fingerprinted now.

But he's already hung up.

"Everyone asks me why I answered the phone," says Mike today. "How could I not answer the phone? I had to take that call. In my mind, I'm thinking that any normal person would be honest—give me some truth. But she gave me the opposite: all lies . . . I couldn't believe she called me, to be honest with you. I was probably her third phone call. Then she's calling me at what she had just told people was *her* house. When I met her, she had a bag of clothes. If she would have done the right thing, I would have helped her—just to be done with her."

But such is the nature of this case that nothing I've covered so far was the biggest bombshell of the day. Because that afternoon, the Boynton

Beach Police Department, primarily Chief Matthew Immler and his Public Information Officer Stephanie Slater, decided to put their video of Dalia being notified of her husband's death at the "crime scene"—the one they filmed just to make it all look authentic—up on the Internet, first on their official website, and then, for good measure, on YouTube. And the Internet did the rest. By that evening, it was starting to trend viral, and by the next morning it was everywhere. I saw it the next evening on Nancy Grace's show on CNN's Headline News network (now HLN).

In their defense, Florida is unique in that it has a very broad Public Records Law, so a government agency in the state is forced to disclose far more than in comparable jurisdictions. For example, it's feasible that police would turn over a 911 call if media made a request for it. According to testimony, the thinking was that since it was a public street, anyone could have made a similar video—as in fact, the crew from *COPS* did—so they were justified in releasing it. (Although the facts were muddied up later on, *COPS* refused to release any footage until the final disposition of the case, in accordance with their long-standing policy and written agreement with the police departments they ride with. Producer Jimmy Langley voluntarily met with me right after I took over the case and showed me the edited version of the show that they planned to air—their first thirty-minute episode dedicated to a single case—but I couldn't use any of it.) And in fact, it's not uncommon for police to post information or even crime scene video on their website in soliciting help from the public. They may have felt a story this compelling and media-ready would leak anyway—they were sitting on an old-fashioned scoop—and they wanted some say in how it broke. The first rule of public relations is to get out in front of the story. And certainly they would have been proud of their efforts and those of their officers, diligently mobilizing over the course of a weekend to save a life in a murder-for-hire plot. From their perspective, it may have looked like a slam dunk.

I have no opinion on whether releasing the video was a good idea or not. I had no previous experience with a case like this, and I suspect neither did they. It was the conclusion they came to and the action they took, at which point it became a fact. I do think if there had been a public records request, which there was not, they would have been justified in denying it on the grounds that the video was part of an ongoing investigation. I also think it was a brilliant idea to stage a fake crime scene. How better to establish intent—and possibly countershock her into a confession—than to convince Dalia that she'd been successful, only to rip the illusion off like a bandage, revealing her true self there wriggling in the bright light of the third degree?

But from the moment I was confronted with this situation, I had two unwavering reactions: (1) I knew it was going to be a problem, since the footage was going to figure heavily as evidence, and now the handling of the evidence had become the story. And (2) How was it that a case this significant, especially one with such pronounced domestic violence overtones, had happened without me knowing about it? I was the head of the Domestic Violence Unit. Although law enforcement is not required to keep the prosecutor's office apprised of its actions, we traditionally enjoyed a very good working relationship. And by including prosecutors at the earliest possible opportunity, police often save themselves problems down the line, since we're the ones knowledgeable in case law—i.e., what kinds of attacks can be made on the evidence or the merits of the case. Here's how I explain it: Law enforcement just needs to establish probable cause to make an arrest—is it more probable than not that a crime occurred?—whereas a prosecutor needs to prove that a crime occurred "beyond a reasonable doubt" in order to secure a conviction. In terms of percentages that means prosecutors are looking for closer to 99 percent certainty, while law enforcement only need 51 percent certainty that a crime occurred. We review search warrants and arrest warrants, and we like to know about sting operations in advance. But it's really better to have everyone on the same page from the very beginning.

When my boss, then State Attorney Michael McAuliffe, learned about the video the next morning, by seeing it on the news and reading about it in the paper, he was livid. As the chief law enforcement officer in the county, he didn't like surprises, he didn't like being blindsided in the press (no one does), and he always wanted to be on top of whatever was going on in the cases that are handled by his office. Now, here, suddenly the burgeoning Dalia Dippolito media circus had hit the trifecta on his worst-case scenario. Since this was a domestic violence case, it was assigned to my unit. So I tracked down the case file and read the Probable Cause Affidavit—two pages that made a compelling case for how I would spend the next two years—and set about the business of issuing subpoenas and building a case. In that document, although he wasn't named, the Confidential Informant's actions were describe in detail, and by now Dalia knew who he was. It was just a matter of time before the media would as well.

By the time I was assigned as chief prosecutor, Dalia was already out on bail. After spending the night in jail, she appeared before a judge on Thursday morning, August 6, for what is known as a First Appearance. The judge's obligation was to determine whether to release a defendant on bail or other conditions, and what that bail or those conditions may be. The court may consider the nature and circumstances of the offense charged and the penalty provided by law; the weight of the evidence against the defendant; the defendant's family ties, length of residence in the community, employment history, financial resources; the defendant's past and present conduct, including any record of convictions, or previous flight to avoid prosecution, and whether she represented a potential threat to the community.

Sergeant Sheridan appeared at the bond hearing, and between him, the prosecutor handling the First Appearance, and defense attorney Michael Salnick, they determined a reasonable bond in the amount of $25,000, with the conditions of house arrest and no contact with her husband. Dalia was also given special dispensation so that she could work, attend church, etc. Since she only needed to raise 10 percent in cash, or $2,500, she was set up at her mother's house with an ankle monitor by the time I knew anything about it.

Over the next week, I reached out to Mike Dippolito through his lawyers and was advised that he felt uncomfortable with the terms of Dalia's bond. He took exception to her claim of employment, saying the only sale she ever brokered at Beachfront Realty was his townhouse, and he indicated he was concerned for his safety—particularly since she was staying less than a mile from his house. I informed Salnick that I planned to petition for a bond modification unless he agreed to changes in the terms of her release: no work provision, church services, etc. She would be enjoined from leaving the house, period—she couldn't even go out in the backyard—except to her lawyer's office or to a doctor or hospital in a health emergency. And they would enter all of Mike's hot spots—home, office, Starbucks, gym, and the usual haunts—into a GPS program, and if she entered any of those "exclusion zones," the Sheriff's Office would be immediately notified that she was in violation. I didn't seek a bond increase because she was essentially locked down. I let him know that if I had to file my motion, I would be forced to inform the court how Dalia actually made her money. Salnick agreed to these terms without comment.

But not before Dalia had made plans to come and get her things from Mike's house, in the company of a house arrest supervisor. Mike would wait down the block until she was through. The night before, Mike's mother helped him box up everything Dalia owned, which he loaded into her car. While he was going through her things and putting them into boxes, he found used tampons shoved into corners and crevices all over the house.

It turned out she hadn't been pregnant after all. Even that was a lie.

CHAPTER 5

. . . .

Burn Notice

Six days before Dalia was arrested and Mike dodged a bullet, a phone call came in to the Boynton Beach police station on a Friday evening. Property Crimes Detective Asim Brown picked up the message from someone named Mohamed claiming he had some important information to impart, and asking him to call. When Detective Brown returned the call, Mohamed claimed he had intimate knowledge of a woman who was planning to kill her husband. The story he told in person that night was compelling enough that Brown alerted Sergeant Frank Ranzie, his superior in the Property Crimes Unit, and Sergeant Paul Sheridan of the Major Case Squad. Mohamed told them a detailed story stretching back a decade about a woman and intermittent lover he knew only as "Delilah" (who nonetheless once bought him a $38,000 Range Rover), the husband she seemed hell-bent on seeing dead, and the reasons why he thought the threat was credible. He obviously convinced them, because they signed him up as a Confidential Informant on the spot. Unlike a lot of CIs, he wasn't paid for his work. Rather, he believed she was serious, and he didn't want to get caught in the blowback.

Mohamed Shihadeh is a thirty-two-year-old Jordanian Muslim born in Jerusalem's West Bank who immigrated to the United States when he was a year old. With his shaved head and intense eyes, he is striking enough to have caught the eye of a producer who, after meeting him in a Miami nightclub, cast him in the USA Network dramatic series *Burn Notice*, where he played (what else?) a terrorist. He had a small empire of check-cashing/

convenience stores around South Florida, where he has lived for the past dozen years, and is a self-proclaimed card counter who claims to have won and lost millions at blackjack in Las Vegas, all the while nursing a vicious prescription Xanax habit. (On some of the police recordings of his phone calls, his speech is so slurred as to be almost incomprehensible.) Thoroughly Westernized, down to his Lexus and the T-Pain remixes he made a CD of for Dalia, he is known to his friends as Mo or, strangely enough, Mike.

Mohamed had first met Dalia over a decade ago when she walked into his convenience store in Boca Raton one day. She was eighteen, five-foot-seven, with jet-black hair and emerald-green eyes, and she looked like the devil's jewelry. She was in and out of his store four times in ten minutes, telling him she was getting her car washed at the Mobil station, and when she flirted with him, he flirted back. They hooked up that night and began seeing each other casually a couple of times a week, whenever it was convenient for both of them, although it was probably more casual for him than it was for her. ("I don't want to say dating, but more intimate friends," he described it in his initial police statement.) But soon enough he saw a less attractive, pushy side of her, this "two-faced personality" where she "all of a sudden throws a tantrum if she doesn't get her way."

She berated him for agreeing to an arranged marriage to appease his traditional Middle Eastern family, claiming her own Egyptian father had tried to force her into a similar situation. (Mohamed says Dalia hated her father, and that he had basically disowned her for breaking up her parents' marriage.) After she showed up at his apartment on a night when his designated bride was also scheduled to be there, and then refused to leave—a gesture somewhere between defiance and obsession—he distanced himself from her, although they continued to rendezvous at hotels and bars occasionally, even after his marriage in May 2003.

He saw her again for two or three months while he was going through a divorce in 2004, taking her to strip clubs and on gambling trips to Las Vegas. Yet for all the intensity of their times together, the porous way that money traveled back and forth between them, and the star-crossed manner in which they exited and reentered each other's lives, Mohamed only ever knew Dalia by her given Arabic name, Delilah; never went to her house;

never had her sleep over at his; and, when pressed, could reveal precious little of substance about her. When she left for California, he didn't see her again for another four years. Their whole relationship was based on lies, he told the police. (According to Mohamed's various, sometimes contradictory accounts, in the interim he went on to meet a woman in Las Vegas four days before she won a $2.3 million Wheel of Fortune slot machine jackpot; began dating her when she bought a house a mile from his in West Palm Beach; ended his arranged marriage, only to have his new fiancée charge him with aggravated assault following a dustup with her extended family—a charge she later recanted, and which was expunged from his record; remarried his first wife two days after he was released from jail; divorced his first wife—now his second wife—six months later; and reconciled with his fiancée, with whom he now has a child. He claims that each of his divorces cost him half a million dollars.)

In late 2008 (possibly on the same trip where she met Mike), Dalia called Mohamed out of the blue and met him for drinks at E.R. Bradley's Saloon in West Palm Beach. She told him she had opened some massage parlors in California, which at first he thought was a joke, and that she was engaged to someone in New York, a rich architect who had given her a $40,000 engagement ring, which she showed him, and a black CLK-class Mercedes. Since they were both involved with other people, they called it a night and promised to keep in touch.

The next time she saw him, months later at the Yard House, a restaurant in Palm Beach Gardens, it was a different story. She had gotten married—not to the guy in New York, but to someone else—and now she was trapped in a nightmare. Her husband was on probation for financial fraud, abusive, scarily violent, a drug dealer, on steroids, insanely jealous, and stalked her everywhere. Mohamed asked her why she didn't just divorce him, or have the marriage annulled, or get a restraining order, but Dalia said he would kill her. At times she was laughing, flirty like he remembered her, and at times she seemed genuinely terrified. Her lack of bruises or signs of obvious trauma made him skeptical of her claims, but she insisted she needed his help—especially after she showed up at his apartment at 6 a.m. the next morning. (Out of it on Xanax and still half asleep, he thinks he may have received oral sex from her, which no doubt helped convince him to help her.) Mohamed ran a check-cashing business and knew how to deal with miscreants. He had been a boxer in his youth and had a concealed weapon permit and two handguns. It made sense she would turn to him.

Mohamed's store, Cross Roads Market & Deli, was immediately adjacent to the Palm Beach Gardens Police substation, and he knew many of the officers who stopped through on a constant basis. He offered to put Dalia in touch with Robert Wilson, an undercover officer working in the narcotics unit, and she came by the store on March 17 hoping to run into him, but had to settle for a phone introduction through Mohamed. According to his police report, Wilson spoke with Dalia a day or so later, whereupon she repeated her claims, adding that her husband routinely sold steroids at the gym. She claimed she could guarantee he would have drugs on him if he was stopped in Palm Beach Gardens—conveniently, within Officer Wilson's jurisdiction—and she offered to pay him for his efforts. He assured her he didn't need any compensation to do his job. He talked to her several more times over the next few days and met with her at least once, but when she persisted in offering him money, he broke off all contact and advised her to contact her local police department.

That first day after they hooked up again, Dalia also asked Mohamed for some Xanax. He had been taking three five-milligram tablets a day for as long as he had known her, prescribed for anxiety and the ensuing insomnia, and it seemed like he wouldn't miss them. This was right before the incident at the Ritz-Carlton in Manalapan in which Mike's car was searched for drugs for the first time. Mohamed revealed that Dalia later told him that in addition to the search with the police dog at CityPlace, which she admitted to orchestrating (she had a friend call in an anonymous complaint), there was an unknown third attempt to have police arrest Mike for drugs, but they missed him by two or three minutes.

Back in touch after a lengthy hiatus, now that she was apparently doing well, Mohamed claims he asked Dalia if she would cosign on a car loan for him, since his credit was suspect due to the extreme fluctuations in the life of a gambler. Dalia didn't want the car in her name, but offered instead to buy the car for him outright. So the next afternoon, in the drive-through of her bank right across the street from his convenience store, she requested a cashier's check in the amount of $38,000. From there, they drove to the Land Rover dealership, where she purchased a used, light-blue recent-model Range Rover for exactly that amount. He claims the car was technically for both of them to use whenever they wanted, but since she still had the Mercedes in addition to her husband's Chevy Tahoe she was driving, he considered it a gift. (He testified that they routinely transferred large amounts of money back and forth between them throughout their friendship.) Dalia confessed to him that the money came from the $200,000 she was supposed to be holding for her husband to make restitution on his stock fraud crimes. She had spent half of it shopping, getting hair extensions, tanning, and now buying Mohamed a car, and the other half was stashed somewhere she wouldn't say. She even asked at one point if Mohamed could help her set up a fake account and forge a wire transfer transaction. He declined.

Within a couple of weeks, Dalia's mood had grown more desperate, and her proposed solution more extreme. Sometime before April 2, Dalia called Mohamed and demanded to see him. He was hanging out at a store called Urban Wear owned by his cousin on a bad corner in Riviera Beach, in the heart of the hood, and he told her to meet him there. Dalia showed up in her Mercedes in a tiny dress and no bra, the promise of sex spilling out of her, unlikely to have attracted more attention if she'd been on fire. She told Mohamed that her situation had become untenable, and asked him if he knew anyone who could kill her husband. She was a live wire, and Mohamed tried to calm her down, telling her she didn't know who these people around them were and what they were capable of. This just inflamed her.

When she got loud enough to attract the attention of some guys hanging out by the counter, Mohamed's cousin tried to make a joke out of it, saying, "She wants him to find somebody to kill her husband."

Except these were members of the notorious Buck Wild gang; this was their corner and the store was their hangout, and now it wasn't a joke anymore.

Buck Wild is an extremely violent African-American gang centered in Riviera Beach that specializes in drug dealing, robbery, extortion, and murder. They hold their tiny, otherwise law-abiding community hostage through intimidation, yet their influence is felt beyond its borders throughout South Florida. Not as organized or structured as the Crips or Bloods, it can best be described as a loosely affiliated crew of ultra-violent street thugs who have exhibited a breathtaking capacity for mayhem, and have been linked to some two dozen shootings.

One of the gang members jumped at the offer, telling her, "Yeah, I'll do it."

Soon the conversation had spilled out onto the sidewalk as they tried to determine whether she was serious, putting Dalia in direct negotiations with Larry Coe, a longtime gang member with a string of violent felonies in his past who surrounded himself with teenagers eager to do his bidding. As Mohamed and his cousin tried to warn her off this line of inquiry, Dalia brazenly told him that she had money, where she lived, what Mike's habits were, and the best time to pull off a hit. In exchange, she offered them $30,000 or the title to a Range Rover (presumably the one Mohamed was driving)—their call. Coe was intrigued enough to investigate further, and since Dalia didn't want to drive her own car and risk being recognized, she agreed to ride with him. The other guys would follow in a second car. Mohamed watched helplessly as they all drove off together, convinced he'd never see her again.

Forty-five minutes later, they all returned, Coe shaking his head. "That girl is crazy," he said, according to Mohamed. The house was equipped with security cameras, motion detectors, and an alarm system front and back. There was virtually no way in without being detected and recorded. Mohamed told them she was trouble; it would get out to everybody, plus there was already a cop involved. He felt like she was his responsibility. Coe told Dalia they weren't interested. Afterward, she tried to get Coe's phone number from Mohamed, who told her he didn't have it; later, she stopped by his cousin's store looking for the gang members. On April 2, Dalia placed thirteen unanswered calls to Larry Coe's cell phone. This was four days after the drug incident at CityPlace, and three days after Mike lost the $191,000 cashier's check to Erik Tal. Police responded to a domestic disturbance call at her house later the same evening. The next week, Mohamed took the Range Rover back to the dealership and settled for a $4,000 loss. He was concerned that Coe would try to take it from him due to Dalia's offer, or otherwise consider it his for the asking, and Mohamed considered it too hot to have in his possession. He checked with one of his cop pals about the legality of accepting a vehicle as a gift, and then used the cash to pay off his divorce attorneys.

For most of May and June, Mohamed was traveling with his daughter in Jordan and the Middle East. When he returned in late June, he claims, Dalia often called him as many as ten times a day. She was on the verge of getting Mike to sign over the house to her in order to expedite his restitution process, and she didn't have long before her husband's suspicions would hit a tipping point. She also admitted she had lied about being pregnant, and had even had her mother convinced. Now it had been four months, and she was worried because Mike had invited her whole family—including her dying grandfather, who was in a wheelchair—to the Philadelphia Phillies–Miami Marlins major league baseball game on July 19, renting a luxury box at his own expense. The wife of one of Mike's friends was also four months pregnant, and Dalia was afraid that the other woman had begun to show while she clearly had not. She tried to get Mohamed to tag along as a friend from the old days, but he begged off. She also offered him $5,000 to find her a street gun, which wouldn't run more than a fraction of that. He tried to ignore her, but she wouldn't let it drop.

On July 31, the day that Mike signed over the deed to his townhouse to Dalia—and the day she discovered that he still owned half of it, regardless of how the title read—she called Mohamed and begged to meet him. They met at a Mobil station near her house. As they sat and talked in the front seat of his new Lexus, she reiterated how she needed his help in finding someone to kill her husband, something there was no way he was going to do. He tried to convince her to just divorce him and walk away. At some point in that conversation, Mohamed went into the station by himself to get a pack of cigarettes and a Red Bull. He took his wallet with him from the glove compartment where he always kept it. That was also where he kept his Glock 9, one of the two handguns for which he had a concealed weapons permit. When he came back out, Dalia told him she had to get something out of her car, and took her purse with her. When he went to put his wallet back in the glove compartment, he noticed that his gun was missing. After some initial stonewalling, she finally gave it back to him. He told her she was an idiot for putting her fingerprints on a gun when she had no idea what it had been used for.

As he left the gas station, Mohamed's mind was filled with conflicting impulses. Dalia's renewed urgency meant that all his advice had fallen on deaf ears. The fact that she would steal a gun meant that she was either ruthless or desperate, and with the house now fully in her name, there was nothing stopping her from going through with it. She could easily be setting him up to take the fall. He called an attorney, who advised him to contact the police. Next he contacted one of the cops he knew in Palm Beach Gardens, who referred him to Detective Brown at the Boynton Beach Police Department, which had jurisdiction (due to the location of the gas station where they had met). By the time he heard back from Detective Brown, it was late Friday evening. At the cops' request, he went and spoke to them, then made an official taped statement once they knew he was serious. He was just hoping to flag down what was turning into a runaway train. He wanted to stop her before she did something stupid and got either one of them in real trouble.

The first night when he came in, Mohamed signed the standard Confidential Informant Agreement. They needed him in order to gain more information—starting with the names of the suspect and the potential victim. For his part, he didn't want Dalia to get into trouble or to find out that he had been the one to intervene. That first night, he never envisioned her getting arrested—he just thought he might prevent a murder from happening. He told the cops he didn't want his name made public, since even as a small-business owner, he often came in contact with an unsavory element, and he didn't need the hassle. They told him it was just a formality and they would protect his identity, which they did. He also believed he would never have to testify in court. But the contract he signed states clearly, "I further understand that I may be required to testify in court cases that I am involved in . . . and to make myself available for court, depositions, or any other action that the court may require."

In that same document, he also gave his consent for the police to "install an electronic listening device or any other device designed for the purpose of monitoring conversation(s) on or about my person, for the purpose of conducting a criminal investigation, and to record those conversations for evidentiary purposes." Those phrases would come back to haunt him.

Since Mohamed had precious little information about Dalia, Sergeant Ranzie suggested they put him in a car on Friday evening and drive him around the neighborhood near the Mobil station, where Mohamed thought she lived, to try to locate her house or car, which would help them identify her or her husband. When that failed to provide any leads, the decision was made for Mohamed to contact Dalia via a controlled cell phone call. By then it was close to midnight, and she failed to answer. The next day, Sergeant Sheridan told Mohamed to contact Dalia on his own and tell her he'd changed his mind about helping her find someone who could do the job for her, and to have her bring $3,000 and a photo of her husband to the Mobil station where they had met last time.

When you have a CI talking to a target, you want everything recorded and perfectly documented, so there is no way for the defense to make some sort of allegation that this was all a setup, or that there were back channels of communication going on behind the scenes. This is especially true in a case like this one, where the CI and the target had a long-standing personal relationship. You also want the CI to appear as normal as possible, even though he's being monitored by a detective around the clock. Most of the controlled calls between Mohamed and Dalia were recorded with a handheld digital recorder or as three-way calls run through the police department switchboard. But the fact that there existed no tape of this first phone call and several other key conversations became an issue at trial.

The next day, Saturday, August 1, he met with lead Detective Alex Moreno at the station to set up a meeting with Dalia that afternoon. When they asked him to wear a wire so they could record the conversation with the subject, he warned them not to put the body mic in his underwear, a common place to conceal it, because when Dalia first saw him, she often went straight for his crotch and performed oral sex on him. They also asked him for the keys to his car and, unbeknownst to Mohamed, set up an undetectable pinhole video camera in the pocket on a shirt he had hanging in the backseat.

Surveillance teams got to the Mobil station early to set up: Sergeant Ranzie and Detectives Moreno and Anderson were staked out at the pumps adjacent to where Mohamed would park his vehicle (Ranzie pretended to be pumping gas for most of the meeting in order to maintain visuals), and Sergeant Sheridan tailed Mohamed to the location and parked where he could keep him in view. Several other detectives were on hand, artfully integrated into the surroundings and listening in on a live feed. Dalia arrived in the Tahoe and got into Mohamed's Lexus, allowing law enforcement to run her tags and establish an ID. When the car came up registered to Mike Dippolito, they figured they had the target.

"I can't believe this shit," he says when she gets in his car.

"Yeah, I love you, too." That was one of their pet sayings, a way to defuse renegade tension and a bemused commentary on their odd, enduring relationship. Before they get started, he tries to give her one last out.

MOHAMED: Honestly, you're not worried about someone getting killed over that much money?

DALIA: It's not even over the fucking money. Like, you don't fucking get it. Like, it's not even about the fucking money. Like, you know, that money, we'll spend it in a fucking blink of an eye. It's not about the fucking money. Like, it's about, like, his fucking friends and all that other shit. Like, the thing is, like, okay, with his wife, like, she didn't have anything. They were, like, renting. So, like, divorcing her, it didn't matter. Like, me going and fucking filing for divorce, like, he'll come after my fucking ass. Period.

A far cry from the grieving widow on display in her interview tape, and, in retrospect, probably as succinct a motive as any other.

DALIA: And all his friends, like, he ran into another guy today at Target that was, like, organized crime, or whatever. Also on probation. Like, he keeps running into all these fucking people is what I'm saying to you. Like, he knows a lot of people.

This is the same argument she will make in more cogent words with the police four days from now.

Mohamed tries to impress on her how serious the hit man is that he has found for her, and how she can't go back on it once she pulls the trigger. She should follow his instructions, get out of town if he recommends it. She balks: she never leaves town; that would be a red flag. They consider which photo to give to the hit man. He brings up the Buck Wild gang, which she brushes aside.

MOHAMED: I told you to stay away from them.

DALIA: I didn't give them anything. What are you talking about?

MOHAMED: Larry and all them, when you walked into [the clothes] store, I told you—

DALIA: I didn't give them any money.

MOHAMED: Well, they told me you did. You told them that you were going to give them my Range Rover or something like that.

DALIA: No. That was bullshit. That guy still calls me. But I told him I'm out of town.

Mohamed changes the subject.

MOHAMED: So, okay, after he's killed him, whatever, your mom and all of them are not gonna, like—his mom is not gonna get suspicious of you or anything like that?

DALIA: Why me? Like, do you know what fucking killing somebody [is]?

MOHAMED: If you say that . . .

DALIA: Yeah, but killing somebody? Come on. I mean, that's fucking, you know—nobody's gonna be able to point a finger at me. But I need him to say, like—remember how you were asking me who's his enemy, who's this, who's that? . . . There's this guy that, like, fucking hates him, hates him, hates him. Like, he snitched them out. Now that family's doing time right now.

She's perfecting her alibi. She wants it done on Wednesday, and Mo assures her it will be because the hit man is flying to Costa Rica on Thursday. He also describes him as former military who is really good at his job. He's improvising now. Mohamed will serve as a go-between on this initial $1,200 to buy the gun, but she'll have to meet with him herself for the rest of it. He also puts the touch on her for $20,000 after the job is completed, for having brokered the introduction—as well as $200 today if she can spare it. She agrees to the $20,000, and promises to try to get some more money out of the ATM, although she knows her account is already overdrawn.

> MOHAMED: I don't want to talk about it anymore. Let's just get this
> shit done with.

We see her hand him the $1,200 in cash on the video, the moment a crime is committed.

> DALIA: . . . And we never talk about it again—ever—do we ever talk
> about it again.

They debate which photograph of Mike they should give to the hit man. Dalia settles on one of Mike with her grandfather.

> DALIA: But take my grandfather fucking out of the picture. Can't you
> fucking cut him out?

They settle on a picture of just Mike instead.

> MOHAMED: Yeah. But start getting your life straight after this. Seri-
> ously. Don't never do this shit again, you know? I'm telling you—

DALIA: You know what? You fucking start getting your shit together, too . . . Don't lecture me.

And one more thing.

DALIA: Wipe my fucking prints off those fucking pictures.

She tells him to smile.

MOHAMED: Fuck this shit. I've been through divorces and problems. And I can't believe I'm even doing this.

DALIA: And who the hell told you never to fucking get married?

MOHAMED: Yeah. Shit happens.

DALIA: I know. Fuck. I ended up in the same boat as you. You're right. We are a lot alike.

MOHAMED: All right. Let me get going . . . Let's not stay in contact the next day or two.

"God forgive me," he whispers under his breath as she's getting out of the car.

On his drive back to the police station, Mohamed gets a call from a friend of his and they chat in and out of English and Arabic.

"I said I'm not going to be able to sleep knowing someone's going to get killed," he says at one point. "I have to get it off my chest, you know." Later in the conversation, he says, "She trusts me like crazy."

Two days later on Monday, August 3, at 11:38 a.m., Mohamed called Dalia and told her the hit man would be contacting her shortly.

"You won't feel comfortable if you go by yourself, right?" he asks.

"Not really, no," she says. He agrees to go with her, and instructs her to keep it close to the vest, do as he says, don't argue about the money, and get out of there as soon as she can. "Straight, fast, quick, clean," he says.

An hour and a half later, he got a message that Dalia was on her way over to talk to him in person. Hastily calling the police department to determine what he should do, particularly since they haven't made arrangements to tape the meeting, Detective Moreno told him to blow her off. "Come on, man, you're a smart guy—think of something," Moreno says. The police tape the phone call. Dalia is driving on I-95 in the Tahoe and refuses to discuss things in the car, instead pulling over onto the shoulder of the highway and pacing back and forth beside passing traffic. (This was the vehicle she repeatedly reported as involved in illegal drug activity, and she fears police may have bugged the vehicle.) Mohammed makes a joke about how long it's taking her to get situated.

DALIA: Whatever. I love you, too.

MOHAMED: I love you, too. But love's one of those really strong words. Be careful how you use it.

DALIA: What? You know I love you. I've known you forever, my God. It's so fucking crazy, I swear. Like, for whatever fucking reason, we always end up, like, I don't know—[she giggles]—we always end up fucking talking again. It's fucking crazy.

Contract murder seems to make her wistful, even philosophical.

She tells him that Mike will be at the bank on Wednesday morning in Boca Raton, where he will withdraw $10,000 from the Bank of America branch as a payment for a business partner.

DALIA: So what I'm trying to tell you is that if our friend or whatever hooks up with him for fucking coffee, he could get a piece of that, is what I'm trying to say. Like, from that fucking money. Even though whatever is taking place, he could fucking give that to you.

MOHAMED (angry): Listen, Delilah. I'm not robbing him. I don't want his money. I'm doing this for you, okay? . . . Let this guy take care of it. He's a professional.

The issue resolved, Dalia returned home to await the hit man's call. At 2:47 p.m., the hit man calls Dalia to tell her he is driving up from Miami to meet with her in a couple of hours, and she should bring $3,000 as a down payment and a key to her house. Although he never gave her a name, this was in reality Widy Jean, a Haitian undercover police officer chosen to match Dalia's imagined profile of a professional assassin, based on her interaction with the Buck Wild gang. Although she was technically guilty of a crime the second she handed Mohamed the $1,200, police officials determined it would be a stronger case if they went through with the hit man sting (and stronger still if they set up a fake crime scene). Dalia agrees to his terms, but immediately calls Mohamed at 3:08 in a panic, wondering if she can pay him less up front, and worried about giving a killer access to her home and possessions.

> DALIA: What if I meet with him and nothing gets done and the key's floating around, and then I fucking get robbed? . . . Why does he need a key to my fucking house? I thought you said this shit wasn't going to get personal . . . I don't like talking all this shit over the phone. It's already fucked up.

In the prosecutor's lexicon, we call this "consciousness of guilt." It's the reason she took her jewelry with her to the gym the next morning. She knew what she was doing, and she was concerned with the consequences. Mohamed tries to look on the bright side.

> MOHAMED: Worst comes to worst, he'll have to give you back the $1,200 if he won't accept the thousand down payment.
>
> DALIA: Okay. Or just give me the fucking shit they were going to use. I fucking paid for it, didn't I? I'm just going to have to get my own man, call somebody I know or whatever.

Around five, Dalia met Mohamed at a Chili's beforehand to go over strategy, although since the police department's backup Unitel recording device wasn't working properly, no record exists of their conversation. The hit man calls along the way and they agree to meet at a CVS near her house, which is virtually right across the street from Chili's. He'll be driving a red Chrysler Sebring convertible. Mohamed—introduced as her cousin "Mike"—gets on the phone briefly to give him directions, after which the hit man asks to speak to Dalia again.

"I know you got somebody with you," the hit man tells her. "He don't got to be in my car, right? This is just between you and I." (Since Mohamed, aka "Mike," had already supposedly given him $1,200 and a photo of the victim, the hit man should have recognized him—if not over the phone, then certainly at their upcoming meeting—a slipup that might have tipped Dalia off if she had realized.)

At 5:55, they pulled into the CVS parking lot, a location chosen for its ability to conceal multiple surveillance teams. Mohamed stayed in the Tahoe while Dalia walked to the Sebring in a light-blue tight-fitting sundress. Once again, the vehicle was wired for sound and video.

"We're staying in here, right?" she asks as she climbs in the passenger side. He says yeah.

The first thing he says to her is, "Damn, you look good." Dalia kind of rolls her eyes but smiles, flattered. Right off the bat, she's got a home field advantage.

The hit man is mostly no-nonsense and straight to the point. He is Haitian with tight cornrows, a two- or three-day growth of beard, and dark wraparound sunglasses that give him a slightly alien quality and no doubt make it hard to read his intentions. A Wyclef Jean comparison would not be out of line. He gets right to it. He tells her that after they talk today, his burner phone is going in the garbage and she won't have any way of calling it off.

HIT MAN: You sure you want to kill this dude?

DALIA: Do we really have to . . . it's just I'd rather be less, you know . . .

She laughs, unable to find the words to discuss not saying certain words. Accordingly, they talk in abstractions. She raises the issue of the money, which she didn't bring with her.

DALIA: And it's not like . . . I have a stash under my pillow.

Surprisingly, for someone who allegedly kills people for a living, he is sympathetic to her plight, despite working for the insider's "lowball" price of $6,000. A conscientious small businessman, he even gives her a cost breakdown of her homicide dollar.

HIT MAN: You know, whatever I get, from whatever money I get from you, most of it goes into planning and getting people the good stuff. . . Twelve hundred went to buying my heat—my gun—okay? A couple hundred for other people to do things . . . I had to get this car. I gotta get rid of this car . . . this phone . . . There's a lot more I have to do.

He tells her she can pay him on the back end if she'll bump the price by a thousand, and she assures him she's good for it. They settle on Wednesday morning, and he volunteers that he'll make it look like a robbery gone bad, since the newspapers have reported a recent crime spree in her area.

HIT MAN: I'm gonna think he's at work, but he's not at work, you know? He gets two to the head, and that's it.

That wasn't abstract.
He asks about Mohamed, who's been waiting in the car, whom she has identified as her cousin, and if she trusts him.

HIT MAN: You know, I'm just saying for you, understand, 'cause I don't know how well you handle pressure . . .

DALIA: I'm a lot tougher than what I look.

HIT MAN: All right.

DALIA: I know you're thinking . . . You're, like, "Oh, what a cute little girl," whatever, you know? But I'm not.

She laughs easily, and bats her eyes frequently for effect.

HIT MAN: Yeah. That you are. You're beautiful.

She tells him Mike will be going to the bank early on Wednesday in Boca Raton, and they discuss possible scenarios and exit strategies. Only this time in the telling, the hit man would get to keep the $10,000, not Mohamed.

HIT MAN: It's like taking candy from a baby.

(Mike claimed the withdrawal was to have been for the purchase of marketing data. Since he was taken into protective custody at 6 a.m., the meeting did not take place.)

Dalia offers to go scout the location with him right then. She also drops the fact that Mike has a Porsche sitting in the garage, if that serves as added enticement. He lays out some possible scenarios, all of which seem amenable to her.

HIT MAN: You're the client. I'm not gonna, you know, do anything without your approval, you understand?

At one point, Mohamed comes to the driver's side window to make sure everything is okay, but the hit man tells him they're fine. He gives Dalia one last out, just to make sure.

HIT MAN: Between now and when it's done, you know, you're not gonna have an option to change your mind. Even if you change your mind, we're talking—

DALIA: There's no changing, no. I'm determined already.

HIT MAN: You definitely want to do this?

DALIA: I'm positive—like, 5,000 percent sure.

HIT MAN: Okay.

The next day, Tuesday, the hit man called Dalia and told her, "The bank thing's not going to work. Be out by six." Boca Raton would mean a change of jurisdiction, meaning the Boynton Beach Police Department would have to work in conjunction with the Sheriff's Office. There was neither the time nor the appetite to try to mount an operation of that magnitude.

After Dalia was arrested, but long before his name became connected with hers, Mohamed received a handful of mysterious calls, all between three and fifteen seconds in duration: On the first one, a male voice said, "You're going down, too." The second and third, there was just giggling and bar sounds in the background.

"I wasn't paying attention to that stuff," he says. "I had a lot more serious stuff to deal with."

After Dalia had been arrested, Detective Moreno took another statement from Mohamed on August 10. As almost an afterthought, Mohamed mentioned to police that this wasn't the first time Dalia had tried to kill her husband. According to her, she had tried to poison him just the week before. After doing research online, while Mike was still laid up on the couch following his liposuction surgery, she stopped by Starbucks and got him an iced Chai tea, then poured half of it out and filled it with a colorless, odorless brand of antifreeze, hoping he was so zonked on painkillers that he wouldn't notice. He took a big mouthful but didn't swallow it, claiming it tasted like gasoline, and immediately spit it out. Mohammed said he assumed she was kidding until the incident with the gun. When Detective Moreno asked Mike about it, he confirmed the incident, saying he thought something had happened with the concentrate and it had all collected at the bottom, where he'd positioned the straw. But for the next ten days he'd suffered diarrhea and stomach cramps, and the inside of his mouth was lined with ulcers. He even asked the doctor who was supervising his lipo if he could have accidentally given him something. His doctor told him he was stupid and that this was something else altogether.

"The money was slowly disappearing," observes Mohamed. "Now that I put one and one together, maybe because he met her through an escort agency. It's kind of weird to marry an escort."

CHAPTER 6

. . . .

Inextricably
Intertwined

With Dalia forcibly detained behind the prison walls of her mother's luxury home and backyard pool, just down the road from the town-house she still co-owned with her victim-husband, it was time to try to put this Byzantine criminal saga into some kind of coherent order.

Every witness or person of interest—from the victim to the reluctant accomplice to the arresting officers—recounted what seemed like a convincing version of the events. But when you overlaid them one atop the other, the cumulative pattern was so much more complex than any one depiction could suggest. Like a lot of full-time criminals, Dalia lavished far more effort and ingenuity on the easy life than she ever would have on a career. Meanwhile, a media wildfire was raging out of control just beyond the battlements, with the release of the crime scene video on the Internet and round-the-clock cable news, and the surveillance videos, bombshell revelations, lurid text messages, and the rest of it ready to set off new shock waves as soon as the cable doyennes and broadcast mandarins knew what I did. Dalia's tour de force performance as the grieving widow was one minute and nineteen seconds of uncut digital adrenaline ready-made for a reality-TV audience raised on the likes of *American Idol* and *The Apprentice* and *Survivor*, adept at spotting bad actors (in both intention and ability) and second-guessing the professionals—a potential jury pool of millions.

Dalia's $3,000 Prada purse contained the keys to a Bank of America safe-deposit box her husband knew nothing about, so that seemed like an excellent place to start, and Detective Anderson obtained a search warrant. At this stage of an investigation, I like to work closely with the investigators on the case—in this instance, lead Detectives Moreno and Anderson and Detective Asim "Ace" Brown (who first fielded the Mohamed call, and concentrated on the elaborate financial transactions)—to obtain evidence. I was on hand to sign subpoenas, review search warrants, or just brainstorm on the evidence we might need to slam the door on any possible defense strategy. (A subpoena is something that a prosecutor signs and issues—to bring a witness to court, say, or obtain certain documents. Some documents can only be obtained via search warrant, which is issued by a judge. In a search warrant, the officer or detective has to set forth "probable cause" as to why they believe that evidence of a crime exists at the place of the proposed search.)

The safe-deposit box contained a number of items that corroborated Mike's version of events, especially the money trail between Dalia, Mike, his lawyer, Mohamed, and Erik Tal. Dalia had saved the March statement from a separate checking account she maintained at her mother's address, which allowed us to obtain a search warrant for her mother's house, a potential treasure trove of additional evidence. At about the same time, detectives got a call from a storage facility where Dalia had rented a unit in her name, on which she had stopped making payments. Mike remembered seeing a duffel bag there once when the couple went to retrieve their bicycles, and the owner considered whatever was left abandoned property. On the way to execute the search warrant on Randa's residence, the officers stopped by the storage facility to see what kind of bounty they might find, only to discover they had just missed Randa, who had ransomed the duffel bag for her daughter. When they arrived at Randa's house, Dalia was in the process of surveying its contents, which included many items related to her escort business: photographs, print ads, photo books, client lists, the dates and times of the "appointments," and other incriminating records, all of which they put into evidence and made copies of for me.

We also got search warrants for Dalia's computers and their content (we were never able to find her laptop), text messages, and e-mails, and subpoenas for her phone records and bank records—trying to cast as wide a net as possible for anything that might track her movements through time. Although the evidence in this trial was particularly compelling—the accused as much as confessed on camera before she was even arrested—it wasn't quite so easy to identify why. She had an enviable life, lots of nice possessions, a husband who worshipped her, and a clearly marked escape route from a sordid past she presumably would want to leave behind—one her husband was fully aware of and neither resented nor blamed her for. It was backward from most of the cases I see: we had all the evidence we needed; we just had to prove a motive. Not a whodunit, but why. And although the State didn't technically have to prove a motive in a case like this, I knew from experience that if I was trying to figure out why, a jury would have the same question. This was why we tried to be so thorough in mapping out Dalia's daily life and social connections. This process continued right up to the first day of the trial.

Mike's legal troubles and subsequent incarceration were well documented, but I found two items of interest on Dalia. One was a missing persons report related to the December 1999 incident where she ran away to New York and was taken off the plane at JFK by local authorities. It wouldn't be the last time she tried to influence the people around her through extreme behavior. The second item was a police report dated June 3, 2002, when Dalia was nineteen. According to the report, a Sergeant DeLong from the Palm Beach County Sheriff's Office was dispatched to assist a Greenacres police officer in interviewing a possible victim of credit card fraud. The man claimed to have gone to Breanne's Photography Club (he spells it three different ways), a retail establishment operating in a strip mall in Lake Worth, just north of Boynton Beach. There he was greeted by a dark-skinned woman named Carmen who "told him that she was going to have him, and that he could not look at any other girls or he will have to leave and never come back." After being made to wait for half an hour, he had sex with "Carmen," claiming at one point she taunted him with a rubber condom filled with coins "to make [it] appear very thick," which she brandished "between her 'pussy' and 'my pole.'" He was eventually charged $230 against his will. Although he claimed to have had sex there between ten and twenty times, she refused to contact the manager, and he was forced to leave.

When DeLong and the second officer went to investigate, they discovered three women on premises, and "Dalia Mohammed seem[s] to be in charge." Dalia described the setup as follows: "Customers come in and use the cameras provided by Brianne's Photo Company to do fantasy photo shoots in these bedrooms on the premises." With her permission, DeLong completed a quick tour of the three bedrooms, at least one of which featured a black light. When he noted that the cameras contained no film, had dust all over them, and did not appear to be in working order, and that there was no evidence of a darkroom or even any photographs on the walls (outside of images from magazines), he questioned Dalia about her earlier statement regarding the cameras and she demonstrated her signature ability to think on her feet, claiming (according to DeLong), "That was one of the fantas[ies] for the customer to use, it's some kind of stage prop while they were acting out their fantasies." He also reports a thirty-gallon garbage can in back "filled to over flowing" with "various pieces of stained ladies' lingerie and other incidental property." No arrests were made, since they saw no evidence of crimes being committed.

We turned Dalia's computer over to a forensic expert at the Sheriff's Office, where we hoped to find evidence of the computer search Mohamed remembered for a lethal, undetectable kind of antifreeze. That effort proved inconclusive, but I did print out Dalia's entire search history—all 3,000 pages of it. A great deal of it consisted of quasi-legal outcall sites like Eros.com (considered the premiere Internet escort site); SugarDaddyForMe.com, which seeks to connect "Sugar Daddies" and "Sugar Babies" for a subscription fee; and the Adult Services Section on Craigslist, which was discontinued in September 2010 following a public furor over illegal ads and child sex trafficking. Dalia also maintained her own escort site with the charming moniker Eyesnatch.com, where she apparently brokered "dates" for other women, and some of her Craigslist postings were marketing notices targeting prospective escorts, making her a madam: "One week free advertisement on www.eyesnatch.com: Increase your clientele and business. Brand-new upscale website targeting high-end business. Your ad goes up within minutes. What do you have to loose [sic]?"

By connecting photos (she rarely posted photos of herself, even on outcalls she answered herself, like the one where she met Mike) and contact e-mails (she often posted real estate ads on Craigslist using the same Hotmail address), and filing subpoenas with the various sites, I was able to document Dalia's career in freelance prostitution. Beginning in 2005 up through September 2008, the ads were all specific to Orange County in Southern California: "Colombian college girl looking to steam things up. Total GFE [Girlfriend Experience, shorthand for "will do anything," although that doesn't sound like any girlfriend I've ever heard of]. Only here for two days. Guaranteed to blow your mind." Or "CUM check out this hot Colombian beauty. Looking for some weekend fun. Only in town for a few days. Looking to satisfy your craving."

By late September, she was posting similar Craigslist ads with the same contact info in Boca Raton, Florida, confirming that she was running girls on the side: "Hot blonde Colombian bombshell ready to CUM to you. W4M. Age: 22. Hi boys! I'm a former swimsuit model all the way from Colombia. Ready to have some fun with you and spice up your life. For some hot, dirty fun—give me a call!" This is the story Mike told in his early interviews. (Craigslist turned over every ad she had submitted, some of which they refused to post due to content.)

In the material recovered from her duffel bag, there was a brown leather notebook with appointments listed in Dalia's girlish handwriting (replete with i's dotted with hearts), including addresses, phone numbers, and directions for her wide array of clients. Over time, I contacted a lot of these men. Most wouldn't give me any information at all, but a couple of them took me at my word that I wasn't pursuing a prostitution case and they weren't in any kind of trouble. I was able to confirm with one of them that he had an appointment booked for the day Dalia was arrested (i.e., the day her husband was to have been executed), but he couldn't remember whether he'd been stood up or not. Her records contained a number of clients in the Washington, D.C., area. The Florida ads continued to run as late as June 2009.

In our early conversations, Michael Salnick, Dalia's attorney, made several references to her as a "battered woman" who was forced to do what she did as a matter of self-preservation—a reference to Battered Spouse Syndrome, where women have suffered such trauma and abuse over time that their only perceived escape is to murder their spouse. This was a likely defense for him to pursue, and one that I found particularly galling, given the nature and extent of Dalia's crimes. So I set about to pick it apart. For example, in many instances of domestic violence, the perpetrator isolates the victim from friends and family. But here, Mike made a point to include her family in their activities. Dalia (allegedly) had her own job and income as a real estate broker, and Mike never sought to control the couple's finances—all red flags. Moreover, if Salnick pursued this line of defense, then he opened the door to whatever proof I had of Dalia's financial independence, including running an escort business before she met Mike and while they were married—an enterprise he accepted, if not exactly encouraged. I made certain to mention my recent windfall from Dalia's private records, and continued to leak this material to him up until the trial—a flanking maneuver that effectively limited his ability to successfully position his client, and may have led him to the defense strategy he ultimately pursued.

Also in California, during the period before Dalia returned to Florida permanently, her Craigslist ads are specific to the town of Santa Ana, about forty miles southeast of Los Angeles, and they all read similarly to this one: "Hottest girls! Hot oil massages by beautiful, exotic therapists. Here to meat [sic!] your needs and desires. You won't be disappointed. Touch us soon." The ads included a street address and the helpful tip "Behind Carl's Jr." (later changed to "Behind Midas"—perhaps trading on his golden touch).

Dalia had two phones—a Sprint phone and a MetroPCS phone, commonly referred to as a burner phone, since the company requires neither a contract nor proof of identity, and calls on such phones cannot be easily traced. Although her MetroPCS account was not in her name, presenting a challenge as to how to enter its contents into evidence, we did discover it in her car, and many of the escort listings led directly back to that number. Mike understood that Dalia's white MetroPCS phone was her escort phone and believed she used it exclusively for business. It explained why she would get texts at inopportune moments and have to answer them, why she received mysterious phone calls at all hours, and why she had to rush out at the drop of a hat. It was the perfect alibi for whatever business Dalia dreamed up, even when that business included getting rid of Mike. We spent hundreds of hours reconstructing her phone traffic and its intricate web of interconnections. In this case, I employed a technique I had used two or three times before, which I named the Phone Game. Such diagrams inevitably spiderweb out into hundreds of dead ends, numbers I don't recognize and have no information on without further subpoenas. So a young lawyer in my office named Lindsey Marcus, who worked with me exclusively on this case and was my third chair—the third lawyer in a trial, who sits at counsel's table in court—spent the three months beforehand doing scut work, including cold-calling numbers that came up at key intersections on our charts. Half the time she thought I was crazy, but my feeling is you never know until you try, and it dislodged all kinds of odd-shaped information that later helped complete the pattern. Even a voice mail greeting could confirm a name, which often gave us a face and an address once we searched online.

When we analyzed the data, we discovered that repeatedly at key junctures, Dalia called three people: Mike, Mohammed, and someone named Michael Stanley (her third Mike, given Mohamed's preferred nickname). Stanley is one of those we cold-called and confirmed through a voice mail message. When I asked Mike Dippolito who Michael Stanley was, he told me he was Dalia's ex-boyfriend whom she had lived with in New York and later in California during the three years prior to Mike and Dalia's marriage. Except that his number came up repeatedly in the weeks prior to the arranged murder. We also found hundreds of texts during that same period, many of an extremely graphic nature. We did a phone dump off both of Dalia's phones, pulling all the numbers, contacts, photos, and texts, and by comparing dates and usage rates, we could tell that a lot of information had been deleted from Dalia's burner phone. But once we subpoenaed Stanley's records, a more complete picture began to emerge.

In Florida, the rules of criminal procedure require that the prosecuting attorney provide the defendant with a list of all of the witnesses that have information relevant to the crime charged and, most importantly, any person that we intend to call at trial to prove our case. We are also required to list and make available to the defense any evidence that we have in our possession that we intend to use at trial to prove the crime charged. Once the defendant is in receipt of that information, he or she is obligated to provide the State with a comparable witness list and evidence. The rules also allow the defendant, through his or her attorney, the opportunity to depose any witness that the State intends to have testify at trial. This took up much of the year before the trial date, which was eventually set for April 25, 2011.

Pursuant to the rules of discovery, I received a list of prospective witnesses from Defense Attorney Salnick that included the name of Michael Stanley. Although he didn't have to, Salnick also turned over the transcript of a fifteen-page interview an investigator had conducted with Stanley on May 17, 2010, in White Plains, New York. The interview was interesting for a number of reasons, not the least of which was that in it, Stanley went out of his way to provide tortuous, implausible explanations of circumstances no one would think to challenge him on. According to him, he had not had sexual relations with Dalia since August 2008. The apparent sexually explicit texting between them was just a case of mistaken identity with Dalia's husband or his anonymous consorts, except when it was some twisted sexual role-playing game her husband expected them both to participate in—using the exact same texts I had turned over to Salnick in discovery. Mike Dippolito's history as Stanley recounted it was coincidentally the same one Dalia had portrayed to the police, with Dalia perpetually the victim of whatever mad whim or demented fantasy had taken hold of her husband. Any misimpression of a murder-for-hire plot was merely some misguided reality TV stunt Mike had forced on those around him (a conspiracy that involved everyone connected to it except Dalia, including the Boynton Beach Police Department). And if he, Michael Stanley, were to have reported this barbarism to a small army of civic authorities, often anonymously, using ethically questionable technology, well, it was merely in the performance of his civic duty.

He seemed like someone who had shot an arrow into the air and managed to split the bull's-eye on his own chest. I couldn't wait to get him on the stand and under oath.

This was also the first glimpse I had of something either so ingenious or so demented that it could only be a trial balloon for some part of the defense strategy—a meta-theory that would seek to transform incontrovertible evidence into conceptual performance, and turn the facts of the case inside out.

It was important for me to be very prepared for Michael Stanley's deposition; to let him know from the beginning that I was running the show and that I had his number. So I spent countless hours learning absolutely everything I could about him. I had obtained a search warrant for his e-mails, and I reviewed them—following up on any information. I had e-mail correspondence between Dalia and Stanley dating back to 2006—including pictures. We contacted his ex-wife and caught her by surprise. She hadn't heard about Dalia's arrest and was more than happy to talk to us about their relationship. I followed up on every detail in their text messages, sent subpoenas to hotels to prove his whereabouts, and lastly, I served a subpoena on his employer, demanding proof that he was using his company cell phone and that it had never been reported stolen. I also obtained business trip expenses, credit card account numbers, and the dates of all his business trips and vacations. I was sending Mike Stanley a very clear message—I would be ready for him and he'd better tell me the truth.

According to the information he provided in his deposition (conducted eleven months after that initial interview, on April 8, 2011), Michael Stanley, forty-one, was a building contractor originally from Connecticut who specialized in the construction of high-end retail interiors in malls. He met Dalia at the Blue Martini, a trendy nightspot in West Palm Beach, while he was visiting for a long golf weekend (he did continuing business with several area malls). She was with her mother and aunt, and he bought them all drinks. Dalia called him back several days later when he was on his way to the airport, and they began what he characterizes as "a long-distance relationship." At the time, he was separated from his wife and living in the basement of his house in Brookfield, Connecticut, which he refused to leave for reasons of "constructive abandonment," which could impact negatively on his impending divorce and custody issues. Stanley describes Dalia's relationship with his daughter as "very strong," even though his ex-wife stated they didn't get along. (She also thought that Stanley and Dalia were still dating, even at the time of Stanley's deposition, nearly two years after Dalia's arrest.) For a beefy lug in his forties whose family was collapsing in slow motion, an attractive, available woman ten years his junior must have seemed like a ray of Florida sunshine.

Within six to eight months, they moved to Los Angeles. Stanley went out a month early and got set up with lodging and employment, and Dalia followed in a month or so. She "spent a lot of time furniture shopping and things like that," according to Stanley, but their relationship did not survive the unfamiliar surroundings, Stanley's long hours, and the trials of their pronounced age difference, and they called it quits six months later. For several months, they tried to cohabit platonically, sleeping in separate bedrooms, but after Dalia went back to Florida in October to visit her mother, she announced she had met someone and would remain there permanently. (This was also the time frame in which Dalia told Mohamed she had been engaged to a rich architect in New York, an assertion that Stanley denied under oath.)

Stanley denies any knowledge of his ex-girlfriend having worked as an escort, in California or elsewhere, even though her Eyesnatch website is registered to a corporation called Eye, Inc., set up in his name—curiously, at a Miami address. When asked about it in his deposition, Stanley volunteered that, based on his experience as a lifelong bodybuilder, having once avoided surgery on his shoulder through a self-administered regimen of stretching exercises and alternative medicine, it was his dream to open a weight-loss, workout, and health planning facility—say, for those with no health insurance who wished to avoid surgery. Unlike Eyesnatch, with which it shared a syllable, Eye, Inc., was to be a walk-in, bricks-and-mortar operation, sounding more like Dalia's massage center "behind the Carl's, Jr." Stanley expressly denied ever incorporating a business on Dalia's behalf, putting money into a massage business, or having anything to do with her escort service (which, at any rate, he was unaware of). His explanation for incorporating the business in Florida using a Miami law firm was that "you've got year-round nice weather in Florida" and "a lot of elderly."

Although Stanley's contact with Dalia after their separation was by his own account limited, he does claim an enduring friendship with her mother and extended family—particularly Dalia's grandfather, now deceased. (He says that he, Dalia, her mother, and her mother's boyfriend once traveled to Peru.) He did see Dalia once, briefly, on her birthday in October—at the dinner at Tremonte's in Delray Beach where Mike Dippolito met Mike Stanley for the first and only time, which Dippolito characterized as "awkward." Stanley spoke with her for several minutes outside the restaurant and then disappeared. With Dalia unavailable to him, he returned to New York and tried to resume his life there.

And so it remained through the long months of 2009—through Dalia's wedding, her economic travails trying to help her husband get off probation, the freakish electrical storm of drama that enveloped them from February on, the huge amounts of money that cascaded through their lives and bank accounts only to reservoir tantalizingly beyond their reach, her reunion and resumed friendship with Mohamed, about which she was apparently happy enough to buy him a car, and all the rest of it—none of which Stanley was privy to. He was out of the loop all the way up to the first week of July, when Dalia called him to discuss their dog Bella, who needed to have several teeth removed, which Stanley offered to help pay for. She first left him a phone message, and then resumed contact via MetroPCS text message on July 9, very quickly covering the open ground between them.

DALIA: Hey its me cll me bck

STANLEY: Im sure ur little toes look great :)

He seems taken by surprise, awkwardly commenting on her presumed mention of a pedicure, but quickly recovers.

STANLEY: Hey you, i almost fell of my chair that u left me a voice mail . . .:), sorry was on a call

DALIA: Really lol i miss u

STANLEY: Im glad, i miss u

DALIA: Happy to hear that im smiling soulmates

STANLEY: :)!!!!!!

DALIA: Muah

STANLEY:??? What is muah

DALIA: A kiss goofy

STANLEY: Haa ill take it :)

Dalia sent her first text at 12:58 p.m., which Stanley responded to at 3:47 p.m. His last text was at 5:10. They are now officially one hour and twenty-three minutes into their reconciliation. But Dalia is not content with long-distance pleasantries after a nine-month estrangement. Eight minutes later, she texts:

DALIA: I want u

STANLEY: Wow . . . I want u

DALIA: Just know no one has ever made me feel the way u have u always spoiled and romanced me and i loved it

STANLEY: I was truly in love w u, so craxy about u and have never felt that before or after u

DALIA: Thank god for that

The next night, after some ineffectual repartee, Stanley says:

STANLEY: Sorry wish we were together . . . I am thinking of u!

DALIA: Me too I want u and hank lol

In the deposition, I asked Stanley who Hank was. At first, he repeatedly insisted it was a "play name." I then read him the postscript to an e-mail he sent to Dalia on September 7, 2006: "Hank agrees with everything above and he wanted me to say more, but I told him to chill out and I was the boss." After an uncomfortably long pause, he claimed that Hank was his heart. He denied it was a pet name for his penis.

She continues:

DALIA: i want to feel u in me

STANLEY: ouch

DALIA: What lol r u speechless do u want my hot tight body all over u

This shocks him, and he writes at 9:41 p.m.:

STANLEY: Yes but the reality is having u, have a nice nite babe

By the next morning at 9:25 a.m., he seems to have worked through his reticence:

STANLEY: The answer to ur question . . . Would [be] HELL YES

Over the next five days, in roughly a dozen texts a day, they keep this banter going: field-reporting their time at restaurants or in rowboats; debating Frank Mir, a mixed martial artist in whom they seem to share an interest; and Dalia's relentless campaign to convince Stanley to come and visit her. With a breathless, minute-by-minute text message buildup worthy of *The Bachelor*, they finally meet on July 15, moments after 12:34 p.m., at the Marriott on Okeechobee Boulevard, less than a mile from the West Palm Beach Airport. In between, Dalia continues to respond to messages from her escort clients, including one from Wellhung Kevin, during the five-hour window she spends with Stanley, at times scrambling to find girls to send out on short notice. Then, at 5:22 p.m., the text trail picks back up:

DALIA: I love u baby

STANLEY: Infinity plus plus? lol, i love u sweetheart

DALIA: Soulmates so happy i saw u baby

STANLEY: Me too! soulmates

DALIA: Really wish u would have cum in me i wantd to feel u

STANLEY: Ahhhhhhh me to im sooo sorry

DALIA: Lol baby I love u and I only want to fuck u I'll be here waiting
for u u have made me smile and laugh haven't done that in forever

In his deposition, Stanley denied that he and Dalia ever resumed a physical relationship. Meeting at the Marriott coffee shop, he says, he noticed a bruise on the inside of her arm that resembled a handprint. When he pressed her on it, the tale she told was a sordid one.

According to Stanley, Dalia claimed her relationship with her husband had turned abusive. He would grab her, push her, and shove her; when he wasn't being physical he was talking down to her, cursing at her, forcing her to do things she didn't want to do. Mike had a "tainted history"—Stanley balked at my use of the word "fraudulent," although he used it himself later in the interview. He had a criminal background, had done jail time, and had bought their house with a bag of dirty money, essentially laundering it through her bank account. Now that she was immersed in his world, Dalia saw that Mike was returning to his old ways, despite bad blood with his former business partners. He was required to pay them $100,000 in restitution for "skimming money from the business." In fact, merely operating his own business was a violation of his probation. During their brief time together, after Dalia met him at a Starbucks in September and married him in February, there had been numerous instances when police investigated him for dealing drugs, surprise visits from his probation officer, a late-night domestic disturbance call that led Mike to threaten her family. Stanley tried to be a good friend and listen, but she wouldn't go to the police, even when he encouraged her to. She feared for her life.

Now Mike was making her take part in a "reality stunt" designed to gain him instant notoriety: In concert with their actor friend Mohamed and his unnamed contacts inside the Boynton Beach Police Department, Dalia would pretend to solicit a professional hit man to murder her husband; when the ruse inevitably unraveled, they would use the media spike to—well, it was never clear. Books, movies—maybe get their own reality series. Fame is like rising water; it lifts all boats. All based on what was essentially a prank.

"He's, from what I understand, pretty savvy with the Internet," Stanley explained. "Whatever his plan was, I mean, it worked."

So by his own admission, over the next several weeks Stanley began calling various official entities, always anonymously, making complaints against Mike Dippolito, trying to provide proof that he had violated the terms of his probation in the hopes that he would return to prison and this long nightmare would boil off like the morning's dew. At Dalia's behest, Stanley called the Treasury Department and reported that Mike had funds for restitution but refused to comply, had paid cash for his house, and should have his accounts frozen. He repeatedly called both the Justice Department and the IRS, but failed to get through to anyone willing to take an interest. He called the State Attorney who'd prosecuted Mike's fraud case in Broward County, alleging violence in his marriage, only to discover that she was out of the country on a two-week vacation. He called Mike's probation officer with accusations of fraud and drug dealing, possibly of illegal steroids. He even reported that Mike had violated his probation by leaving the county to take Dalia's whole family to the Marlins-Phillies baseball game in Broward County, including her dying grandfather who had never been to a baseball game before, renting them a luxury suite at the stadium to watch the game for $3,000.

Stanley also claimed to have a personal reason for waging his procedural jihad, aside from taking revenge on the man who stole his wife-to-be and rescuing the woman of his dreams from imaginary dragons: when Dalia left California, somehow Stanley's Eye, Inc., corporate documentation inadvertently left with her, and now she claimed Mike was illegally using it for tax purposes.

"My phone calls were general phone calls so the authorities could conduct their investigations as they see fit," claimed Stanley. "I was not calling and making direct and slanderous accusations. I was calling to let them know that they may want to look into this because there may be these potential issues."

Of course, in all his concentrated efforts to derail Mike's celebrity juggernaut and return him to prison for violating the conditions of his probation, Stanley never once thought to pick up the phone and call the FBI, the DEA, the Sheriff's Office, the Producer's Guild, Stone Phillips, or anyone else, to say, "This sociopath plans to hijack world attention with a fake murder plot; that can't be legal."

Stanley claimed he thought nature would take its course: "They would say this is a joke and go from there." I dared to point out that we were now two years into this thing and this was the first we were hearing about it. Stanley became defensive and claimed that his address and phone number was the same as it had always been, and that he was willing to speak to anybody. (Nancy Grace's producers reached out to him after the release of the texts, but he refused to comment.)

There was also no mention of this elaborate hoax in any of Stanley and Dalia's private text messages, even though they didn't display any qualms about discussing even the most intimate or furtive matters. On July 18, after missing Stanley on a lunchtime call, she writes:

> DALIA: Just tried cllg got vm just wantd u to know i love and miss u
> and cant wait to fuck ur hard cock love u im crazy about u

On July 27, after his second daylong junket to see her in Florida, Dalia writes at 8:24 p.m.:

> DALIA: Im so attracted to u lovd fucking u it blew me away i love
> having ur hot cum in me

On July 17 at 8:35 p.m., there appears this exchange:

> DALIA: So how much do you want me
>
> STANLEY: Dalia, i have always wanted u, ir my unicorn . . .
>
> DALIA: What u said was beautiful i startd crying ur the man of my
> dreams my prince charming

On July 24, in anticipation of his imminent arrival, she asks at 5:19 p.m.:

DALIA: What time will u be here i want us to start baby making

And a day later, while apparently standing him up at the Blue Martini, where they first met (he goes to see *The Hangover* instead), she texts at 7:11 p.m.:

DALIA: Soulmates is what we r we r meant to be together do u know i have baby names pickd out i want ur child in me

That's not to mention those moments that might sound collusive or insidious if viewed in the wrong context, such as these, all from July 27, the day after their second illicit rendezvous:

DALIA (1:38 p.m.): The sooner his shit gets fuckd up the better

DALIA (1:55 p.m.): The sooner he gets jammed up the sooner we can be in paradise island baby

DALIA (5:38 p.m.): I love u just want my life w u lets get this mother fucker arrested im so tired of his shit

DALIA (5:50 p.m.): He has some here at the house too but i want to put x pills and coke in the car and xanax

DALIA (7:45 p.m.): Me too lets get this shit handld and well have it all i really hate him and want to c him rot

DALIA (8:32 p.m.): Then lets put his lying ass back in jail

But it turns out Stanley had an explanation for this, too. Along with his domestic threats, incorrigible criminality, deceptive finances, and casual business betrayals, Mike was also a sexual deviant and tyrant. Dalia confided that "he's very sexually demented in nature, and he thinks it's hilarious to fuck with my ex-boyfriend." Since they shared a phone, "Some text messages are going to come from him and some are from me, directed by him. You need to understand they're not real. It's part of this charade, this game that he wants play." Dalia said that Mike had been "arrested for prostitution or excessive credit card use and sex calls." Soon Stanley began receiving inordinately provocative texts from Dalia—gratuitous, sordid declarations that would have been totally out of character for her. Often when he would call the number back, Mike would scream obscenities at him, or there would only be room sounds or music. Once, a strange woman answered and said, "No, Dalia's not here, why don't you talk to me," which he found both amusing and embarrassing, and which quickly devolved into the preliminary stages of phone sex.

By carefully going through all forty-nine pages of Dalia's MetroPCS phone records and having Stanley designate who he thought each text was coming from, I was able to determine the following: Whenever the text messages appear casual or benign, they are from Dalia. When they reveal emotion, but are still platonic, they're also from Dalia. When they are sexual but respectful in tone—"I want you"; "You always spoiled and romanced me and I loved it"—they're most likely from Dalia, but with Mike there directing her. And if it was overtly prurient—"sexting"—it would be Mike in the throes of his particular mania. Quickly triaging his incoming messages, Stanley would merely respond in kind. Through this elaborate and seemingly inscrutable ruse, Mike sought to lure Stanley in, keep him close, and study him, as he would any rival or mark. A secondary benefit of Stanley's system is that it completely exonerates him of illegal behavior.

This is most problematic in the final days leading up to the planned murder. On Friday, July 31, at 2:16 p.m., Dalia reports:

DALIA: Did the tranfr but he said because were married i cant sell it
    w out his signature even though its in my name

This sends her into an apparent spiral: throughout the afternoon and evening, she sends Stanley a number of fraught, increasingly desperate messages:

DALIA (3:19 p.m.): I want my life w u rite now wed be gettn our party weekend startd

DALIA (7:01 p.m.): I love u ur my world help me figure this out love of my life we have alnt of catchn up to do

DALIA (7:04 p.m.): Im so unhappy and empty w out u i cant stand being here u should be here not him

DALIA (9:27 p.m.): I cant stop crying

DALIA (9:34 p.m.): Im upstairs and i cant stop im falling apart w out u

DALIA (9:42 p.m.): I love u im such a mess rite now i lockd mysf up here

This is the day she tried to steal Mohamed's gun, inadvertently sending him to the police. Stanley appears increasingly distraught at his inability to console her.

STANLEY: . . . need to cleen up ur mess baby life is waiting

The next morning at 10:53 a.m., after a phone call between them, Stanley declares:

STANLEY: Baby I was blown away, stars are lining up for us love!!!!

That evening at 6 p.m., after Dalia has met with Mohamed to arrange for a hit man—and after Dalia and Stanley have spoken by phone before and after that meeting—there appears a brief text exchange between them in faux gangster-speak, with a kind of forced merriment grating at the edges:

DALIA: Wud up dawg lol does that sound impersonal

STANLEY: Yo yo chillin, tierd heading to ct, lol

DALIA: Tell yo peeps holla lol

Then just fifteen minutes later, at 6:21 p.m., comes the following:

STANLEY: Hey thanks for the service my confidence is so much better and I think I may start seeing somebody very serious I talk to girls so much better now :)

DALIA: No problem im glad the roleplaying has helpd u good luck and stay in touch

STANLEY: Thank you I feel more comfortable expressing myself now

Despite Stanley's elaborate explanation of the role-playing protocols governing these text messages, with Mike Dippolito the unseen puppet-master governing everything for his sexual gratification, this appears to be a new category of messages between them: as part of her escort outreach services, Dalia has been texting with Stanley—including intimately—to build his confidence and bolster his self-esteem. Any implied intimacy between them, even emotional intimacy, is merely situational and contractual ("good luck and stay in touch"). Dalia hasn't been sexting with Stanley; she hasn't even been pretending to sext with him—she's been giving him sexting lessons.

Michael Stanley's deposition lasted roughly nine hours. At one point near the middle, I had to excuse myself and leave the room to keep from laughing. I told Salnick during one of our breaks, "I *hope* you put him on the stand—I'll have him up there for days." By the end, Salnick looked absolutely defeated. Perhaps he had thought Stanley was going to be his star witness. But once I had the witness locked into these answers under oath, if he diverged from them during the trial, he would be impeached with his prior statement. Everything Stanley testified to was based on what Dalia told him—he had no independent knowledge of anything. The legal term for this is hearsay—an out-of-court statement repeated in court and represented as the truth. If reproduced during the trial, it would be self-serving hearsay on Dalia's behalf in its most obvious form. I ended the deposition by asking him if he knew what perjury was. He had come to Florida voluntarily for this deposition, only to expose himself to possible criminal prosecution. Such is the power of love.

And the law says a lawyer cannot knowingly put on perjured testimony; if a witness plans to perjure himself, you are forbidden to ask them questions, leaving them to testify in the narrative. Meaning Salnick would be hard-pressed to carry forward with this. If these were Stanley's answers— and they were clearly the answers Dalia wanted him to give, since she was the only one who stood to benefit from them—I think he was worthless as a witness the second he sat down across from me. My belief is that this deposition knocked Michael Stanley off the playing field, and it kicked a leg out from underneath the defense they had planned.

In the end, I chose not to call Michael Stanley to the stand. My focus was on proving Dalia guilty of the crime of Solicitation to Commit First-Degree Murder with a Firearm. Although he may have been integral to the motive behind it, I never saw any direct evidence that Stanley was involved in that crime, and in fact, when Dalia suggested he call the Treasury Department and pretend to be Mike in order to trip him up, Stanley refused to commit fraud. The best I had was circumstantial evidence linking him to efforts to frame the victim, or possibly misrepresenting himself on the phone. I felt at this point his presence would only make the trial more of a circus than it already was.

Stanley denied that Dalia had coached him or influenced his answers in any way. "Dalia is very sensitive about the case, so we don't speak about it," he said. He visited her after the arrest and sent flowers, and freely admits he gave Randa several thousand dollars that she would logically have applied to Dalia's bond. "Her mother is going through a trying time right now and she needs the support of her friends," he says. "I'm happy to help her."

Stanley's plight brings to mind Charles Dickens's *A Christmas Carol*. If Mohamed Shihadeh is the Ghost of Dalia Past, the one who saw through her opportunism and sexual bravado from the outset and thought she would stop somewhere short of the edge, until she didn't; and Mike is the Ghost of Dalia Present, someone who even through the hard rains of adversity believed he had found his destined love, and is now paying the price; then

Michael Stanley is the Ghost of Dalia Future, who in spite of all logic and proportion to the contrary, still believes he'll be the one to take the prize home from the fair. I fear he is in for a rude awakening.

On the same day as the Michael Stanley deposition—April 8, 2011—the judge in the case, Judge Jeffrey Colbath, granted my Motion to Introduce Evidence of Prior Bad Acts as Inextricably Intertwined Evidence with one exception. I was not allowed to talk about Dalia's fake pregnancy in any capacity. In most trials, previous criminal acts, or uncharged bad acts are not admissible as evidence of a crime charged. Otherwise, every accused repeat offender might automatically be found guilty just based on their history—if they did it before they would do it again, or that they are a dishonorable person. That would be prejudicial to a criminal defendant. So we as prosecutors work within the parameters that all cases should be tried on their own merit, and plan our strategy accordingly. But sometimes one's past actions are necessary to explain a motive, provide context, or otherwise inform the crime at hand. In the state of Florida, you can introduce evidence of prior bad acts in certain situations, such as if it's intertwined, or inseparable from the crime charged. With Dalia, calling or directing others to call the IRS, Treasury Department, Inspector General's Office, or Mike's probation officer, trying to plant evidence on him, engaging the Buck Wild gang, stealing a gun, serving him antifreeze, and the rest of it, while certainly prejudicial, were necessary simply to make sense of her crime. Otherwise I would be trying the case in a vacuum.

In Dalia's case, she had a tendency to become inextricably intertwined with everyone and everything around her.

CHAPTER 7

The Three Ps

The easiest way to define your defendant is to define your victim. If a jury can put itself in the victim's place, then a prosecutor has a much better chance at conviction. But if the victim is a lowlife, a scumbag—"no angel," as the prosecution often tries to spin it—then the defendant just moved a whole lot closer toward grabbing the brass ring of reasonable doubt. I knew this and Defense Attorney Michael Salnick knew this (the fourth Mike in Dalia's inner circle, for those keeping score). So before I settled on a courtroom strategy, I needed to meet with Mike Dippolito and see what I was dealing with. Plus, I knew firsthand that anyone who heard Mike's story was alternately mystified about the money and outraged by how he had been treated.

I met with Mike Dippolito at the State Attorney's Office within days of getting the case. All I knew about him on paper was that he was a convicted felon, a shyster, and a con artist who was still on probation and owed roughly $200,000 in restitution for money he had taken in some sort of boiler-room foreign-exchange fraud. All of this represented baggage, the last thing you want in a key witness, much less a victim. Mike had done two years in state prison—it wasn't really enough money for the Feds to take an interest in—and I didn't pull his case file ahead of time, in the interest of seeing him through fresh eyes, as a jury would.

I walked downstairs to find a stocky, spiky-haired Philly-born Italian whose tight T-shirt accentuated a muscular frame and the tribal tattoos entwined on his biceps. Rather than ask a lot of pointed questions to see how he would stand up under pressure, I just had him tell me his story, start to finish. Some parts, I had him tell me two or three times, slightly reframing my question so I could see how his answers lined up. My goal was to catch him in a lie, or at least to highlight the inconsistencies. As a prosecutor, I naturally assume everyone is lying to me; that may seem cynical, but it saves me a lot of time. Everyone has secrets, and I would prefer not to discover his on the witness stand.

I told him the best way he could help me was to be completely truthful, regardless of what he thought the consequences might be. I said, "Listen, I invited you here to speak to me but now that you are here I'm basically forcing you to give me all of this information. So I promise not to use it against you. I'm not going to turn around and report it to your probation officer." There is no prosecutor-witness privilege analogous to the attorney-client privilege, but since I was acting as Mike's advocate in the service of justice, I had to pretend for the moment that there was. I knew from his police statement how he and Dalia had met, and I was encouraged that he volunteered this fact himself. After hearing Mike's story (and confirming it from the court record), I understood that his crime was neither smart nor complex: he basically sold foreign currency by phone to credulous investors and then pocketed the money. Fraud implies a certain level of ingenuity and cunning to which his crimes failed to rise. As long as stupidity continues to be legal, about the best you could call it was theft enhanced by sheer audacity. His explanation—by no means a justification or excuse—was that he was so high he basically didn't care. The bank account he used was in his name; he never changed his phone number. It was like the first half of a Ponzi scheme: take everyone's money, but forget to pay some people back.

Opening up did not come naturally to Mike. He had the opposite of the con man's easygoing confidence and glib delivery. Here was a guy whose parents were both drug addicts, the grandparents who raised him were functioning alcoholics, he took his first drink at the age of eight, and most of his longtime friends were from recovery groups. The legal system, of which I was his latest appointed contact, had sentenced him to court-ordered supervision for three *decades*, a punishment that would not have seemed out of place in *Les Miserables*, and a succession of lawyers had taken his money with precious little to show in return. Now the woman who had methodically made herself his true love and soul mate had tried to have him killed. This is not a life trajectory that engenders trust. Not to mention that testifying honestly could send him back to prison. And since he was on probation out of Broward County, one county over from the State Attorney's office in Palm Beach County, I had no say on how they handled it. All I could do was document the theft of the restitution money and bring it to their attention.

For the record, I can tell you that hearing his story for the first time, I was no less baffled than any other law enforcement professional who was convinced they'd heard it all. He had to tell me three times, and I still had him write it down so I could pass it along to the detectives for their report. But I discovered fairly early on that as unbelievable as his story seemed, the parts that I could verify all checked out. Other police departments weighed in to confirm his version of the events in Manalapan, West Palm Beach, and Palm Beach Gardens, and all the forensic information I could marshal, either about Dalia's circumstances or his own, matched the story he told me.

The other insight I gleaned from speaking with Mike in person was that he was a creature of habit—literally. You don't experience long-term drug addiction without accepting the primacy of routine. Often, the solution is to lose the drugs and focus on habit. When I met him, Mike was ten years sober, minus a few bumps in the road, and he regimented his life in excruciating detail: up at four thirty, to the gym by five, work out for exactly an hour. It was this obsessive nature that Dalia exploited, and which she later characterized to anyone who would listen as Mike's controlling, threatening nature. By putting guardrails on his day, Mike lessened the chances that he would inadvertently pitch headlong into shadow, where most of his troubles awaited. The only problem is, once you're outside your comfort zone—say, if your wife goes out of town and you wander onto an escort site with an evening to kill, or if the old obsession becomes a new one, like getting off probation—it clouds your reason and dismantles your judgment. All I had to do was listen to that jailhouse call where Dalia tried to manipulate Mike into taking her side against the police and, ultimately, himself. Their whole history was in that phone call, as was his before he ever met her. Mike was a runaway train, something Dalia could have spotted before they ever left the station, as well as the perfect victim on whom to practice her dark magic.

She probably thought he had more money than he did, the way he spent it like a drunken sailor, but that just meant she was operating on a shorter time line. She'd have to have sex with him and make him believe it, but that wasn't a problem: her real estate license aside, having sex for money was the only job she'd ever had. I think her path was laid out for her the moment she first laid eyes on him—a few months' work, topple the dominoes, divorce him while he's in prison, and she'd have his house, his cars, his bank account, and the bragging rights on a game brilliantly played. It would be the easiest money she ever made.

Later on, when we were e-mailing about some court documents, Mike wrote, "Liz, I know you are doing a lot of work for me. Thanks. Just please get this girl what she should get. She killed me without killing me, with all the probation on me still, and fighting me for [my] house and just basically playing mind games with me for our whole marriage."

Like most people in my position, I consider myself a pretty good judge of character. I started out as a victims' advocate. Watching the way Mike laid it all out, his hangdog, blindsided delivery adding to the accretion of outrage that even the casual listener couldn't help but share with him, I thought we were going to do fine. I told him, "You will have good days and bad days throughout this process. Just try to focus on the positive and rest assured I am doing everything that I can to hold her accountable and bring her to justice."

Realizing the kind of impression he would make on the jury, I made the somewhat controversial decision to lead with Mike as my opening witness. To everyone else, Mike looked exactly as he had to me at first—like someone we needed to distance ourselves from. But that's exactly what I was doing. This showed that we had nothing to hide. Mike's history was a matter of public record, and Salnick was a resourceful, capable adversary; it was coming into evidence with my blessing or without it. Mike takes full responsibility for what he's done and has paid his debt to society—or is trying to, if he could get his money back. I had spent enough time with him to know that he could take it. I explained to him that it was better to get the information out on direct examination and then to get hammered on cross-examination, and he got a little taste of what it would be like going up against Salnick in the deposition. He understood what he was up against. With so much of the case on surveillance video, Salnick's only real shot was to beat on Mike Dippolito for fifteen rounds and hope a cut opened up and his credibility leaked out. And the longer Salnick kept Mike in the hot seat, the more he helped my case, since the greater risk he ran was looking like a bully. In my experience, that's the one thing a jury will not tolerate.

The trial date was set for April 25, 2011. As with all trials, both the prosecution and the defense filed pretrial motions for the judge to rule on, so we could know what would be admissible as evidence and what would not. The judge assigned to the case was Judge Jeffrey Colbath. I had practiced in front of him in 1999 as a relatively new Assistant State Attorney in Domestic Violence Court, and in my experience he was scrupulously fair. He's known for his sense of humor, and usually opens each day of court with a word of the day or "this day in history" reading, but I've seen him put attorneys in their place when need be. He's also not afraid to hand out a tough sentence.

In addition to the State's Motion to Introduce Evidence of Prior Bad Acts as Inextricably Intertwined Evidence described in the last chapter, I filed a Motion in Limine to prevent the defense from making mention of certain topics in the presence of the jury without first obtaining permission from the court. This was a complicated case, in that it had a lot of moving parts and a lot of information the jury had to hold in its head at one time. Any red herring or rogue elephant thrown into the mix could quickly derail the proceedings. So I put a lot of work into it ahead of time to make sure there were no issues that would unfairly prejudice the jurors against the State. I didn't want the defense bringing up any issues that were irrelevant or immaterial to the case. The guiding principle was "you can't unring the bell."

The hours of depositions Salnick took gave me a pretty good indication of the issues he might try to focus on in the trial, so I tried to plan accordingly. I sought to bar any discussion of events surrounding several waivers Dalia signed to appear in an episode of *COPS*, which apparently figured into the defense strategy, or of a related investigation into Sergeant Paul Sheridan by Internal Affairs on his part in obtaining Dalia's signature for the producers. My position was that anything Dalia did after her arrest had no bearing on her guilt or innocence. I sought to exclude any mention of Mike's prior drug use unless they could show it could have altered his memory and perception of events. (Although I brought it up during Mike's testimony, this allowed me to control how the subject was introduced.) I asked that there be no mention of Mike soliciting prostitutes in the past, even though he had admitted to as much with Dalia. I sought to prevent any claims that the defendant suffered from Battered Woman Syndrome, since as provided by the Florida Rules of Criminal Procedure, the name of no such expert witness had been provided by the defense thirty days prior to trial.

I wanted there to be no allegations that Mike had laundered money, that the money earmarked for his restitution came from illegal means, or that he had any obligation to pay the entire amount of restitution if he had the means to do so. I asked that there be no mention of any paternity suit filed against Mike. (A week after those initial surveillance tapes were released to the media, one of Mike's former lovers resurfaced with an eleven-year-old son she claimed was Mike's. After paternity tests proved conclusive, he accepted this unintended consequence of fame and now pays child support.)

I requested there be no mention of Dalia's mental health (outside of an insanity plea, which she had not alleged and which at any rate would require an expert witness), her age (which could incite sympathy), any penalty that she could receive if convicted (ditto), her lack of prior arrests, her claims of innocence, proof of prior good conduct, any self-serving hearsay statements made by the defendant to any person—especially the testimony of Michael Stanley regarding alleged statements made by the defendant, since his entire testimony was inadmissible pursuant to the rules of evidence— and any statements by the defendant that would indicate remorse (not that I was aware of any).

I also wanted to preclude mention of any prior plea offer or conversations regarding a possible settlement in the case. Salnick had approached me early on and suggested that his client shouldn't do more than a year. I didn't laugh in his face exactly, but I did indicate we weren't interested in a plea bargain. Then, in Mike's deposition, when Salnick asked him what he wanted to happen in this case, Mike said, "[I]f she fixed my mess, they could let her go. I'm fine with that . . . I don't care if they send Dalia on a trip to Vegas and let her go. All that does nothing for me. I wouldn't gain nothing by it." When Salnick sought to follow up, I said in an e-mail that if Dalia were to accept responsibility for her actions, pay Mike back the money she stole from him, relinquish any rights that she has in the house, and grant him a divorce, I would bring that information to the State Attorney. But until such time as the money was in Salnick's trust account (and I wasn't holding my breath), the whole thing was speculative. I didn't want him bringing this up at trial to persuade the jury that Mike didn't care whether Dalia was convicted or not. In a hearing several weeks before the trial started, Salnick asked the judge if he would entertain what is known as a pre-plea inquiry. This is where a defendant asks the court to commit to what sentence they would receive if they were to plead guilty to the crime. Both sides proffer what they believe the evidence would show at trial, and the defendant presents any mitigating information. A lot of judges won't do it because they don't want to be in the business of negotiating with the defendant. Of course, Dalia could just have pled guilty and received the sentence she was due, but she chose not to do that. Judge Colbath refused to entertain a pre-plea inquiry.

Finally, I wanted there to be no extralegal ploys or procedures to circumvent the established evidence: no random comments by any witness on anyone's credibility, psychiatric history, or character; no mention of witnesses who didn't testify, evidence that wasn't presented, experts that weren't qualified or coconspirators who remained uncharged; and no use of jury pardons (basically asking the jury to walk the defendant in spite of the evidence because they disagree with the law or are sympathetic to her plight), no "voluntariness" defense (claiming that the defendant was coerced to act by another party), and no hypothetical questions *in voir dire* (jury selection) that might contaminate the jury through misdirection.

Some of this may have been to send a strong message that just because I felt confident in my evidence, it didn't mean I wasn't going to present an aggressive case. Salnick agreed to many of these motions, since the law supported each issue. The rest were granted by the court.

I was also presented with a hurdle I had not anticipated that took a bit of legal maneuvering to get around. I had planned to call to the stand Todd Surber, the lawyer who executed the quitclaim deed to transfer the house into Dalia's name the week before she was arrested. Although this was a simple clerical procedure, I thought it important to highlight it for the jury's benefit, preferably linked to someone besides Mike. But when I contacted Surber at Independence Title to get copies of the documentation and arrange for his deposition, his response was, "I'm sorry, that's attorney-client privilege." Since he had technically represented both Mike and Dalia in the transaction, he didn't think it appropriate that he answer any questions, much less testify in court against either one of them. Mike could always waive his right to attorney-client privilege, and in fact did so in the case of Michael Entin, the other attorney he had met with in this case. But that wouldn't help with Dalia, who also enjoyed attorney-client privilege with Surber. So I filed a motion to override attorney-client privilege based on the crime-fraud exception. This says that there is no such privilege when the services sought or obtained constitute fraud. A lawyer can advise his client on the consequences of committing a crime; he cannot participate in a crime himself. Under the statute, it was immaterial whether Surber knew this to be a crime at the time fraud was committed, which he most certainly did not; it only mattered that the client knew their actions constituted fraud.

The motion necessitated a separate evidentiary hearing to establish Dalia's intent. The standard of proof was whether she could show with a preponderance of the evidence—meaning just enough evidence to make it more likely than not that the fact that what we are seeking to prove is true—that there was a reasonable explanation for her conduct. This effectively put Dalia in a position where the only way she could explain her actions was to take the stand, and I knew Salnick would never allow that to happen. Once she took the stand, I could ask her practically anything I wanted related to the alleged fraud, which would have been an entire trial in itself. Instead, I argued that there was no attorney-client privilege here, but even if there was, Dalia's only reason to transfer the property into her name was to defraud her husband.

I cited her text messages to Michael Stanley: "The sooner his shit gets fucked up the better," and afterward, "Did the transfer, but he said because we're married I can't sell it without his signature, even though it's in my name."

Mike had told me this was the advice he'd gotten from Surber, so I called him as a witness at the hearing to say as much. Since there was no evidence to contradict him (Surber wouldn't testify until made to do so; Dalia knew better), the judge ruled the quitclaim deed had been created for fraudulent purposes, attorney-client privilege was overridden (if it even existed—he never said), and Surber could be deposed and testify at the trial.

Salnick also filed a number of motions of his own. Soon after Dalia was arrested, he claimed that a leather-bound journal seized during the execution of a search warrant at her mother's house was protected under attorney-client privilege. Salnick claimed that in it, Dalia had taken three pages of notes during their initial meeting that were important to their defense. The motion was granted, the pages were photocopied and placed in a court file under seal, and the notebook was returned to the defendant. Salnick filed a motion to compel Mike to turn over his bank records and business and personal tax returns, as well as his own Motion in Limine to prevent the prosecution from referring to the defendant as an escort, prostitute, or call girl, which was granted, even though the subject was now a matter of public record.

In the end, there were three major topics that I did not address at trial, which I labeled the Three Ps and instructed witnesses not to mention: Prostitution, Poison, and Pregnancy. Both Dalia's alleged prostitution and her claimed pregnancy were off the table due to the judge's rulings. On the issue of Dalia and the poisoned iced tea, I consulted a doctor and did a lot of research online, and the potential side effects experienced by someone who has been poisoned with antifreeze were not consistent. Mike claimed in an early police interview and in his discussions with me that he had developed mouth ulcers afterward and suffered from diarrhea for two weeks straight, but the research was inconclusive as to whether these were recognized symptoms. The court had ruled it admissible as one of Dalia's many Prior Bad Acts, and I had multiple witnesses offering circumstantial evidence, but in the end, I felt that it might offer her an appellate escape hatch if she could convince a higher court my claim was a stretch. The prostitution and the poison both figured heavily in press accounts, and were widely discussed outside the courtroom. As far as I know, Dalia's aspirational pregnancy has remained a secret until now.

In Florida, a capital crime, which this was not, merits a twelve-person jury. All other cases, including first-degree felonies like the one Dalia was accused of, are decided by a jury of six. As a prosecutor, I've seen juries do a lot of crazy things, and as far as defenses go, from the hints I was picking up from Salnick, this would be among the wildest I had ever personally witnessed. My biggest concern in selecting a jury was that any thinking person was already inundated with the facts of the case and would be tempted to disqualify themselves. TV outlets used any pretext to rehash the case history and rerun the videos, and between the *Palm Beach Post*, the *Sun-Sentinel, Broward and Palm Beach New Times*, and *Nancy Grace*, it was a constant drumbeat leading up to the trial. This was the single biggest case to hit the Palm Beach County Courthouse since the William Kennedy Smith rape trial in the early nineties, and that was before the omnipresence of the Internet.

Consequently, Salnick filed motions requiring a bigger-than-usual jury pool—sixty instead of the usual forty—based on our pretrial publicity, and a specialized *voir dire* protocol to guard against the "media blitzkrieg" presenting what he termed "the prosecution's version of the case."

This included Mike's appearance on *The Today Show*, which he says he only did to get the rest of the media to stop calling him. I disagreed that we were the source of any of this pretrial publicity, since reporters were simply harvesting morsels from pretrial motions on both sides, which is what reporters do. But I did agree that we needed a modified voir dire process in this case. Traditionally, the lawyer singles out a potential juror from the panel (those citizens of voting age under consideration) and asks specialized questions to determine that individual's sympathy or susceptibility to his case. If those questions include sensational aspects of the case outside the purview of the court, then they've just tainted the jury pool. Perhaps it would make more sense to question jurors individually at the bench, where the judge has a button labeled "white noise," or one at a time in the jury room. But the judge denied Salnick's motion for individual voir dire.

Jury selection is my least favorite thing to do in a trial. People say I'm good at it, since I can usually talk to anyone and make them feel comfortable. But if trying a case is surveying the evidence, selecting that which is most conducive to your argument, and controlling the story, then jury selection is the place where you have the least control. It's not just that juries are automatically a tough audience, it's that you have to explain to them how to be an audience, since very few of them have ever done it before. I've learned over the years that jurors will lie to you: they'll either tell you what they think you want to hear, or else they'll lie to get out of jury service. Either way, you have to shepherd them toward what you need from them. You have a very short period of time to make a judgment about a person based on limited information and interaction; you have to study their body language while taking into account their life experiences, employment history, family situation, and expressed opinions to determine whether they're right for your case. I want to ask the right questions and explain the legal principles I need to, but mainly I want to let them do most of the talking. The more they talk, the more I learn.

So I start by telling them I'm simply looking for someone who is fair and impartial. It's not a contest, so they shouldn't take it personally if they're not selected. Not everyone is right for every case: if this was a DUI case and their sister had been killed by a drunk driver, that wouldn't be fair to the defendant for them to be placed on the jury because of their obvious feeling about DUI drivers. I want people who are able to make decisions. Someone's life or liberty hangs in the balance, and a lot of people can't pull the trigger. So with women, I ask, How easy is it for you to decide what dress to buy? Do they make their purchase and then continue looking in other stores or do they buy what they like and never look back? Or for guys: When you go out to a restaurant, how long does it take you to decide what to eat? Do you change your mind when you hear other people at the table order? The analogies may be trite, but it humanizes the question, and it gives me a snapshot of them as a person. I need a person who can make an informed decision and stick with it.

I also have to deal with what I call the CSI Effect. So many people are familiar with the legal system through its portrayal in courtroom dramas, especially on television with the latter-day procedural dramas that rely heavily on forensic science. They're primed for high drama, courtroom reveals, and magic-bullet DNA evidence, and if they don't get it, they're disappointed. It's something you actually have to address in the courtroom. For instance, I had them fingerprint the money that Dalia is seen giving to Mohamed on tape to pay the alleged hit man. My lab techs told me it was a waste of time, since fingerprints rarely register on money, but again, I didn't want the defense bringing it up and making a nonissue into an issue. It also pointed up the difference between reality and what you see on TV, no matter how skilled the professionals have become at confusing the two, which helped me address the defense strategy.

For the Dalia Dippolito jury, I needed to know if anyone was offended by graphic language, because they were going to hear a lot of it on tape. I asked them if they could rely solely on the evidence presented in the courtroom and refrain from speculating about inadmissible testimony or evidence. I didn't want them getting frustrated whenever I objected to a particular line of inquiry. Could they believe testimony from a witness who was unlikable, or one who had lived a less than admirable life? Could they believe the testimony of a convicted felon, or believe that he could be the victim of a crime? Would they accept the testimony of an admitted drug addict? This was all designed to head off attacks on a witness's credibility. For his part, Salnick spent a great deal of time finding out what reality shows the jurors and their families watched.

In the end, I felt like I got the jury I needed. I wanted as few men as possible. You could argue that no one would be more sympathetic to Mike as a victim, or more appalled at his wife from hell, than a man. But as far as I could tell, Dalia had successfully manipulated every man she'd ever met. I didn't want the spectacle of her batting those giant palm-frond eyelashes at the jury box and having my jurors keeling over with the vapors. Of the six, four were women. (One of them was the wife of a chief of police I knew. I think Salnick kept her on the jury because she said *Dancing with the Stars* was her favorite show.) And one of the two men was a Marine, which is as close to law and order as you can reasonably get.

The trial lasted two weeks, with a week off in between. Here is how I began my opening statement: "I know what you're thinking: 'What a cute little girl.' But I'm not. I'm a lot tougher than I look."

I could see confusion in the jury's eyes. Was I talking about myself?

"That's what the defendant—Dalia Dippolito—said to the undercover police officer from the Boynton Beach Police Department on August 3 of 2009. She meets undercover agent Widy Jean because she wants to kill her husband, Mike Dippolito. He asks her, 'Are you sure you want to kill him?' Without hesitation, as if she had ice running through her veins, she says, 'There's no changing. I'm determined already. I'm positive. I'm 5,000 percent sure. When I say I'm gonna do something, I'm gonna do it.' And then she laughed. She laughed when agent Widy Jean asked, 'Is this someone you're married to?' She laughed because she'd been married for exactly six

Dalia Dippolito entering the courtroom.

months. She laughed because she was good at manipulating her husband, Mike Dippolito, and he had no idea of what she had planned. She laughed because she thought she could fool him, and she thought she could fool everyone else and she could get away with having him murdered."

I could sense the momentary fear receding, this awkward jolt I'd created in them, like a sharp poke in the chest. By allaying that fear, answering the unasked question, I set the jury on solid ground—a path they could walk in confidence all the way to the end of the trial. And I felt like they never left me. I walked them through the evidence, using an aerial photograph that showed all our locations within a three-mile radius, a map that subconsciously connected the characters, their motives, and their fate like a spider's silken threads. I noted Mohamed's unlikely bout of conscience, and how it peeled back this privileged view on the police department's rapid response, the videotaped evidence, bags of cash and jewelry, Dalia's big scene, the big reveal at the police station, the first blooms of her alibi, the text record, and all the rest of it. I also tried to frame in subtext what I thought would be the jury's biggest question: How could Mike Dippolito have fallen for all of this? How is that even possible?

My answer, which I would present during the trial, was simple: Mike. Mike in all his contradictions—the nice guy and the ex-con; the go-along, get-along guileless patsy; and the obsessive, hyper-motivated Internet hustler who brought in millions—legally, well after he'd done his time. Mike, warts and all. And the longer Salnick kept him on the stand, the more he was forced to withstand the cold hard glare of the justice system, then the more it became a simple calculation of the odds. I was betting that if you put Mike and Dalia head to head, a jury would find Mike the more credible of the two. After all, isn't that what reality TV is all about? It lets the audience decide who wins and who loses, who's good and who's evil, who's telling the truth and who's lying through their carnivore's teeth and claws. All I had to do was get out of the way.

In contrast, Michael Salnick's opening statement finally gave us a first peek at this intriguing defense strategy we had been getting wisps and glimmers of in the months leading up to the trial. Here is how he began:

"We live in a world where the media has proven time and time again that it is used by people from all walks of life as a means to an end. We live in a world where the line between the reality of TV and people's real lives get blurred. We live in a world where people seeking their fifteen minutes of fame lose all sense of judgment and common sense. The power that people give to the media, no matter who these people are, can have an impact on how they live their lives. And in this case, the evidence will show that people tried to use the media to hopefully gain exposure and that brief moment of fame that they can turn into opportunity and money.

"The evidence will show that Mike Dippolito enjoyed watching reality TV. Mike will tell you that he watches *Jersey Shore*, that he finds it amazing—*amazing*—that people make money doing this. But he thinks it's cool. He was a fan of the show *Cheaters*. Now that's the show where one person in a relationship suspects the other of infidelity, and the show basically investigates the suspicion. The show plants a hidden camera and stalks the suspected partner until there's enough footage for the confrontation episode. The cameras roll, and they roll to catch the emotion and the drama that springs from the confrontation. Michael claims to have actually purchased for his wife, Dalia, a boxed set of all the episodes of *Cheaters*. It also came with a tank top with the logo of the show on it for her to wear.

"Now, the evidence will show that for many, reality TV shows depict the worst of our society: They're superficial. They're artificial. And they're filled with attention-getting hokey drama. For others, reality TV has become a way to launch a center-stage career. Reality TV has evolved from letting real life play out in front of the camera to a meticulously produced program packaged to hold the viewer's attention. The evidence will show that reality TV is not as real as it's portrayed to the public. Producers sometimes engineer situations to activate the desired reactions from the actors, who are often carefully chosen through casting calls. Sometimes people just act as they go through what they believe to be a reality TV moment. Producers pore over footage, splicing it together to create the most attention-grabbing entertainment episodes. Almost anybody can go to a website and read about how to make a reality TV show. The trick is to come up with a unique idea that will be picked up by a real producer and a real production team. The evidence will show that when Dalia Dippolito was younger, she was actually an extra on a reality TV show. It was called *Jamie Kennedy's Experiment* and ironically, the episode in which she was an extra involved a fake hit on someone. The evidence will show that reality TV often glorifies what we call bad behavior that appeals to the gullibility of people. The evidence will show that the plot of the contract killing of Mike Dippolito was never real. It was a stunt, a hoax, a ruse—a plan that Mike Dippolito, whether he'll admit it or not, hoped to capture the attention of someone in reality TV. And while he'll never tell you this, the evidence will show you that his motives were very clear.

"The evidence will also show that as it so happens, one of the original and possibly the oldest reality shows on television is also involved in this case. The TV show *COPS* was coincidentally in South Florida to ride with the Boynton Beach Police Department during the week that Miss Dippolito was arrested."

He goes on to link the incidents at Manalapan and CityPlace, the "cloak-and-dagger-type note that was left on his windshield," with "the liposuction, the orthodontic braces, the expensive clothing, a Porsche, a Corvette, trips to the tanning salon, lots of cash, and a beautiful young wife" to prove "an orchestrated stunt to get Mike Dippolito in front of the cameras."

"He'd come up with this story and plan for reality TV, which was absolutely crazy," said Salnick. "She thought this was ridiculous, but maybe as a way to stop him, attempting to violate his probation might put an end to what Mike wanted to do. She was scared, and she didn't know what to do." By denigrating what was essentially his own defense strategy and then attributing it to Mike, he was using its sheer unlikelihood as his strongest selling point. The more outrageous the idea, the faultier its logic, then the crazier Mike was, and the more likely his guilt.

That must have appealed to Dalia, the long-shot gambler. She must have liked these odds, since they defied reality even as you were staring straight at it. It's the same ploy she used on Mike in her jailhouse call: "You know me!" Who are you gonna believe? And because it gave her an unobstructed shot at the jackpot—the house, the money, all the possessions, and the biggest score of all: walking out of the courtroom, free and clear, past the bailiff and the TV crews and her assembled fans.

One hand, heads up, all in.

Bring it on.

CHAPTER 8

Reap the Whirlwind

So I put Mike Dippolito on the stand.

My main goal was to portray Dalia as the mastermind of everything—the missing key in explaining all of these inexplicable events in Mike's cloistered world, culminating in his narrowly averted death and transition to a more circumspect way of life. For Dalia to emerge as the victim, they would have to redefine Mike as the ringmaster, the mad scientist of this elaborate social experiment whose ultimate payoff was still unclear two years later. I didn't know how the defense planned to get there, but I instinctively felt that the jury wouldn't go with them if they could see Mike the way I saw him. So I put him up and I let him talk.

Mike gave us a snapshot of his life now: Selling construction supplies online, diamond blades that would cut through cement blocks. How he filed for divorce a week after his wife's arrest (a process that would continue until several months after the end of the trial). The details of his previous marriage, to a loyal girlfriend who had stayed with him all during his time away, and the compounded guilt he felt for ending their life together so suddenly. And the flip side of that coin—his meeting and marrying Dalia, this whirlwind that dropped out of the sky into his highly structured existence and blew everything that wasn't battened down to the outer edges.

Here's Mike on his marriage to Dalia:

It was exciting. I had fun with Dalia; it was interesting, we got along well, seemed to share the same interests in things . . . I thought we had

a good marriage. We had some issues, but I was in love with my wife,
I married her and I wanted a future with her.

In plodding detail, I walked him through all of those issues I knew
Salnick was sharpening his knives to dissect: Mike's criminal history, time
in prison, dysfunctional childhood, baroque drug legacy, stints in rehab,
flouting the terms of his probation, the cache of money he had squirreled
away, his health problems, superficial self-improvements, profligate spending, flashy trappings, and all the rest of it. If it was embarrassing and potentially character-destroying, we covered it, hour upon hour, through the rest
of that first day and the morning of the second.

The monotony would be broken up by objections from Salnick, which
would often require a sidebar at the judge's bench. These were usually about
the admissibility of evidence or to argue some point of law. As we got further into Salnick's cross of Mike and later Mohamed, Judge Colbath grew
increasingly annoyed at the repetitive nature of the cross-examination. But
given that the trial could easily come down to what the judge allowed the
jury to hear, there were relatively few objections on either side. Although

©The Palm Beach Post/ZUMAPress.com

Mike Dippolito being cross-examined by Defense Attorney
Michael Salnick.

it often seemed like we were mortal enemies in the courtroom, we actually had a very smooth working relationship. At one early hearing, Salnick told Colbath that if we got along any better we could serve as co-counsels. Salnick's defense wouldn't have made any sense without his reputation as an intense, accomplished trial attorney. That's what kept everyone on their toes—this ingenious strategy and wondering what he knew that we didn't.

According to Florida law, the defendant is allowed to approach the bench during all sidebars, and this was the closest I ever got to Dalia. She wasn't allowed to speak, but I was very aware of the jury watching us and tried to be deferential when I could. I prefer the practice, since the defendant is aware of every issue at trial and can't claim later they were misinformed or were denied due process.

This was my first big national case, and my parents flew in to attend the trial. Because of the notoriety, local TV stations were streaming the court proceedings, and my brother Jeff was watching live in New York City. Sometime during the first couple of days, he saw a shot of my parents in the courtroom and got so excited that he called to leave them a message that I was doing great. Except that my Dad had forgotten to turn off his cell phone, and as I was preparing to ask a question, I heard it go off in the middle of the courtroom. I knew it was him because he has "The Entertainer" as his ring tone. The bailiff ran over to help him get it silenced. It took them forever, while I stood frozen with my head bowed, trying not to laugh.

Near the end of the six hours I kept Mike on the stand, after I'd walked him through the tightening circles of intrigue converging on the morning of his ersatz assassination, after he was spirited into the upside-down world of police stations and holding cells and everyone he met looking at him like he was a dead man walking, I asked him how it felt seeing Dalia in police custody, a dangerous animal boxed into a tight corner, pleading with him through an open doorway. He struggled to put the experience into words.

MIKE: It didn't feel good watching it. It didn't feel like . . . I'm not
    getting any satisfaction out of this whole thing. I felt bad for her.
    Not that I could do anything, but I didn't want to see it—talking
    to her, asking her questions, [her] sobbing.

PARKER: You say you felt bad for her—why did you feel bad for her?

MIKE: How could somebody be that stupid? I'm a person who has been in trouble, and all I talked about was wanting to get out of trouble. I thought we had a pretty good thing going in life. To do something like that? That's one of those things to me. I broke the law, I understand, but on the other hand, I'm not out hurting people. It's violence . . . violence. I don't get it. So stupid. I don't understand. So stupid.

I asked him a series of blanket questions about reality TV to stake a claim for when the defense began to unfurl their shadowed theory:

PARKER: Did you ever try out for a reality show?

MIKE: No.

PARKER: Do you have aspirations to be on a reality show?

MIKE: No.

PARKER: Did you speak to a producer about an idea?

MIKE: No.

PARKER: Did you talk to the Boynton Beach Police Department about having a reality show?

MIKE: No.

PARKER: Did you write a script for a reality show?

MIKE: No.

PARKER: Did you act out scenarios with Dalia Dippolito for a reality show?

MIKE: No.

I asked him about his appearances on television news shows (he appeared on *The Today Show* on August 10 and November 20, 2009), in case the other team presented that as some kind of unrequited craving for media attention—establishing that he was never paid for his appearances, cataloging his reasons, and trying to determine how it made him feel.

> PARKER: Why did you go on *The Today Show?*
>
> MIKE: They just—nobody would leave me alone. The phone keeps ringing, ringing. They're in front of my house almost two, three days. Ringing the bell, ringing the bell, ringing the bell; my phone's ringing, ringing, ringing. I thought if I just said something, not saying nothing, it would take it away from me. And that's not exactly what happened, but that was the idea.
>
> PARKER: Did you read any articles or see any news reports that painted you in a bad light?
>
> MIKE: Yeah, lots of 'em.
>
> PARKER: And how did that affect you?
>
> MIKE: I mean, it's uh . . . it affected me, but I know that's nonsense and I try not to let it bother me. But being approached left and right, and reading stupid things that people write in the news. I'm not here because I want to be here . . . I'm gauged to be a fake gangster, a thief, a convicted felon, a wife beater—all these things that were said. And I'm none of that. I'm a convicted felon, I report to my probation officer every month and report, but I hold my head up as high as I can—I feel, rightfully so. So to just let people bash and bash and bash me, I didn't feel it was right for me not to maybe say something.

Finally, I had Mike read transcripts of a series of texts between him and Dalia in the days and hours leading up to the event, while she was putting the final pieces of her plan into place, to demonstrate Mike's complete obliviousness to the events unfolding around him:

On July 26 at 11:31 a.m.:

MIKE: Okay, pills make me feel sick.

DALIA: I'll be there soon [and] take care of you. I'm sorry, love.

MIKE: I'm fine. I'm watching *The Hulk*.

DALIA: Nice. Thinking of you. You were great last night.

MIKE: LY ["Love you"].

And on August 4, the day before, at 1:28 p.m.:

MIKE: [Can you] see when the soonest will be that we can go to Fort
    Lauderdale to see a doc? Want him to drain my back.

DALIA: 'Kay. Why? What's going on?

MIKE: This isn't going down, and when I sit it bulges into my side and
    hurts. Just want it drained, you know?

DALIA: I'm sorry. I love you so much. I'll call them right away.

MIKE: No biggie. Just see when we could go, okay?

As far as Dalia knew, in another seventeen hours her husband would
be dead. Mike began to tear up a little bit as he read this last part.

I asked him if he had known anything about a plot to have him killed on
August 5, 2009, and he said no. And with that, I had no further questions.

After a break for lunch, Michael Salnick began his cross-examination
of Mike Dippolito. In his opening statements, he had laid a substantial
amount of groundwork establishing Mike's reality show gambit. I was really
looking forward to seeing how he was going to pull that off, and I think the
jury was, too. But whatever sleight of hand was going to come later, his one
unwavering approach to the two days he kept Mike on the stand could be
boiled down to a single declarative sentence:

"Mike Dippolito is a liar."

He gripped it like a golden chisel and hammered at the edifice of
Mike's credibility wherever he thought it might warp or crack, only

letting up when I objected and the judge sustained it, which he did fairly consistently.

> SALNICK: You talked about some kind of thing you had to wear when you were in rehab a long time ago, like a feeling thing or something?
>
> MIKE: Yes.

(According to Mike, when he was fifteen, he did his first stint in rehab, trading six months of getting in touch with his feelings for another five and a half years of sobriety. One of his tasks was to wear a "feelings wheel," with which he could dial in to his dominant emotion on a minute-by-minute basis.)

> SALNICK: Okay, if you were wearing that today, how would you feel?
>
> MIKE: Sad.

Salnick started off by enumerating Mike's crimes—Organized Fraud, Unlicensed Communications as a Telephone Seller, Unlicensed Commercial Telephone Seller, and Grand Theft—forcing him to acknowledge them as "crimes of dishonesty." (Mike called them "the dumbest thing I did in my life.") When Mike volunteered that he knew how wire transfers worked (and thus knew Dalia was lying), Salnick couldn't resist getting in a dig: "And you're familiar with how this wire process works from scamming other people."

Although Mike readily admitted his actions, taking full responsibility wherever he could, Salnick went through an itemization of how that money was spent:

> SALNICK: Did you use pay-by-the-minute chat rooms with the money that you withdrew?
>
> MIKE: Can you elaborate?
>
> SALNICK: Sure. Did you withdraw money that you stole from people from ATM machines?
>
> MIKE: Yes.

SALNICK: Okay, did you go into psychic hotlines and sex hotlines, chat rooms, with that money?

MIKE: Yes.

I tried to object on grounds of relevance, which was sustained, but Mike had already answered.

Salnick focused on the mechanics of purchasing the house, suggesting that because the cashier's check was made out in Dalia's name, it meant that he was trying to shield his assets from those seeking restitution. This brought on the first dustup of their contentious exchange.

SALNICK: Okay, so let me talk about this now. Just so that I understand, you told the jury before that it wasn't until you supposedly talked to this fake lawyer on the steps of the Miami Dade County Courthouse that you were advised by someone on the phone to hide your assets, right?

MIKE: Later on, down the road, we're talking. Not where you started.

SALNICK: Okay, listen to my question.

MIKE: You went from here to eight months later. I'm confused.

SALNICK: Does that make a difference to you?

MIKE: You confused me.

SALNICK: Does that change the truth?

MIKE: I don't even know what you're asking me at this point.

Salnick got them back on the rails and then returned to seven months earlier, when Mike purchased his house with "money that you didn't tell probation about."

SALNICK: So that check for the house says Dalia Mohammed.

MIKE: I don't know where she would get the money from.

SALNICK: I didn't ask you that question, but I appreciate your sharing that with me.

This brings a chuckle from Mike.

MIKE: Yeah. Sure.

SALNICK: What I asked you is: that check, if someone were to look at it, has the name of Dalia Mohammed as the person who purchased it. Correct?

MIKE: Yes.

Salnick was scoring points, but they were coming at a price. He used Mike's drug history to festoon more lies on his tainted legacy:

SALNICK: You certainly didn't run in and tell your probation officer that when you got out of prison you were using drugs again, did you?

MIKE: No.

SALNICK: You certainly didn't go in and say, "I've got a drug problem, I need a little help," did you?

MIKE: No.

SALNICK: What did you use when you were on probation?

MIKE: I did cocaine.

SALNICK: And you just didn't get caught, is that correct?

MIKE: Yes.

Salnick spent the better part of an hour meticulously detailing Mike's income during the months he was on probation, from January 2008 until August 2009, always contrasting his $2,800 in declared income with the much larger sums that were porously flowing in and out of his bank account—income and expenditures that Mike deemed "a lot of frivolous spending and nonsense." He ran through a litany of the five separate lawyers Mike has hired to guide him through his legal morass—pointing them out in the courtroom as he went. He detailed tanning salons and fashionable restaurants as possibly fraudulent expenses, itemized the money Mike lavished on luxury sports cars, and noted that he once threatened suicide in order to get insurance to pay for another stint in rehab—one more in a lifetime full of lies.

Almost four hours into his cross-examination, Salnick finally reached the topic of Erik Tal, and with it a possible motive for Mike's behavior.

> SALNICK: You testified that this fella Erik Tal got involved in this matter when you were at the attorney's office, Mr. Entin, attempting to pay off your probation, right?
>
> MIKE: Yes.
>
> SALNICK: And according to you, after your wife had somehow lost the $100,000, Mr. Tal was someone that you were going to utilize to come up with the full 191?
>
> MIKE: That was presented to me, yes.
>
> SALNICK: And you told me just a little while ago you had never met Mr. Tal before.
>
> MIKE: Before that, no.
>
> SALNICK: And at some point, you went to the safety deposit box when your wife was questioning you about money or something and you got an additional $90,000 in cash?
>
> MIKE: Yes.
>
> SALNICK: Let me ask you this: let's put ourselves in the month that you were at Mr. Entin's office. And you're in a situation now where you're hoping that that $100,000 will come around, and your wife was supposed to get $91,000. This was before you went to your safe

deposit box. How much cash did you have in your safe deposit box at *that* time?

They haggled over how much money Mike could put his hands on at any one time, and finally settled on Salnick's hypothetical 160. The longer Salnick belabored following the money, the more it seemed like he was trying to intentionally confuse the jury. After a while, it started to sound a little bit like "Who's on First?"

SALNICK: You still had a significant amount in there, right?

MIKE: I guess if I took ninety, that left me . . . yeah.

SALNICK: And that's all in cash, right? All in green? No cashier's checks?

MIKE: No—cash.

SALNICK: All right. And you gave that money to your wife, but then you say your wife gave it back to you?

MIKE: No, you're way off on the story.

SALNICK: I'm way off.

MIKE: You're one day to the next to the next. You're back and forth.

SALNICK: All right. At some point your wife gives it back to you, right? When you give it to her?

MIKE: The $90,000? Yes.

SALNICK: That's before Mr. Tal, right?

MIKE: That's when I meet Mr. Tal.

SALNICK: All right. And when you met Mr. Tal, you gave him the $90,000?

MIKE: No.

SALNICK: What do you give him?

MIKE: I meet Mr. Tal and I get my ninety that I just gave my wife that day back.

SALNICK: From your wife?

MIKE: Yeah. Mr. Tal had it; she gets it.

SALNICK: No, wait, wait—did Tal give it to you or did your wife give it to you?

MIKE: She grabbed it from Mr. Tal.

SALNICK: All right. And where's all that going on?

MIKE: The parking lot of my lawyer's office.

SALNICK: And after she gets it from Mr. Tal, you say, she gets it from you?

MIKE: Yes.

SALNICK: Okay. Why didn't you just give that to the attorney?

MIKE: Because it wasn't the full amount.

SALNICK: If you had $160,000 in your safe deposit box, why didn't you just give that to the attorney?

MIKE: I should have.

SALNICK: Okay, I understand. But why didn't you, Mr. Dippolito?

MIKE: Because I was getting a check the next day for the full amount.

SALNICK: But you had almost exactly the full amount in your own cash, didn't you, sir?

MIKE: Almost.

Salnick took off his glasses here to emphasize his point, but he's near-sighted, and he looked momentarily at sea.

SALNICK: Isn't it because you really didn't want to pay back the restitution that you didn't give them your own money?

MIKE: Absolutely not.

SALNICK: Well, you talked a little bit about hoping to negotiate the amount, didn't you?

MIKE: That's how I went into it thinking.

SALNICK: Thinking that maybe you could pay a little bit less to some of these victims, is that right?

MIKE: That was my rationale at the time, yes . . .

SALNICK: From January 2008 up to August 2009, when MAD Media [Mike's online marketing company, which stood for Michael A. Dippolito] was making all this money, why didn't you pay back your restitution then?

MIKE: Because like I said, I had made arrangements to have it paid. Why would I go lose another hundred-some thousand dollars on top of it?

SALNICK: Well, wait a minute. You had all of '08, before you ever met Dalia Dippolito, to pay that restitution back, didn't you?

MIKE: I was saving money.

SALNICK: You were saving money. Money you didn't want to give to the victims, right?

MIKE: Saving money so I could give it to the victims.

SALNICK: That's why you cashed checks and put them in your safe deposit box, right?

MIKE: Well, that's part of it, yeah.

SALNICK: That's why you got the Porsche, and that's why you got the trappings to the Porsche?

MIKE: What's the question?

SALNICK: Well, that was the question.

MIKE: That's why I got the Porsche?

SALNICK: That's why you got the Porsche, because you wanted to pay restitution?

At this point, they were just bickering, so I objected to the line of questioning as argumentative, which Judge Colbath sustained. Salnick repeated the question more calmly.

SALNICK: Is that why you got the Porsche?

COLBATH: I just sustained that objection.

SALNICK: I thought it was just the argumentative nature. I'm sorry, Judge.

He repeated the question, articulating it carefully so as to appear overly courteous. This just came off as mocking, and the courtroom laughed.

SALNICK: No, I'm being serious.

COLBATH: And I was, too.

Colbath was not amused. It looked like Salnick might have just overplayed his hand.

SALNICK: Okay. Understood. Thank you. I'm sorry . . . You were saving money supposedly to pay restitution, right?

MIKE: Yes.

Salnick quickly tried to divert the testimony back onto more solid ground, returning to the subject of Mike's expenditures with money he could have used to repay his victims—a $20,000 condo for his mother, with full furnishings—but getting him to admit he bought his mom an apartment is probably not the best assault you could mount on a witness's character. Very quickly, the judge moved for a recess and we broke for the day. The damage had been done.

The next morning, Salnick returned to the topic of Erik Tal, contrasting the approximately $140,000 Mike allegedly lost to Tal with the fact that he never filed a lawsuit or reported Tal's actions to the police. Mike claimed he accepted Dalia's word that Tal was legitimately trying to correct the problem, and considered any talk of a lawsuit premature with a trial pending. But then, as if on cue, we interrupted Salnick's cross-examination to hear the testimony of Michael Entin, Mike's probation attorney, who was unavailable to testify any other time.

Entin is a former prosecutor and has been a criminal defense attorney for thirty-three years, so he knows his way around a courtroom. He made it clear early in his testimony that he would not be here had his client not signed a waiver to the attorney-client privilege, and he spoke carefully and exactly throughout. He explained that nowhere was it stipulated that Mike pay his restitution according to his ability to do so, and that in fact it would be an "issue of futility" if he tried to get off probation without the full $191,000 available, since he would lose whatever leverage he had. Because the lead investigator, the original district attorney, and Mike's probation officer had all agreed not to oppose termination of his probation if restitution was paid in full, it was essential he place the entire amount in Entin's trust account before proceeding further.

> ENTIN: My concern at the initial meeting was that the money had to be clean money, which would not be tainted by any type of—it's called "nebbia" [Italian for fog or mist], but basically that the money could be shown to be from legitimate sources if it was questioned. I explained to him I wasn't going to launder money to pay these people back, and that the money had to come from lawful means.

By Entin's account, as the issue with Dalia's wire transfer stretched into days and then weeks, despite daily calls from his secretary and no documents to support her evolving claims, he doubted the money had ever been sent, and he had already decided on severing the relationship by the time they showed up at his Fort Lauderdale office with the checks.

PARKER: Why did you do that?

ENTIN: Why did I terminate my relationship with him?

PARKER: Yes.

ENTIN: That's a big answer but I'll tell you. There were several issues. Number one is I was retained to do something which is a very simple task. It would take normally four or five hours of my legal time to complete the whole process. Get the papers, talk to the people, do the motion, and go to court and get the money. It turned out that this thing dragged on for months. There was always a reason the money wasn't showing. There was always an argument between them as to why the money wasn't there. There was never any conclusion to the fact the money was getting there. And then what happened was there became a collateral representation where I started to assist him with no additional fees, which became very time-consuming, where he told me on several occasions there were drugs he thought planted or found in his vehicle, which needed attention, because he was on probation and he didn't want to violate probation. So what started out being four or five hours of work became twenty or thirty hours of work, and I just didn't like the case anymore. I just wanted to get out.

The drama with the cashier's checks merely validated his instincts. Two days later, Mike called to say he was on his way down with a legitimate check that would fix everything. When collateral documents arrived by fax from an attorney named Richard Blake representing someone named Erik Tal, it was the straw that broke the camel's back.

ENTIN: I am exclusively a criminal attorney. I have no knowledge of civil law. Anything civil, *I* would go to a lawyer. I get a fax, which suggests I have some legal ability to review mortgage documents and balloon notes and something of that nature, and it was sent to me for my review as an attorney, for validation for them to sign.

He immediately fired off a letter to this effect to "whoever Richard Blake is" and gave Mike the number of another lawyer "who had more time and patience for this."

"I wasn't going to have any part of it," Entin said.

On cross-examination, Salnick made the point of acknowledging that he and Entin had taken the bar together thirty-two years ago, and there appeared to be an easy rapport between them—not uncommon in a small fishpond like South Florida. Salnick successfully laid in some of the foundation for why Mike needed Dalia to front the restitution process for him.

> SALNICK: And even if the full amount were not paid, if the state or the prosecutor or probation were to learn that he contributed money to this, they might have the right to try and take it.
>
> ENTIN: That would open up a can of worms on that issue, yes.
>
> SALNICK: All right, then it was probably a smart thing for Mike Dippolito to stay out of providing money, is that correct?
>
> ENTIN: Yes.
>
> SALNICK: Would you ever, as an experienced criminal defense lawyer, encourage Mike Dippolito to write checks to his wife so she could cash them or put them in her bank account for him to use as restitution?
>
> ENTIN: No.
>
> SALNICK: Why not?
>
> ENTIN: (long pause) I don't know, I just wouldn't do it. It doesn't sound right.
>
> SALNICK: Doesn't pass the smell test.
>
> ENTIN: Yeah, it doesn't pass the smell test.

During cross, speaking of Mike, Salnick asked Entin, "Did he seem pretty smart to you?" to which Entin replied, "Yes."

In my redirect, I took direct aim at this assertion, pausing for effect, even if it meant winging my chief witness in the process. From there, we got pretty thick in the weeds.

PARKER: Mr. Entin, is Mike Dippolito one of the smartest clients that you've ever had?

SALNICK: Objection! I don't see how that's relevant at all.

COLBATH: I think it's fair in redirect, given your questions. Overruled.

ENTIN: No.

PARKER: What is your opinion about his knowledge of the system and what was going on in his life in 2009?

SALNICK: Objection. You're asking a question on a question—I guess that's a compound question—and I'm not sure if it's relevant or . . . relevant.

COLBATH: Overruled.

ENTIN: (grinning) Can you break that down for me?

PARKER: Well, I don't know. What is your opinion about his ability to understand what was going on in his life back in 2009?

SALNICK: That calls for a lot of speculation.

COLBATH: I'll sustain.

PARKER: Well, how about the other question I asked—can I ask that one again?

By this time, I was giggling.

COLBATH: Yes.

PARKER: Do you have an opinion about Mike Dippolito's ability to understand what was going on with his probation situation back in 2009?

SALNICK: I'm gonna object to this probation situation. Again.

COLBATH: Sustained.

PARKER: I don't have any further questions, Your Honor.

I also spoke with the elusive Erik Tal during my investigation, as well as his wife, Kerrian Brown, and I was there when investigators questioned them both on October 26, 2010. Like Mohamed Shihadeh, Tal was of Middle Eastern origin—in his case, Israeli—as well as the owner of a small convenience store in North Miami. Asim Brown (no relation) reached out to contacts in the North Miami Police Department and discovered that Erik had filed a stolen vehicle report for an All-Terrain Vehicle. I drove down with Eric Hutchinson, an investigator from the State Attorney's Office, and detectives from North Miami Beach called Erik and told him they had recovered his ATV and needed him to identify it. When he arrived at the police station, they put him in a room and we basically ambushed him.

In the interview, Erik spoke with a marked accent that emphasized English as at least his second language. He was balding, dressed in a dark T-shirt and slacks, and he fidgeted throughout. He understandably seemed a little startled at first, but was willing to answer our questions despite being told he could leave at any time. For the most part, I sat quietly and took notes. Erik claimed he was familiar with Dalia's case from the TV coverage, but only knew her through his wife.

ERIK: She's a little bit like crazy . . . crazy like she is always hyper, or she'll be your friend and then disappear for like two or three years.

But soon enough, his story began to drift. He only met Mike once, when he loaned him $20,000 in exchange for receiving a $20,000 profit. Mike offered Dalia's ring and the title to his car to sweeten the deal, but Erik pulled out when the lawyer refused to execute a lien against Mike's house. Except that he also received a $30,000 cashier's check from Mike, which he cashed. And maybe $20,000 in cash that Mike gave him, which he returned. His wife paid Dalia back the $30,000 over time with gambling proceeds. He also gave Mike a cashier's check in the full amount of $191,000, but later he took it back. And asked the bank teller to lie and tell Mike the money was frozen, so Tal could get out of the deal. Any large amounts deposited in his account were cash his father sent him from Israel to invest in real estate properties. Maybe Dalia tried to take Mike's money and is blaming other people. At any rate, for none of these transactions did Erik keep any receipts.

HUTCHINSON: That sounds reasonable to you?

ERIK: I mean, what receipt I gonna give him? I have no receipts. Like to write something?

HUTCHINSON: (after reiterating Erik's position) . . . So, you didn't have the dates—a journal, nothing you wrote down that shows that?

ERIK: I'm bad with writing. I'm bad with spelling—so even if I write, I wouldn't understand it. That's why I don't write stuff.

At one point during his interview, Erik said, "You can ask my wife, too. She's downstairs." So when the interview was concluded, the investigator went downstairs to see if Kerrian Brown would consent to speak with us. I was left alone in the interrogation room with Erik, who asked me what was going on with the case. I ignored him and got on the phone with a detective to come escort me out of the room.

Kerrian arrived with a Gucci handbag almost as big as she was and wearing a silly print hat that on her looked charming. She is thirty-five, but looks much younger, the rigors of multiple childbirths showing nowhere on her delicate frame. She told us basically the same story Erik did about the money, in much less detail but with a good deal more consistency. About Mike, she said, "[H]e started looking like he wasn't wound too tight."

But from the start of the interview, it was clear there was more to the story than she wanted to tell us. She started to smile uncomfortably at times, like she was nervous, but not about herself. More like she knew a secret she had promised she wouldn't tell.

HUTCHINSON: Just relax.

KERRIAN: No, I am relaxed. I'm just seeing where to start from. Me and her had a little break. We were friends, on and off for years, but we had a little break for about two months, and then I saw her on the TV. So there was a two-month break in there.

HUTCHINSON: What was the reason for the break?

KERRIAN: Oh, I don't know. She started acting weird. And like I said, the relationship was on and off. She'd start to get on my nerves and get too clingy. It's always something with female friends. You know, I'd give her a break and walk off. Too much drama or whatever.

Kerrian said Dalia constantly complained about Mike—he was abusive, obsessive, had a temper, kicked the dog—all of which seemed at odds with the nice house, beautiful engagement ring, and sumptuous lifestyle he lavished on her, as far as her friend could tell.

KERRIAN: She was saying she couldn't leave him, and he knows people and stuff. The problem was, I had met him—not much, but a few times—and I didn't see him the way she was saying to me. You understand? And like I said, I know her for years on and off—so, I know when she's working me.

I could tell she was close to spilling, so I jumped in to see if I could knock her off point a couple of degrees.

PARKER: We know what she did for a living, if you're talking about that. We know she was a female escort.

KERRIAN: She probably was, on and off—I don't want to confirm or deny that.

PARKER: But that's why you're smirking.

HUTCHINSON: You're like a politician.

KERRIAN: I don't . . . gosh . . .

HUTCHINSON: You're blushing.

KERRIAN: It's a nightmare. I just thought I'd never see her there, but she never said to me—honestly, she didn't say to me, for example, "I'm gonna try and kill him." She never said that. With that being said [she giggles], she's a complicated girl.

We both kept at her for several minutes, advising her to ease her conscience, since it was clear that's what she wanted. Eventually, that did the trick.

PARKER: You know what? Just say it. I know you have things to do, places to go.

KERRIAN: You know, she did say to me one time, "Do you think there are any undetectable poisons?" She did say that to me. Honestly. And I said to her, "Are you kidding? Are you crazy? Don't talk to me about stuff like that!" And it was shortly after that, that we . . . That was probably the most detrimental . . .

They talked once more about six weeks prior to Dalia's arrest.

KERRIAN: I called her and she told me she was pregnant . . . she said, "Well, everything is okay," but I knew it wasn't. I could tell it wasn't. Something was ticking there. Something wasn't right, but I never called her again, and then I saw her on the news a couple of weeks later.

Neither of them testified at the trial. I didn't put Erik Tal on the stand because I believed he was guilty of a crime, and if forced to testify, he would receive immunity for his crimes within the jurisdiction of Broward County. And once I decided not to use Dalia's original murder attempt with the poisoned iced tea, Kerrian's one big revelation was no longer relevant to the case.

Kerrian turned up again in March 2011 in the final stages of our investigation. Among those items discovered in Dalia's safety deposit box was a receipt for the alleged wire transfer from the Cayman National Bank, which we knew to be false. It was faxed to a 305 number (Miami-Dade) printed on the top of the page, it was handwritten, the handwriting matched Dalia's, and her phone records indicated she had contacted the bank in question five times in the forty-eight hours before the fax was sent. So I had my assistant, Lindsey Marcus, send an official fax from the State Attorney's Office to the number of origin listed on the transfer, asking them to contact our office. I had a hunch it would be Kerrian Brown, purportedly Dalia's best friend, and since we had met, I made a point of leaving my name off the fax. Whoever it was, if they called us back, then we'd know, and if they didn't, then we'd know they had something to hide. Sure enough, within a day Kerrian called, asking what this was all about. We made something up in case we needed to call her as a witness if Dalia testified, and she was apparently none the wiser.

After lunch, back in cross-examination, Mike Dippolito and Michael Salnick started in bickering again like they'd never let up.

SALNICK: Mr. Dippolito, you told me yesterday the reason you didn't file a lawsuit against Erik Tal, or you didn't file a police report, was because you didn't think Erik Tal stole the money, is that right?

MIKE: Didn't say that either.

SALNICK: What did you say?

MIKE: I said my wife told me not to file a lawsuit.

SALNICK: Well, I don't think you said your wife yesterday. I asked you if you filed a lawsuit, and you said you haven't filed a lawsuit. Is that correct?

MIKE: Maybe that's what I said, but I didn't file one, and not for the reason you just stated.

On Mike's stated reasons for his Vegas getaway:

SALNICK: I'm asking you something very simple: Did you say to the jury that it wasn't really business, you just met him?

MIKE: I might have, but maybe you misunderstood the way I said it.

SALNICK: I misunderstood you?

MIKE: If you're wording it the way I think you're wording it, that doesn't make any sense.

SALNICK: I'm not wording it at all. I'm just repeating the words that you used.

MIKE: Well, maybe we misunderstand each other.

And about his restitution:

SALNICK: Were you concerned about the money?

MIKE: Yes. I told you that yesterday.

SALNICK: You were concerned about your money, the source of your money?

MIKE: No, I didn't want to have to go through fifty hoops just to get off probation when I had the money to pay it.

SALNICK: That's not what I'm asking.

MIKE: Isn't that an answer?

SALNICK: Well, it's an answer, but not to this question.

This culminated in a discussion of the CityPlace incident. Salnick had seized on a line Mike used in direct—"A weird guy was staring at us the whole time"—that he used to describe their experience at Starbucks before they returned to the parking garage.

SALNICK: And what's significant about a weird guy staring at you in Starbucks?

MIKE: I just found it odd. We both looked at each other and the guy wouldn't stop looking at us, and I didn't know what it was about. It was just very strange. That was the only reason I said it.

SALNICK: Can you describe him?

MIKE: I think he was wearing like a button-up shirt, maybe a . . . See, I'm thinking like he's the guy I see there all the time. He *is* a police officer, but I'm not 100 percent sure. He walks around, it seems like it's his patrol, he's always smoking a cigar. He's almost bald. I see him now often, and I'm pretty sure it's him. But like I said—honestly?—I don't know. It just happened. If there's a connection to whatever, I don't know. But that's how that started.

SALNICK: First you said it was a weird guy. Now you say it was a weird guy who might be a police officer. Are you just guessing?

MIKE: I don't know if it's him exactly or not. I'm just trying to tell you the story the best I can.

SALNICK: When you say it's a weird guy, that implies one thing.

MIKE: He was weird because he wouldn't stop looking over at us, you know? If you were staring at me, I'd think you were a weird guy.

Salnick snaps his head up with his eyes wide open. He looks like an owl.

SALNICK: Okay. Well, I'm staring at you now, so am I weird?

MIKE: No, you're like a parrot.

SALNICK: A parrot?

MIKE: Yeah.

SALNICK: What does that mean? I've been called a lot of things. What's a parrot?

MIKE: You know. Come on.

People were starting to giggle, including some at the prosecution table.

SALNICK: You're winking at the Judge. He doesn't know what you mean. What do you mean?

MIKE: "Did you do that on probation? Were you on probation? Did you do that on probation? Were you on probation?" You know what I'm talking about. I'm just having fun with you. Come on.

By now the entire courtroom was cracking up.

SALNICK: You're having fun with me? Well, let me ask you something: Is this fun, Mr. Dippolito?

MIKE: This sucks.

SALNICK: Okay. Was it fun when you got arrested?

MIKE: No.

SALNICK: Was it fun when you went through court?

MIKE: Horrible.

SALNICK: Okay. So is there anything funny at all about this proceeding, Mr. Dippolito?

MIKE: The questions you're asking me, some of them, yeah.

SALNICK: You don't like them, do you?

MIKE: It's ridiculous. We're not here because of me. You might as well put me up next. I mean, what are we doing here?

In the final hour of the two days he kept Mike on the stand, Salnick finally broached the subject of reality television, the putative linchpin of his defense strategy. He got Mike to admit that he liked *American Chopper* (which Salnick tried to call *American Family*), *Cheaters* (which Mike claimed was Dalia's show), and especially *Jersey Shore* (even though it first aired in December 2009, four months after Dalia had been arrested), and that "it's crazy how these people are making money." Under continued prodding, Mike also admitted to being a YouTube fan, but it didn't seem like this was something he was especially trying to hide. Salnick tried to resurrect the subject of Mike's appearances on *The Today Show*, but my objection that this line of questioning had been asked and answered was sustained. Finally out of ammunition, Salnick stared up at the ceiling, apparently lost in thought, and then delivered what seemed like his coup de grace:

SALNICK: You're certainly a celebrity now, aren't you, Mr. Dippolito?

PARKER: Objection. Argumentative.

COLBATH: Sustained.

SALNICK: I don't have any other questions.

In my redirect, I tried to put out a lot of little fires, but most of the heavy lifting had already been done for me. I got Mike to explain that he had discussed the Erik Tal situation with the Boynton Beach PD, and at one point even picked him out of a lineup.

On the subject of the Marlins game that Mike took Dalia and her whole family to at his own expense, which Salnick used as an example of how he had squandered potential restitution money and defied the provisions of his probation, I just let Mike expand on his motivations for a moment.

PARKER: Besides being a Phillies fan, was there another reason you took the defendant's family to that Marlins game back in 2009?

MIKE: Yeah. I was sitting on the couch at her mother's house with Paprique, her grandfather, and the old man always watched baseball. And he didn't speak that great English, but we would talk as best we could. And I asked, "You ever been to a game?" And the old guy, somehow I understood, he says, "No, I've never been to a game." So then I started researching games, and I saw there was a Phillies game, and the old man, basically we took him. It was for both reasons. Basically for him, though. It was a good reason to go to a baseball game.

And on the pretext of explaining his demeanor at the police station, which Salnick suggested proved he knew about the bust ahead of time, I basically just let Mike walk the jury through what he was feeling on the morning his world turned upside down. His response was not especially articulate—it was barely even coherent—but as far as putting the jury inside his head and letting them take that ride, I thought it was pretty close to perfect.

> PARKER: Why were you so calm that morning at the police department?
>
> MIKE: I just, I mean, I didn't really, you know—I was in shock. And, I mean, I was in shock. And also, all of this stuff that had been happening to me in the months prior, it just kind of fell into place with it. But I, you know. 'Cause you have to understand: I thought I was crazy for the longest time. 'Cause I know, it's just . . . every time I go to the car, the truck, I'm just waiting for something to happen. And then this happens on top of it, that's why I froze at the door. I didn't know how to react. And, uh, you know, everybody's just talking to me, talking to me, talking to me. And I'm hearing 'em, but I'm really not hearing 'em. And I guess I just got quieter. I don't know. But maybe my reaction wasn't like everyone else's would be. I was a little shocked, obviously. And the other part, honestly? At that point, I mean [deep breath] when that happened, after all that's been happening and all I've really been trying to do, I'm thinking to myself, I am just so much in trouble now. And this just even makes it all the worse, that it's my wife. So my hopes of getting my money for probation obviously were smashed. I realized that that was not going to happen.
>
> PARKER: Okay, how did the incident affect how you thought your life was going to be in the future?
>
> MIKE: It just smashed me. Everything was done. That was it.

Expanding on that, I referred Mike to one of his last lines to Dalia in her jailhouse call to him: "Don't say [shit]. I just said I'd help you, okay?"

PARKER: Why do you tell her to stop talking?

MIKE: She just keeps lying to me: "I didn't do it, I didn't do it. It wasn't me. It was someone who looked like me. I didn't do it. I love you, I love you." I mean, how much do I have to . . . It's fourteen pages of it. It's ridiculous. I'm trying to talk to her and be nice, and she's just telling me how she didn't do anything.

For the first time, I noticed Dalia smiling in court. But I also thought she looked like she might cry.

PARKER: In that entire transcript that you just reviewed, did she ever at any time say in the phone call to you that this was a reality show stunt, and you need to come clean?

MIKE: No.

PARKER: I have no further questions.

Salnick opted for a recross, citing a few small points, like noting Mike's comment at the end of his phone call with Dalia—"I'll fix it. I'll help you."—presumably as a coded reference to the reality plot. But really, I think, he just wanted to get to the following:

SALNICK: And this reality thing didn't work out the way you wanted it to, did it?

Mike looks confused.

PARKER: Objection, your honor. Beyond the scope.

SALNICK: How is it beyond the scope? It's the last question she asked you.

COLBATH: Overruled.

SALNICK: (suddenly stern) This reality thing didn't work out the way you wanted, is that correct?

MIKE: What reality thing?

SALNICK: And this reality thing would have gotten your probation violated because of the way it went down. Is that correct?

MIKE: What reality thing?

SALNICK: And this whole reality thing was actually orchestrated by you, wasn't it?

MIKE: I don't know what you're talking about.

SALNICK: Was your wife ever on a reality show?

MIKE: Not that I knew of.

SALNICK: She never told you about *Jaime Kennedy's Experiment*?

This was an MTV *Pranked*-style reality series that Dalia claims to have appeared on as an extra, although I've watched it half a dozen times and I can't find her. In the sketch, Kennedy, doing a bad Pacino in *Scarface*, orders a hit on a hapless party guest.

MIKE: No.

SALNICK: Your wife never told you she was on a show that had to do with a fake hit?

PARKER: Objection. Beyond the scope.

COLBATH: Overruled.

SALNICK: And you certainly wouldn't lie about anything—you'd come clean about everything. Is that right?

PARKER: Objection. Argumentative.

SALNICK: Would you say anything that wasn't true under oath?

MIKE: No.

SALNICK: Would you say anything that wasn't true to your probation officer?

MIKE: Yes.

SALNICK: Thank you.

And with that, Mike finally was able to step down.

One thing Mike did during the trial—I still don't know if it was intentional—was to consistently refer to Dalia as "my wife" rather than Dalia or Miss Dippolito. It made it seem like he was still in love with her, which I guess in some way he must have been. After his testimony was finished, Mike didn't attend the rest of the trial.

MIKE: I glanced at her, but I didn't stare. I didn't mad-dog her or any of that stuff. People were like, why aren't you in court every day? I'm like, what's the point—to give her dirty looks? It was just weird. Her reactions were just not normal—any of them. At one point, I'm on the stand talking about how she was acting—"It wasn't me . . . It was her . . ."—and I glanced at her, and she was laughing. I'm thinking to myself that she was laughing quite a bit in court, and—if I'm sitting there? You wouldn't see me laughing. I wouldn't laugh once. What's comical about any of this?

CHAPTER 9

Tacks in the Carpet

After three days of Mike on the stand, I put up a series of witnesses who could back up his version of the story, front-loading the line with expert witnesses, individuals in uniform, and physical evidence and documents, following Mike's experiences chronologically, hoping their cumulative weight would hit a tipping point that would be impossible for the defense to recover from. These were the tacks in the carpet, to hold the story line in place until my major witnesses could document Dalia's master plan and motives before the defense had a chance to come in and pull the rug out from under all of us.

First up was Sergio Calderon Obregon, the paralegal who met Mike and Dalia on the courthouse steps in Miami to receive legal papers related to Mike's administrative probation for the lawyer Dalia had so graciously hired for Mike. Sergio was actually a luggage salesman from Columbia living in Miramar who went to Randa's church. We got his identity by tracing the text number on Dalia's phone and determined that he lived in Broward County and had a child custody case pending in Palm Beach County. I had him served with a subpoena to appear at the State Attorney's Office, but purposely omitted my name, Dalia's name, and the case number in order to preserve the element of surprise. He called wanting to know what this was all about, and my assistant, Terri Bramhall, successfully stiff-armed him, arranging for us to meet at a designated place and time. When investigator Glenn Wescott, Lindsey Marcus, and I met him in Broward at a Dunkin' Donuts near where he worked, he was convinced he was about to be blindsided on his custody hearing. I started out by confirming his phone number and then asked him how he knew Randa.

Halfway through my questions, as I was concentrating on how well he knew Dalia (he met her once at a birthday party), he stopped and asked me, "Is that why you're here?" He'd been living in a media bubble and had no idea she had been arrested. He was so relieved that he was prepared to tell me anything.

According to his testimony, he was contacted first by Randa and shortly after by Dalia in July 2009 asking if he would be available to meet Dalia and her husband on the courthouse steps in Miami and pick up some papers from them—he remembers it as a handwritten letter to a judge. He exchanged a handful of texts with Dalia instructing him to dress professional and where they would meet him. She told him that if questioned he was just there to get the paper to give to the lawyer named Richard. Mike tried to ask him questions during the handoff, but he played dumb—not a stretch, given how little he had been told.

PARKER: And did Randa tell you what to do with the paper after you left the courthouse?

SERGIO: I called her and she told me to just throw it away.

He had no idea who Richard the lawyer was. The fact that he seemed completely in the dark about his role in any larger design worked in his favor on the stand. He just confirmed his piece of the jigsaw puzzle and stepped down.

Next I put up four cops, one after another: Williams, Wilson, Hooper, and Gilbert. Officer Paul Williams was one of the Manalapan police officers who responded to the Ritz-Carlton event. Williams, a thirty-two-year veteran of law enforcement, testified that police received an anonymous complaint from a woman identified only as "Sandy" who gave the license number and a description of Mike's Tahoe and claimed someone was dealing drugs out of the vehicle in front of the Ritz-Carlton. Sandy never met them in the lobby like she promised. When they approached him,

Mike appeared shocked but immediately gave his permission to search the vehicle.

Palm Beach Gardens Officer Robert Wilson is the officer Mohamed introduced to Dalia in mid-March at his store, Cross Roads Market & Deli. Mohamed repeatedly identified him as ICE (U.S. Immigration and Customs Enforcement), but in fact he belongs to the Tactical Crime Unit, working as an undercover narcotics agent. Although he often wore long hair and a beard and moustache as part of his cover identity, for his testimony Wilson was clean-shaven and kempt. He told me how Mohamed, whom he knew only as Mike, set up a first call with his friend Dalia.

> PARKER: When you spoke with her on the phone, what did she say to you?
>
> WILSON: She explained to me a situation she was having with her husband. She said he had a violent temper, he was on probation, and that he frequently brought illegal narcotics into the city of Palm Beach Gardens, in particular the Yard House Restaurant. She then went further to ask my assistance in arresting him for possession of illegal narcotics in Palm Beach Gardens.

The fact that Mohamed put Dalia in touch with an undercover narcotics officer from the appropriate jurisdiction to arrest Mike shows me they were plotting to get him arrested for drug possession and dealing from day one. Wilson met with Dalia in person a week later at Mohamed's store, where she reiterated vague concerns for her safety but exhibited no signs of abuse. She also continued to offer to pay him if he would arrest her husband, practically guaranteeing he would have drugs on him.

> WILSON: Each time she would say that to me, I would explain that it was my job, and that I would not take any money for any type of investigation—it's part of what I do.

When she continued to offer him compensation over the space of several phone calls, he referred her to the Boynton Beach Police Department, since that's where she lived, and severed all contact with her. After he saw her arrest on the news, he notified the BBPD. Wilson confirmed his phone number and the dates and times they spoke. On cross, Salnick noted that in his deposition, Wilson identified Dalia as "a thin woman with blonde hair," although it didn't seem to have any impact on the jury.

West Palm Beach Officer Mary Hooper, extremely buff and by the book, was the officer who took pity on Mike during the CityPlace drug search and cut him loose. She had eight years on street patrol, most recently with the weapons and narcotics Quick Response Team, and before that was with the Army CID Drug Suppression Team. Her experience told her the bust was too easy, noting the suspect appeared polite but clearly shocked, while his female companion mainly seemed annoyed, and she used her discretion accordingly.

On cross, Salnick pushed back against the notion that a suspect's surprise at an officer finding drugs on him was proof of innocence, but Hooper stood her ground.

SALNICK: But he convinced you that he wasn't aware, correct?

HOOPER: He did not convince me.

SALNICK: Well, he obviously did, because you didn't arrest him, right?

HOOPER: No, my training and experience convinced me.

She challenged his use of the word "upset" to describe Mike's state of mind, preferring instead "concerned," and noted that Mike confided to her that his ex-wife, Maria, might be responsible.

"The call was that there was like a kilo of cocaine under the tire in the back of my truck—not a baggie with a gram and a half in it," says Mike today. "I mean, I don't even smoke, and it was stuffed in a cigarette pack . . . All she had to do was put it in the glove box." Mike also notes that during the trial, Hooper spotted him in the hallway and confided that the reason they let him go was because they knew it was Dalia. Her reaction had been all wrong.

Finally, Officer Douglas Gilbert of the Boynton Beach Police Department, ex-NYPD, was dispatched to Mike and Dalia's townhouse on the morning of May 27 after they had discovered the threatening note on their windshield as they were coming out of the gym.

> GILBERT: From the moment I met Mr. Dippolito, he was very nervous speaking to me about the occurrences. Looked a little paranoid, troubled, a little anxiety.
>
> PARKER: Who do you think was in charge that day?
>
> GILBERT: Because of Mr. Dippolito's demeanor, I want to say Dalia was more in charge of what was going on. She was able to communicate the story better to me . . . She was concerned, but more calm than he was.

Dalia wrote Mike's statement when he seemed too overwhelmed to do so. Gilbert filed the report as a suspicious incident, but later amended it to phone threats after hearing details of the phone call and the death threats made against Dalia and Mike. Dalia neglected to tell Officer Gilbert that she was the one who had called the number on the note.

Next I called to the stand Meir Cohen, the owner and president of TelTech Corp., based in Toms River, New Jersey. Meir was my expert witness on the phenomenon of "spoof calls," a term Dalia had used ("it seems like somebody just like spoofed the call") to describe her phone call from the mythical Detective Hurley during her conversation with Detectives Llopis and McDeavitt on their ride to the police station. A "spoof card" allows the caller to protect their privacy by masking their Caller ID, substituting any other number in its place, which is the spoof part. Although I could have just subpoenaed the TelTech records and admitted them into evidence with a business records affidavit from the custodian of records for TelTech, I needed someone to explain the records and how a spoof call is made, so I flew Meir in from New Jersey. A good-natured, unflappable character on the stand, Meir claims to have been involved with the spoof card's creation, so I'll let him do the honors:

PARKER: How does a person go about spoofing a call?

COHEN: So they would buy the spoof card on our website, SpoofCard. com, and then they would be provided with an access number and a PIN number. And they would call that access number, very similar to a regular calling card, then they would enter their PIN number in, and they would be presented with an IVR [interactive voice response], which is a whole bunch of automated options. It will first ask them for the number they want to call, then it will ask them for the number they want to appear as a Caller ID, and it will ask them if they want to change their voice, if they'd like to record the call, and then the call will be put through.

PARKER: . . . Is spoofing illegal?

COHEN: Spoofing is legal as long as it's not done with intent to cause harm or obtain anything of value. People use it to protect their privacy. Obviously, it could be misused, but if it's used in the proper way, it is legal.

As an example, I asked him if he could place a call from the phone on the judge's bench and make it look like it was coming from the White House. He was confident that he could.

During my investigation, once I had figured out who Mike Stanley was, I pulled his phone records to see who he was involved with and what he was doing. The day the records arrived, I started digging into them and was up most of the night. When I compared them against a time line, I discovered that around the time "Richard" (the lawyer) was calling Mike offering to set up administrative probation, Mike Stanley was repeatedly calling a number in Big Sur, California—an odd number with a lot of zeros in it. I thought it might be a business number, so I dialed it at 3 a.m. It picked up immediately and a recorded voice said, "Enter your PIN number." If it were a commercial business, there would have been some pro forma greeting. It could have been simply a voice-mail service. But when I did a Google search on the number, it took me to TelTech's "SpoofCard.com" page.

The next day, I contacted Detective Ace Brown and asked him to see what he could find out about the company. He drafted me a subpoena, since phone companies are pretty specific about what they need from law enforcement requests. When we contacted the company, they told us to provide them with the phone numbers in any combination—destination number, spoof number, or number of origin. They got back to us in less than a week with details of an account Stanley had established on July 22, 2009, which he paid for by credit card.

In cross, Salnick continued his campaign to discredit my witnesses, attempting to tar Cohen, his company, and the technique itself as both amoral and ridiculous. After Cohen had explained the company's extensive safeguards, noting that it keeps comprehensive records and is generally sympathetic to inquiries from law enforcement, he detailed other services the company offered, including a Trap Call app that unmasks blocked calls, a Liar Card that applies a voice stress test that is reportedly over 90 percent effective, and the ability to disguise your voice by gender simply by modulating the pitch.

SALNICK: But you've got another one you didn't talk about. You've got a Love Emotion Card, don't you?

COHEN: That's correct.

SALNICK: Okay, tell me a little bit about the Love Emotion Card.

COHEN: The LoveDetect.com is very similar to the Liar Card: it uses voice analysis to determine different algorithms within the voice to determine different emotions, extract emotions—whether there's love or passion or excitement in somebody's voice.

SALNICK: So, wait a minute. If I'm calling somebody up on the phone, they can tell if I'm feeling passionate or excited or emotional?

COHEN: That's correct.

SALNICK: And who uses that product?

COHEN: Anybody that is looking for love, I guess.

SALNICK: Looking for love in all the wrong places?

Cohen laughed.

Before he was done, Salnick got Cohen to concede that calling a spoof number from another spoof number would render the caller effectively anonymous, making any conjecture as to his identity or intentions moot. (Salnick noted that the spoofer would then become the spoofee, inspiring a rare moment of laughter from Dalia in court.) On recross, I verified Mike Stanley's phone records with Cohen, which proved that did not happen in this case. There were any number of incidents that spring and summer prior to Michael Stanley reentering Dalia's life that probably employed a spoof number: the anonymous calls to Mike's probation officer that he was dealing ecstasy and steroids, the call from "Sandy" that led to the Ritz-Carlton event in Manalapan, the similar tip-off prior to CityPlace, all in March; the call from a neighbor reporting a domestic dispute at their apartment in April; and the call May 1 from the mysterious Detective Hurley of the Boynton Beach Police Department, whose outgoing call registered a unique four-digit extension, even though BBPD calls only show the main trunk number. I subpoenaed TelTech records multiple times with many different phone numbers, but I could never figure out who the callers were in any of those situations.

What I could prove was that Mike Stanley placed calls to Mike Dippolito from a 305 number—that of the Miami-Dade county courthouse—at the exact times Mike said he was contacted by "Richard," the lawyer advising him in the intricacies of administrative probation. I asked Mike about this when I had him on the stand.

"The first guy I spoke to started talking about . . . he wasn't going down a path that made sense," Mike said. "This and that; going nowhere. I told my wife this guy isn't making any sense, so she had another lawyer call. This lawyer was in Miami and he started talking about administrative probation and how he thought he could get it for me."

Mike Dippolito claims that Dalia had canceled three or four appointments with her OB/GYN for the two of them to discuss her pregnancy with her doctor. The following text string occurred between Dalia and Mike Stanley on July 17 at roughly 2:30 p.m.

DALIA: Need u to cll me and act like doc just ask me y I didn't come and how im feeln

STANLEY: K I will cll from private num in 15 min

Fifteen minutes later, at 2:42, she asks:

DALIA: Do u know how to spoof a cll

STANLEY: ??? Pretend to be doc?

DALIA: In two min cll the other phone . . . Yes dr emerick sound proper

STANLEY: Ill try

DALIA: K in one min cll

(Stanley admits making the call, but claims that Mike was aware of the ruse, and that the call was staged for the benefit of Mike's mother, who still believed Dalia was pregnant.)

On July 22 at 8:15 a.m., the day before they were supposed to meet their lawyer's paralegal on the courthouse steps, Dalia texts Stanley:

DALIA: Hey baby whats the earliest u cn make the cll I wana prep u before u talk to him

At 1:30, she texts:

DALIA: Cll my other phone w the spoof he wants to drop the paper tell me tomm call now please with the spoof 561 num

And then the next morning at 10 a.m., she texts him:

DALIA: I need u to spoof the cll and tell him that he needs to meet ur paralegal at 230 at the courthouse and that since ur vacation u live at the courthouse. ur paralegals name is sergio if he asks

and u apologize for the inconvenience but ur filing it tomm and
need to revise the documents before and just in case its the miami
courthouse on flagler 2:30

From the texts, we know that Stanley made additional spoof calls to
Mike, once on July 27 (again apparently originating from the courthouse)
that informed Mike his administrative probation was in the works, with a
possible answer by week's end (or August 1, four days before the planned
hit), and once on July 30 recommending he transfer his house solely into
Dalia's name because of the amount of restitution Mike owed.

When I asked him in his deposition, Mike Stanley said he knew what
a spoof call was, and claimed that it was Dalia who had steered him to
the TelTech website. I asked him specifically about the spoof calls to Mike
Dippolito.

STANLEY: The spoof call to Mike Dippolito was done [with] my spoof
account but not made by me.

PARKER: Who had your cell phone at the time when that phone call
was made?

STANLEY: Friend of mine made that phone call.

PARKER: Did that friend pretend to be Richard?

STANLEY: No.

PARKER: Were you there when your friend had your phone?

STANLEY: He walked away from me. I didn't stand next to him and
see him make the call, no.

PARKER: Who is this friend?

STANLEY: This guy Joe from the deli around the corner from my office.

I asked Stanley what was Joe from the deli's last name, address, phone
number; whether his work cell phone had been stolen, and if his employer

knew he was loaning it to acquaintances for personal calls. He could not give me any of that information.

> PARKER: Did you give the phone to him and ask him to make a spoof call?
>
> STANLEY: I gave the phone to him and said, "Make this phone call." I said, "Offer advice to this person and say that they can file papers on their own. That was it."

According to Stanley (i.e., according to Dalia), one attorney had already dropped Mike as a client over issues of fraud, and four or five subsequent attorneys recused themselves because they knew the first one, South Florida being the fishbowl that it is. Mike had asked Dalia to find him a Dade County attorney to help with his administrative probation, a situation Stanley had advised her not to get mixed up in because it seemed fraudulent on the face of it. He called the DA (actually called State Attorney in Florida) to determine the proper course of action, but the DA was out of the country for two weeks. So the spoof call was simply to suggest that Mike file the paperwork himself, and to stall until the DA returned. Problem solved.

> PARKER: We'll go back. So you told Joe at the deli to pretend to offer legal advice to—
>
> STANLEY: No, no, no—I did not say that. I told him basically just call and just offer advice that you could do this on your own; don't take money, don't give him any legal advice, just go to the courthouse and do this on your own.

At this point, Salnick entered the deposition room and I told him we didn't have a last name or address for one of his potential witnesses, Joe from the deli.

Salnick, ever witty, said, "It's kind of like Larry the Murderer."

I asked Stanley if he was aware that it was a federal crime to spoof a call to someone by use of fraudulent means.

STANLEY: Not understanding that, I'm sorry.

PARKER: It's either yes or no. Did you know that it is a federal offense for you to use the spoofing card—the numbers, the spoofing system—to commit fraud in any way . . . maybe to get somebody to sign their house over to someone else, to misrepresent things?

STANLEY: Right, if you were committing fraud, I would assume that's a federal offense.

For me to prove that he committed a crime, I would have to show that he had prior knowledge of the solicitation of murder, and that he was complicit in her plan, meaning that he furthered it in some measurable way. Even if he knew what she was up to, that alone didn't make him a conspirator in her crime. I ultimately decided I didn't have the evidence to prove that. Do I believe that he was involved? Buy me a drink sometime, I'll tell you what I think.

After Meir Cohen, I called to the stand Dawn Hurley, a representative of Bank of America, to help make sense of Dalia's bank statements, and proof of ownership and visits to her safe deposit box. In what I'm sure was excruciatingly boring testimony for the jury, I walked Miss Hurley through nine months of transactions: Documenting how Dalia deposited Mike's initial $100,000 meant for restitution; demonstrating her spending habits, the Range Rover she bought on a whim for Mohamed, the bank branch she withdrew that money from, which was right across the street from Mohamed's convenience store in Palm Beach Gardens. And especially how quickly she tore through the money—$700 to King Jewelers in Aventura; $1,175 to the Ritz-Carlton; $1,250 to Lulu, a clothing store in Bal Harbor; hair extensions, fake eyelashes, tanning sessions—six figures in five months; her checking account was overdrawn at the end of practically every month.

"It's not even about the fucking money," she told Mohamed in the front seat of his Lexus when she was ordering up a hit man a la carte. "We'll spend it in a fucking blink of an eye."

I tracked Dalia's money trail from before she was married up until the day she withdrew her last $1,200 on the way to meet Mohamed in the parking lot of the Mobil station as a down payment on the gun. The sheer fact that she spent his money with such abandon and disdain is the best proof that she thought she'd get Mike's probation revoked, and soon all the money would be hers.

Next I called Todd Surber of Independence Title in Delray Beach, the lawyer who supervised both transfers of the house title—adding Dalia to the deed soon after they were married and putting the property solely in her name just before her arrest. Surber testified that on July 31, he executed a quitclaim deed for the couple, a streamlined type of deed transfer, often between spouses.

The one question people continually have about this case is how Mike could have fallen for Dalia's betrayals so consistently. It's like Charlie Brown and the football: the inevitable conclusion seems to be obvious to everyone but Mike, and in the end it cost him all of his money, the best of his friends, briefly his sanity, and almost his life. Nowhere is this more apparent than in his willingness to sign over property to her. Here is Mike from his initial police interview with Detective Moreno.

> MIKE: I purchased the home, and then we put it in half her name, half my name, a month after the fact. Because she would say things to me, a little pressure here and there, so fine, I did it. You know, it's my wife, I'm not thinking anything's wrong, man.
>
> MORENO: . . . Why did you transfer your title to her?
>
> MIKE: She was saying maybe it's better that it's in her name. And I was nervous, too, because I had all my other business [to get] straightened out, everything's upside down, I thought, "Okay, I'll just do it."
>
> MORENO: Well, that's what I'm trying to understand. By her having the house under her name, how would that help?
>
> MIKE: I don't know. I don't know. It makes as much sense as what she tried to do to me, man.

In the end, Todd Surber's bombshell testimony had him explaining that, despite the fact that the house was now in Dalia's name, she could never sell it without Mike's consent and participation because it was a marital asset.

What we forget is that Dalia had a real estate license going back to 2006. She worked at Beachfront Realty in Aventura and sold him his house. As far as he knew, this was her job and designated area of expertise—she left the house twice a week to show houses to prospective clients. He was lucky to have the in-house counsel. Not only that, but it was her real estate commissions with which she was going to resolve their financial impasse and repay the debt of his restitution money. It's what kept him in the game, and why he repeatedly gave her the benefit of the doubt. It was only after she was arrested that he discovered the only house she ever sold her whole time at Beachfront Realty was Mike's. These twice-a-week meetings with prospective clients were how she could carry on affairs with Mohamed, Michael Stanley, and who knows how many others. It was a ready-made cover story, in that it bought her space and time—the things she needed most to set her myriad traps.

And so close to the end, she hectored Mike into putting his house entirely in her name, wrongly believing that title and possession were the equivalent of ownership.

It was her inability to grasp even this most basic concept of property law as much as anything that put her over the edge to literally pull the trigger.

Mike wonders why she went to all the trouble. "Right now those houses are going for 150 grand," he says. "You couldn't sell it if you were lucky."

Randa Mohamed was up next. She was questioned by my co-counsel, Laura Burkhart Laurie. I handpicked Laura as one of my Felony Assistant State Attorneys for the Domestic Violence unit because she was a talented trial lawyer who had a true passion for protecting victims of crime. She is tenacious and a hard worker, and I was blessed to have her as my second chair. Immediately prior to the testimony, our third chair, Lindsey, took Randa into a nearby conference room and played each jailhouse call from Dalia in succession, so that she would be familiar with their contents, and had her initial each CD. On the stand Laura established how Randa knew

Sergio—they attended the same church—and got her to identify Dalia's voice in the jailhouse calls so that we could enter those as evidence. Laura also confirmed Randa's phone number so we could link her to Sergio and Sergio to Dalia. I could have had Mike do that, but too much of this case was riding on his word as it was. Since Randa was a witness for both the State and the defense, after the Rule of Sequestration was invoked she was not able to sit in the courtroom and hear the testimony of other witnesses. This was an added benefit of her testifying. The last thing I wanted the jury to focus on was the suspect's grieving mother sitting in the front row weeping.

I was never able to effectively determine Randa's role in Dalia's plans. But from the text record alone, I think her hands aren't completely clean. On July 22, at 3:50 p.m., Dalia had the following exchange with her mother:

DALIA: Need someone professional to meet me and mike at the miami courthouse at 2 and act like a legal secretary and take a paper from us . . . They just need to say they r takn it to the attorney and thanks for meeting us they were in dipositions all day. Ill pay them 500

RANDA: What lawyer r they representing? And what happens 2 the papers after. R they talking 2 anybody besides u and Mike

DALIA: Me and mike r giving them papers they cn trash it later. Let me know if u have someone that looks professional they just need to meet us in front of miami courthouse and take a paper from us and say they will mke sure the attorney gets it and sorry for the inconvenience thats it . . . He thinks were handing it to an attorneys legal secretary. Ill give u the money then u cn put it in there acct when they meet us

RANDA: K I got a guy give me all the details. Including address and what is the lawyers name

DALIA: Does he look professional

RANDA: Yes he will

In the middle of this, as long as she's thinking about it, Dalia sends Stanley a booster text:

DALIA: Love u sexy

I flew Linda Taylor-Vincent in from Texas. She is the Custodian of Records for MetroPCS, and I needed her to help make sense of Dalia's phone and text records. They're highly confusing to follow—more than once Mike went silent on the stand for ten or twenty seconds trying to figure out the printout in front of him to answer my question—and so much intrigue went on behind the scenes via text or furtive phone calls that I didn't want an officer or detective to try to reference them without an expert to lead the jury by the hand. This allowed me to get all the phone records into evidence, which offered a ready-made blueprint for all the connections in this case.

Next I put up David Banks, Mike's probation officer since February 2009, or roughly the duration of his marriage and beyond. So much of Salnick's efforts to impeach Mike's credibility rested on his failure to comply with the terms of his probation that I felt I needed to reinforce what those terms actually were: there was no condition he must pay restitution in full if he could, merely that he make the stipulated payments; he was free to travel with the approval of the court. Banks had been some form of probation officer for over thirty years and seemed by the book. When Mike went to see him on August 10, five days after Dalia's arrest, Banks informed him that on four separate occasions in as many months, he had received anonymous phone calls alleging that Mike was dealing ecstasy or steroids, that there was a steady stream of kids in and out of his garage. According to his testimony, this is what inspired the late-night raid on the evening of March 12. Officer Banks made about a dozen visits to Mike's house between February and August. (On July 28, corroborated by his phone records, Mike Stanley called Banks to report that Mike owned a business he was not reporting the profits from; Stanley was even considerate enough to provide the business ID number.)

In cross, Salnick itemized Mike's lies to his P.O.: that Mike owned his own business, the considerable proceeds it generated, all the exotic ways

Mike could think of to spend his money, how his Vegas junket was hardly a business trip at all. I didn't think much of it stuck. At the end of his testimony, Banks shrugged off these new armor-piercing assaults on Mike's character. As he noted, "I'll be Mike Dippolito's probation officer until 2032. He's gonna be with us for a while."

CHAPTER 10

Delilah

And then we put on Mohamed to round out the first week.

When Mohamed first approached police on July 31 and agreed to go undercover to meet with Dalia—whom he called by her Arabic name, Delilah—he signed the standard Confidential Informant agreement guaranteeing that police would make every attempt to safeguard his identity. In his mind, that meant that the case could proceed without him and his participation would never be acknowledged. And, in fact, the police protected his identity all throughout the arrest and Dalia's first appearance in court—leaving his name out of the probable cause affidavit, not identifying him to Dalia during her initial interview, or to Mike in his subsequent police interviews, and shielding him from the street and the media. Contrary to popular opinion, the police did not release the surveillance tapes of Mohamed and Dalia negotiating a hit man, or Dalia and Officer Widy Jean arranging for Mike's early dispatch, both of which went viral. (Once they were given to the defense, the news media was entitled to copies, and publicized them accordingly.) As the chief prosecutor, I knew his identity, but I intentionally kept my distance and didn't make him part of my initial strategy, in accordance with his wishes and expectations.

Generally, a source is kept confidential so that the person who is charged cannot identify them or attempt to dissuade them from testifying. In a typical drug case, for instance, a CI might be someone in a privileged position to know the details of a drug buy, someone privy to the word on the street, or someone looking to extricate themselves from their own bad bust or a professional snitch looking to advance in their profession like anyone else. Here, Dalia knew immediately who the confidential informant was, because Mohamed was the only one she had discussed her intentions with in depth. Even Michael Stanley, her would-be paramour and last-ditch collaborator, was given an elaborate set of justifications that diverged significantly from reality and applied logic, which he took at face value. Mohamed was the one person she had known the longest, the one who could call her on her nonsense, and the one around whom she eventually dropped all pretense about her true plans. It's only when those plans threatened to sweep him into the pit along with her that he was forced to take action.

Dalia Dippolito on her way to the courtroom.

In Florida, we have a very broad public records law that says that any document, regardless of physical form (tape, recording, photograph, or film), made or received by an agency in connection with official business is available for copy or personal inspection by any person. According to the statute, documents or evidence related to a trial not considered a work product is a public record. With the release of the staged crime scene video by the Boynton Beach Police, media interest was already on high alert, and every imaginable print and broadcast outlet had their requests pending. I was not obligated to provide them with material until I formally released it to the defense attorney under the rules of discovery—I had thirty days from when the defense filed its motion—and I was getting in new documents almost daily. In the back of my mind, I never thought this case would go to trial, since the evidence was so overwhelming: a great deal of it is captured on surveillance video, in taped phone calls, bank records, and text messages. If you're suitably wired, you can watch it unfold practically in real time. I thought that Dalia would have no choice but to throw herself on the mercy of the court and accept responsibility for her actions, so I tabled the discovery as long as I could in order to keep Mohamed out of the mix. But once it became evident we were going to trial, my hands were tied. Although I probably could have tried the case without him, Mohamed was an integral part of my case.

I released everything on November 16, 2009, including Mohamed's name as a witness, where he showed up in Dalia's phone records and text messages; her bank records that showed the purchase of the Range Rover with Mike's money; and particularly, a discovery CD with all the audio and video elements I planned to enter into evidence. Once the defense was in possession of this material, I also had to provide copies to every media outlet that requested it. The videos were uploaded to YouTube almost immediately, igniting a second media firestorm, and Mohamed's world changed overnight.

Mohamed was adamant that he had been promised anonymity. Although he knew he was wired for sound, he had not been told a camera had been placed in his car prior to his meeting with Dalia, and his first clue to that fact was when he viewed himself online. Even though the contract he had signed authorized police to record his actions in the service of their investigation, they chose not to complicate the moment by burdening him with their decision. Legally, he had no realistic expectation of privacy, but it was no less a body blow when the world came down around him. Now, not only was he a public figure—and I would characterize the media attention in South Florida as radioactive—in his world, he had just committed the one unpardonable sin. Here was a person who had two guns and a concealed weapons permit, spent much of his time reporting stolen checks to the IRS, and by necessity kept one foot in the world of ballers and bad men; and through his actions, gang members and street thugs were in danger of getting dragged into a crime they didn't commit. Larry Coe, whom he had identified to police, confronted Mohamed at his store the day after Dalia was arrested, called him a snitch, and threw the newspaper in his face. For someone like Mike Dippolito, sudden notoriety had been disconcerting and more than a little embarrassing. But for Mohamed, it could actually prove fatal.

When I contacted Mohamed a year and a half later, after Salnick made plans to take his deposition, he was less than thrilled to hear from me. Contrary to the defense's claims that Mohamed was a failed actor who craved the public spotlight, he could not have been more reticent. He declined all media requests for interviews. And he was livid that, in his eyes, the cops had given him up—he called them and screamed at them for having filmed him surreptitiously. When I finally met with him, I told him I was sympathetic to his plight, but that Dalia had refused to take a plea, she didn't think she had done anything wrong, and although I was asking him nicely, it wasn't really an invitation. If I had to go to extremes, I would have held him in custody as a material witness until trial.

Mohamed traveled on his own dime from California, where he was then living, to Boca Raton, where he had business to attend to, and we conducted the deposition at the State Attorney's Office. Mohamed showed up with an attorney, Ian Goldstein, who had once been Salnick's law partner, which created a minor wrinkle. The deposition lasted for six hours, and it was brutal—Salnick kept hammering at him incessantly. By the end, Mohamed was exhausted, but I couldn't take the chance that he would disappear back to California and not show up for the trial, so I had him served with a subpoena for trial before the deposition ended. I felt bad, but he seemed fine with it, although he informed me there was a chance he would be out of the country at the time of the trial. His mother was quite ill, and he was considering returning to his native Jordan indefinitely to work in the family business. A week later, I contacted Mohamed to find out what his status was for trial. He told me he was certain that he would be out of the country on April 25, 2011, with no return date.

After some deliberation, I filed a motion to perpetuate his testimony, which means that if a witness is unavailable for trial, their testimony can be prerecorded and played for the jury at a later date. The session is set up exactly like at trial: The witness is sworn in and a court reporter takes down the proceedings. Both sides make objections as they would before a judge, the witness goes ahead and answers the question, and then prior to trial the judge rules on each objection and the video testimony is edited accordingly.

The motion was granted, and testimony was taken a month later, on March 7, 2011, in the training room, a big room in the State Attorney's Office. We were seated at a long table, Mohamed posed against a gray back-drop with Salnick and me both just inches away from him on either side. Both our co-counsels were in attendance, as was Dalia, who had the statu-tory right to face her accuser, and whom Mohamed had not seen or spoken to since her arrest. This was the first time that Dalia and Mohamed had seen each other since her arrest. Dalia wore a tight low-cut white blouse and sat close enough for him to reach out and touch her, and the heat was palpable. I thought she was flirting with him. He would look over at her and giggle, especially when he had to describe something graphic, like her giving him a blow job. I could tell it must be excruciating for him, but it was also funny, just because the situation was so absurd. There were also times when he couldn't look at her because he felt bad about the things he was saying. He hadn't wanted to hurt her. He'd honestly believed he was helping her, and now he was driving the nails into her coffin. I believe he genuinely cared for her. Whatever else, they had history together.

The problem with prerecording testimony is that you have to formulate your questions before you're fully ready to go to court. The last few weeks in any major trial are crucial because everything is just coming together. You're finally seeing the pieces that don't fit, and these often show you the flaws in your strategy or inspire a new understanding of the facts. Questioning him a good month early, I didn't know where he fit with my physical evidence or my lineup of witnesses, nor did I have a clear picture of how he fit into the defense strategy, or even what that strategy might be. I thought if I had interviewed him in court live before the jury, in real time, it might have gone more smoothly. But there was a ragged hole in Mohamed's story—the privileged conversation he'd had with Dalia at the Chili's across the street from the Mobil station immediately before she met with the alleged hit man. That conversation wasn't recorded because the surveillance equipment failed, and I had visions of the defense linking Mike and Mohamed in some sinister plot, portraying Mike as coercive or having threatened Dalia into compliance, all of which hinged on this suspicious half hour of silence. It was my eighteen-minute gap, or the motorcade passing behind a sign. If Mohamed was out of the country and couldn't answer such charges, it could blow up on me. So I forged ahead the best I could and tried to do some preemptive triage.

Once we were closer to the trial date, I checked with a contact at ICE, who provided me with a copy of Mohamed's travel itinerary. These showed the dates he flew to Tel Aviv and then Jordan, with no return flight. He told me he would be in Jordan indefinitely. He did call me a week before our trial date to say he'd be willing to return to testify if we paid for his flight. I contacted Salnick, who agreed to pay for his return flight, but ultimately Mohamed changed his mind. Once we knew he wasn't coming back, Salnick and I met and agreed to what portions of his video testimony should be redacted, based on previous court rulings, a little give-and-take and the law, and Judge Colbath wasn't forced to rule on our objections.

I played Mohamed's prerecorded testimony in court on the Friday of the first week, after the lunch break. It ran a little over four hours. We had a projector screen set up right in front of the jury box with a special sound system; it was like he was sitting there facing them. On videotape, Mohamed appeared casual—drinking soda, chewing gum, smiling on occasion. On paper, his comments often seem confused or slightly flustered, but he has a natural magnetism that somewhat counteracts that in person. A jury could see him and Dalia as a natural couple, which hopefully would emphasize the price he was paying for following his conscience. It was also obvious he didn't want to be there.

Mohamed testified that Dalia had initially told him she was in an abusive relationship, that Mike beat her and she was scared of him, but that quickly gave way to a more benign version: Mike was "a nice, nerdy guy" and she could "pretty much do whatever she needs to do to him"; she had inadvertently spent his probation money and "needs to replace it"; and more precisely, "She doesn't like him and she wants him to go to jail." Mohamed had the distinct impression that "she can't stand him and she wants him violated." He was "a musclehead," had OCD, and "he wouldn't let her out of his sight."

Besides asking if he knew "an officer or someone" who could help get her husband's probation revoked, "she wanted to know how to transfer money or get a fake receipt showing that the money got transferred into Western Union or a bank account" (he declined to help, since he was audited by the IRS virtually every month). She also asked to borrow $200,000 and gave him details about a Cayman Islands account that he remained sketchy on. As noted previously, she also confessed that she had lied about her pregnancy, repeatedly called the police on Mike, admitted she tried to poison him with antifreeze, and, on more than one occasion, expressed her desire to have him killed. In fact, Mohamed claims that after he had inadvertently introduced Dalia to the potential hit man Larry Coe and his crew from the Buck Wild gang, they called him repeatedly trying to determine if she was "legit." By his account, he may have saved Mike's life more than once:

> I told them . . . let things cool off and let her deal with her problems her own way. I told them I already had an officer involved, so if you guys do anything to that house or do anything relevant to her, you guys will get caught and will be in trouble. And I think they backed off.

She later apologized to him for trying to go behind his back in hiring them.

Mohamed traveled to Israel with his daughter during early summer, returning June 20. By the time Dalia tried to steal his gun at the Mobil station on July 31, he'd had enough. He believed that by approaching the police, he might scare her straight—wave her off of a course of action that could prove cataclysmic. But he never intended for her to be arrested. He only agreed to wear a wire after they convinced him he might be implicated if she actually went through with it. Outside of two phone calls, he never knew police were listening to his conversations, or that they were being recorded, and certainly not that he was being videotaped.

"My whole point was to try to help her and get her out of the trouble she was in," he said. "I didn't know it was going to get to this point or any fake crime scene or anything that they did. Like, I just really wanted to help her at that time. I don't know if she was really feared [afraid] from the people she showed the house to or she wanted her husband killed. So I figured maybe the officer can help her. I didn't think it was going to get this far."

If Salnick's cross-examination of Mike could be boiled down to the sentence "Mike Dippolito is a liar," then his cross of Mohamed could be summed up in the question: "Are you high?" Mohamed's grasp of detail and his general concept of time were elastic at best, and Salnick was looking to exploit every inconsistency he could find in Mohamed's testimony. This is from Salnick's opening statement:

> The evidence will show that Mr. Shihadeh will be asked about a number of things he claims to have knowledge of. You'll notice inconsistencies in his statements. You will hear him contradict himself. And in some instances, he says he has a photographic memory, and then he'll tell you only what he chooses to remember. He gets dates, times, and places wrong, and then tries to explain it away with excuses. The evidence will show that Mr. Shihadeh's memory of significant events is not good.

Yeah, tell me about it.

The difference between depositions and trial testimony in general is that the first is expansive and the second is constrictive. Much of the material that surfaces in a deposition is inadmissible because the goal is to get the witness talking and keep him talking. In a criminal deposition, an attorney wants to lock a witness for the prosecution into a particular version of events—the more detailed the better. Then, on the stand, corral his answers in ways that seem to contradict his initial version—get him confused, intimidate him, screw up his memory—all in order to challenge his credibility. That was the entirety of Salnick's strategy with Mohamed. In Mohamed's deposition, there was a prolonged section at the end that sounded like a personality test out of the *Diagnostic and Statistical Manual of Mental Disorders*:

> Do you think you're good at influencing people? . . . Are you modest? . . . Are you cautious? . . . If somebody dared you to do something, would you do it? . . . Do you get embarrassed when you're compli- mented? . . . Do people tell you you're a good person? . . . Can you talk your way out of anything? . . . Do you like to be the center of attention?

And on and on. This would not have been out of place in a film like *The Master* or in a sidewalk personality inventory administered by the volunteers at the Scientology Center. In fact, Salnick was trying to peg Mohamed as a narcissist and borderline personality—presumably to cast him in some nefarious role in the reality TV conspiracy defense he must have been formulating at the time. He seems to have abandoned that strat- egy by the time he got to trial. Here, he was only interested in documenting Mohamed's lapses of memory.

SALNICK: Do you have a bad memory, sir?

MOHAMED: No, I don't have a bad memory, but so much happened to me during the past two years.

And later on:

SALNICK: But you did tell me previously that you're the kind of per- son that has a great memory, is that correct?

MOHAMED: Yes, when it comes to things that I want to remember.

Mohamed routinely consumed a quantity of prescription Xanax to treat his anxiety, an admission I got on the record up front; there are tapes of phone calls he made to Dalia that are virtually incoherent. Detective Moreno told me that on one occasion, he was standing next to him supervising one of these calls when Mohamed fell asleep in the middle of the conversation. By pinpointing Mohamed's confusion over dates and times, nit-picking every time he misspoke in now four separate attempts to recount his experiences, and attempting to put him at odds with the police over whether or not he was a willing witness, Salnick hoped to push him over into the red zone, make him angry or frustrated enough to render him unsympathetic to a jury, or if Salnick got really lucky, provoke him to walk out on these proceedings and refuse to participate in the case.

"So it's your testimony that you didn't lie to the police," Salnick asks at one point, "they didn't ask the question the right way. Is that what it is?"

Salnick found disparities in the date Mohamed first met Dalia (between 1999 and 2001), how long they initially dated (between fourteen months and four years), what month they reconnected (February, March, or three weeks before her arrest—i.e., July), and where they first met (Palm Beach Gardens Mall, adjacent to the mall, on the plaza, etc.).

> SALNICK: So if you told me in your deposition that you only heard from her three weeks before, that would have been a mistake, right?
>
> MOHAMED: I probably misunderstood your question.
>
> SALNICK: You probably weren't listening to my question.
>
> MOHAMED: Misunderstood your question.

And he spent an inordinate amount of time on whether Mohamed was driving the Range Rover or the Lexus when Dalia tried to steal his gun, since he returned the former the day after Dalia offered it as an incentive to Larry Coe (whom Mohamed calls "a really bad person who lives in Riviera Beach") to kill her husband, contributing a finite time line to the events as he described them. Under Salnick's ceaseless probing, Mohamed is uncertain whether the gun incident took place in the Range Rover or the Lexus, outside his cousin's Urban Wear store or the Mobil station, whether it was serious or a joke, six weeks or six days before she was arrested, whether he left the car to talk to his cousin or for Red Bull and cigarettes, and whether there were people around or they were alone.

And by the way, if Mohamed felt so strongly about Dalia's threatened actions that he would squander a friendship and affection of a decade's standing to go to the police, why is it that he couldn't understand the simplest instructions in the agreement he signed with them?

SALNICK: You're a smart man, aren't you?

MOHAMED: Yes.

SALNICK: Owned a lot of businesses?

MOHAMED: Uh-huh.

SALNICK: Owned a lot of cars.

MOHAMED: Uh-huh.

SALNICK: Did the police speak a different language that you didn't
   understand?

On redirect, I tried to make sense of all of this. On the table in front of him, I placed Mohamed's 225-page February 3, 2011, deposition; the 25-page transcript of his first July 31, 2009, police interview; and a second police interview, conducted August 10, a week after Dalia's arrest, which clocked in at 20 pages. Lining them up there in front of him like a three-dimensional bar graph, it was easy to demonstrate how the deposition would have been far more detailed than the police statements, which were by necessity both broad and rushed. His disagreements with the BBPD aside over his having to testify, I easily established that he sat for both his deposition and perpetuated testimony, answering every question asked of him, even at personal risk, and in the latter case, traveling from California at his own expense to do so. I got him to freely admit the discrepancies in dates and times, which he attributed to the passage of almost two years. Beyond that, I could peg the date that Dalia tried to steal his gun to the day of his first police interview (which it inspired), his travel abroad to his cell phone records, and I was able to explain the uncertainty surrounding the gun incident by proving it was actually two separate incidents:

PARKER: Now, the day that she took the gun from your glove compartment—if I remember correctly, she went to her car to bring the gun back to you after you questioned her about it. Is that right?

MOHAMED: There was a time before that, where, you know . . . killing her husband was not serious. I didn't think it was serious at all. It was before the poison or anything. She was like, well, you have a gun here, you know—use it. Let me take it. I took it back and I put it back in the glove compartment. That's where I got confused. I said, "Don't put your fingers on a gun." And the time at the gas station, when I left the car and I came back and the gun wasn't there, that's when I told her to give it to me. And then she went to the car and got it.

It was apparent that none of his confusion was intentional—he had never set out to deceive the police, the defense in his deposition, or the court here today. I also let him go on at length about how the police manipulated him into wearing a wire. His reluctance in testifying added weight to the substance of his testimony: here was someone who came forward to prevent a murder, and any actions by the defense attorney to obscure that fact now looked merely threadbare and somewhat churlish. I thought at the end of the day, he came off both likeable and credible.

Salnick took one more bite at the apple in recross:

SALNICK: You're a college-educated person?

MOHAMED: Yes.

SALNICK: You have a diploma, I think you told me the last we got together?

MOHAMED: Yes.

(I objected here as beyond the scope.)

SALNICK: You understand English? You don't have any problems speaking English, do you?

MOHAMED: No.

SALNICK: You know what the truth is, is that correct?

MOHAMED: Yes.

SALNICK: Okay, I'm done.

The following week we were in recess. Early Thursday morning, I got a call from Fred Laurie, my co-counsel Laura's husband, who is an officer with the Boca Raton Police Department. He woke me up, and the first words out of his mouth were, "I have Mohamed."

I said, "My Mohamed?" My Mohamed, according to ICE, the government organization tasked with knowing these things, was in Jordan for the duration of the trial. I had just spent an enormous amount of money to perpetuate his testimony and broadcast it for the jury. Certainly not my Mohamed.

"Yes. Mohammed Shihadeh. I have him right now. He's under arrest for DUI, and he asked for you." Fred knew we had just entered his testimony into evidence, and without saying as much was obviously concerned that Mohamed's arrest would create headaches for us.

He couldn't change the facts of the case, but he could give me a heads up. At the time of his arrest, Mohamed had over ninety Xanax in his possession. He was booked for DUI, but it could have been for trafficking if he hadn't had a valid prescription. I assumed he had just arrived from overseas and had his prescription refilled.

The next morning on my way into the office, I notified Salnick, who didn't seem overly concerned, although I did some research anyway in anticipation of this becoming an issue. Remarkably, there was no case law pertaining to this specific issue, which came down to Dalia's Sixth Amendment rights: whether she would have the opportunity to confront and cross-examine her accuser. What I discovered was that, as long as those opportunities had been afforded her—and they certainly were during Mohamed's perpetuated testimony—then I couldn't be held responsible if a witness lied to me about his whereabouts. I told Salnick I was willing to bring Mohamed back to testify in court if that's what he wanted, but he assured me that was not what they wanted.

When I finally viewed the police report, I discovered that Mohamed had been staying at a hotel in Boca Raton. Late at night, he drove to a gas station across the street to get some food for himself and his girlfriend and her son. In the parking lot, he struck up a conversation with a shirtless guy in a pickup truck about the hip-hop CD he was playing. Mohamed offered to buy it from him for ten dollars, and they got into his rented white Saturn 4-door SUV. Mohamed gave him a $20 bill and set his wallet in the cup holder. The man said he'd have to get change from his girlfriend, who was waiting in the truck. When the truck took off in a hurry, Mohamed realized his wallet was missing, containing $4,500. Mohamed set off in hot pursuit and got involved in a minor accident, which he left the scene of to continue the chase. When he flagged down a passing police officer for assistance, the officer noticed his glassy eyes, slurred speech, and lethargic manner and detained him. Officer Fred Laurie was called in to conduct a DUI investigation, which ultimately led to Mohamed's arrest. The entire incident—transient hip-hop, robbery, high-speed/half-block pursuit, hit-and-run, and potential drug bust—seemed like just another one of those only-in-Florida stories or some wild bar tale. But knowing Mohamed's prodigious Xanax intake and the fact that he used to make Dalia mix tapes made the whole thing sound bizarre yet entirely plausible.

I followed up with Fred, and Mohamed's whole story checked out on surveillance video and in witness statements. The detectives assigned to the case were able to run the license plate of the pickup and tracked it to a local residence. The man confessed and showed them where he had buried the wallet in the backyard, minus a small amount of cash. The following Monday when we resumed the trial, I asked the judge if we could approach to discuss the matter. I informed him of Mohamed's status, that my co-counsel's husband was the arresting officer, and that I had notified Salnick as soon as I learned of Mohamed's return. Salnick said he understood that Mohamed was "done, finished, history" as far as my case went, and that his client had no objections to using the prerecorded testimony as his sole testimony. Dalia confirmed that in the sidebar. We agreed that if Dalia testified and I needed to bring Mohamed in for rebuttal, we would discuss the parameters of Salnick's cross, which would certainly include details of his return and arrest. I told Judge Colbath I certainly hadn't seen this one coming.

"Oh well," said the Judge. "What can you do?"

For his part, Mohamed called me afterward to explain his changing his mind again, but I told him that henceforth, I could only communicate with him through his attorney. Given that he had testified under protest, and that his appearance before the jury was now officially complete, I guess it should come as no surprise that he hadn't alerted us he was back.

Delilah. From the Hebrew word meaning *weak, poor, or displaced.*

She was the lover who laid Samson low, and who betrayed the secret of his strength to the lords of the Philistines for 1,100 pieces of silver, fifty times the haul of Judas. Who left him blinded, alone, and in chains.

"English is Dalia and Arabic is Delilah," states Mohamed. "She told me her father is Egyptian, so I figured I got her—you know, Egypt. It's an Egyptian name: Delilah."

I asked Mike how he felt about Mohamed, who knowingly pocketed the proceeds from a luxury vehicle bought with Mike's stolen money, but who probably saved his life on more than one occasion, and whether they had spoken since.

"I don't feel the obligation to reach out to him," Mike said. "He benefited plenty—he got some of my money. Let's leave it at that." He quoted himself from one of his later TV appearances: "'He banged my wife, so we're even.' The guy doesn't get a Citizen Medal, but he did do the right thing."

CHAPTER 11

. . . .

Dinosaurs

A t the beginning of the second week, after we got the business with Mohamed sorted out, I called Jim Eddy to the stand. Sergeant Eddy was a member of the Lantana Police Department who also served with the Palm Beach County Sheriff's Office Violent Crimes Task Force, where he was an authority on the Buck Wild gang. Prior to Sergeant Eddy taking the stand, Salnick had been successful in getting the court to prohibit him from discussing would-be hit man Larry Coe's specific crimes, so I used him merely to confirm Larry's cell phone number, which I was able to prove Dalia called thirteen separate times on April 2, three days before her arrest. (Only two of the calls connected, for less than two minutes apiece.)

While not going into the details, Eddy was comfortable on the stand referring to Larry and his crew as killers. He also informed the jury that Larry was currently on trial in the adjacent courtroom as one of five Buck Wild members charged with racketeering, conspiracy, and related crimes under the RICO (Racketeer Influence and Corrupt Organization) Act. These included Larry's younger brother Quamaine Falana, an honor student who received fifteen years for conspiracy to commit racketeering and grand theft. Larry was acquitted of all racketeering charges, but sentenced to twenty-five years on a related gun charge—Possession of a Firearm by a Convicted Felon—due to his violent past. Palm Beach County Prosecutors Greg Kridos, Cheryl Caracuzzo, and I compared notes, including the contents of Coe's cell phone. Cheryl and I have been friends for years, and she kept joking about offering Dalia a deal to testify.

On cross, Salnick established that the Metro PCS cell phone Larry used was actually registered in a woman's name—a seed of doubt I successfully countered on redirect: he posted the number on MySpace to promote his burgeoning rap career, tapes of which were on sale at Urban Wear, the Riviera Beach store owned by Mohamed's cousin. Whether predominantly from the worlds of incipient hip-hop or Gold Coast criminal affinity, contacts in Larry's cell phone included the following: Boogie, Brain Crip, Bug, C-clip, Chew, Chops, Clete, Creep, Dent, Doy, Drako, Easy, Face, Fat Boy, Flake, Fluff, G, Gangster, Gangsta Face, Gboi, Hen, Honkey, Ja, Joc, K-cool, Lil Bit, Lil John, Lil Larry, Lil Q, Lil Taye, Lip, Lock, Lo Lo Lo Lo, Maut, Nard, Nay, Nelly, Niq Niq, Nookie, Noz, Puma, Ram, Raylo, R.J., Saucey, Scoobie, Ski, Skittles, Stew, Tatoo, Tootie, Trap, and Yella.

Next to the stand were three cops: Detective Asim "Ace" Brown, Sergeant John Bonafair, and Officer Carlos Reinhold. Ace Brown fielded Mohamed's phone call that set the whole case in motion, but he also became one of my trusted investigators. Under oath, he confirmed Mohamed's actions on the day he contacted police and continuing through his initial interviews, and he explained the particulars of the standard Confidential Informant contract. Since Detective Brown specialized in financial crime investigations, I had him speak to further details of the Cayman wire transfer and those subsequent financial transactions involving Erik Tal, including that the money deposited in Tal's bank account was soon after wired to Israel. On cross-examination, Salnick focused on a fifteen-minute discrepancy in the times Brown listed for the first Mohamed phone call in his official reports, and hammered him on his initial impression that Mohamed's information was "sketchy" and that he was unable to identify the victim's full name. He also tried to get Detective Brown to admit to promising Mohamed anonymity, which he wouldn't.

Sergeant John Bonafair headed the surveillance teams at both the Mobil station with Mohamed and Dalia and the CVS with Dalia and "hit man" Widy Jean. Deep-voiced and sporting a goatee, he testified that he and Detective Sheridan chose Widy Jean for the role of the hit man because he was able to braid his hair (everyone else sported a military cut). He testified that although informants are generally told when recording devices are placed in their vehicles or on their person, here notification on the upgrade to video somehow slipped through the cracks. On cross, Salnick once again had a witness reiterate that the Chili's meeting between Mohamed and Dalia just prior to her meeting with the hit man should have been recorded.

Lead detective on the surveillance equipment was Officer Carlos Reinhold, responsible for placing the surreptitious video feed in the backseat of Mohamed's car. Throughout an eight-year career, he estimated he had placed electronics in the field probably 200 times. As to alerting Mohamed to the technology onboard, he said, "We don't like to get too specific. We try to keep our trade secrets." He explained a discrepancy in the time code for the CVS surveillance tape as due to the fact that the batteries are removed from the Unitel recording device after every use. On cross, Salnick seemed most interested in his interaction with the *COPS* crew at the staged crime scene, which was minimal.

Next I called Boynton Beach PD Public Information Officer Stephanie Slater. Her background was as a newspaper reporter, so her efforts to secure the department some decent press made perfect sense to me. According to her testimony, their involvement with *COPS* began in September 2008 when she contacted Bryan Collins, a producer for the syndicated series, at the behest of Chief Matthew Immler. (Immler appeared on *Nancy Grace* to discuss this case after Dalia's arrest.) *COPS* had recently done ride-alongs with the Palm Beach County and Martin County Sheriff's Offices, and at Slater's invitation, they spent a week in April 2009 riding with Boynton Beach patrol officers to test the waters. When that went smoothly, Collins requested eight weeks with the BBPD beginning on August 11. *COPS* later moved their start date up a week, and on August 4, 2009, producer Jimmy Langley (nephew of series creator John Langley) and Miami-based cameraman Chris Flores showed up at the station to start prepping. As confirmed in an e-mail, *COPS* agreed not to air footage related to any case prior to its disposition in a court of law (a standard policy designed as much to shield them from liability as to ingratiate them with local police departments). Sometime during the day of August 4, Sergeant Paul Sheridan, head of the Major Cases unit, approached Slater with the brainstorm that *COPS* film the Dalia Dippolito staged crime scene the following morning, despite the fact *COPS* focuses almost entirely on patrol officers and random events, not on detectives during an open, active investigation. All parties agreed that the actual crime in question—Solicitation to Commit First-Degree Murder—had already been committed, during Dalia's meeting with CI Mohamed Shihadeh on August 1 when money changed hands. Since anything else was gravy, they felt there was no real harm in commemorating some superlative police work on tape. From there, things moved very fast.

> PARKER: After your conversation with Sergeant Sheridan on August 4 of 2009, what if anything did you do next?
>
> SLATER: Well, as soon as he had said it, I thought it was a great idea, and went up the chain of command to the lieutenant of the detective bureau, then to the major and then to the chief, and then we had conversations about what the parameters would be.

COPS agreed that on the morning of the bust, after they filmed Mike being notified of what was happening, they would be cordoned behind police barricades as if they were members of the regular press, in order not to alert the suspect.

I also asked Slater why she posted the scene to YouTube.

> SLATER: That was posted. A discussion was had, and we realized that it was going to be on a public street, and on a public street there is no expectation of privacy. Anyone could have filmed that video. It just so happened that the police department did, and we decided that someone else could have posted it on there, so we were going to take the proactive approach and post it on there ourselves, and explain the entire case in the process.

Immediately following Slater I called Detective Frank Ranzie to the stand. Ranzie was born and raised in Brooklyn, and the borough's brash manner had never entirely left him, even down here in our sun-blasted paradise. He's physically ripped (that's him in the video telling Dalia her husband has been killed) and tightly wound, with an almost comical propensity to speak his mind. He's on the cusp of fifty and coming up on thirty years in law enforcement, but unlike a lot of other cops his age who see the past through a halcyon glow, he wears his slights like battle scars, and makes no secret of having outlived his era.

"I drove a cab," he says today. "I got robbed at gunpoint, took a really bad beating within an inch of my life. Almost got stabbed by a group of guys who set me up. And there wasn't a cop around when I needed one. Sounds cliché, I know." When a buddy got a job as a New York City transit cop, Ranzie took the test and aced it. Very quickly, he was pipelined straight into the Police Academy and then worked as an NYPD Housing cop. Four years later, when a colleague took a job in Boynton Beach and was asked to recruit some of his friends, Ranzie came south for a two-week vacation and never left.

Ranzie was the first guy Ace Brown called when he originally fielded the call from Mohamed. He sat in on that first interview and called Sergeant Sheridan to alert him to the situation. And since Mohamed didn't have a full name for the suspect, and therefore no way to identify the victim, Ranzie spent hours that first night driving him around Boynton Beach in the hopes he would recognize "Delilah's" residence. He claimed it was the first time in twenty-six years someone had walked in the door to interrupt a murder. Although Ranzie believes Mohamed's story—"he just had no other purpose in coming to us"—he also doesn't find him without fault.

"My vibe was this," says Ranzie. "Not only was Dalia in a relationship with this person, for some reason she believed Mike Dippolito was worth, I don't know, a gazillion dollars and had all this stuff that she could somehow acquire. And I believe the boyfriend, the informant, somehow thought that somewhere down the road he would be the beneficiary of all this luxury when she gets rid of this guy. Initially, it was just leave the guy, get rid of the guy, have him sent back up the river. But when it got to where she was saying 'Do you love me?' kind of stuff—'pull the trigger'—he's thinking 'Whoa, there's limits on this. I enjoy the luxury, I enjoyed the free Range Rover, and hey, it would be nice to live in that house. But I don't want to go to jail for murder.' I think that was the block that hit his conscience. Despite him being an unsavory character in a lot of ways, he's not a murderer."

Ranzie was there the next day at the Mobil station when Mohamed met with Dalia—he was pumping gas the whole time at one of the islands—and I used him to introduce the surveillance tape into evidence and play it in court. He was also on the stakeout in the CVS parking lot the day that Dalia met with her "hit man," doing standard surveillance as well as countersurveillance. "For all we know, she has two guys in a car following her in because she's going to rip or kill this guy," he says. "You have to prepare for it all." And he planned and executed staging the crime scene, where he was the point man on interacting with the suspect. This allowed me to finally play the crime scene video for the jury, as well as a second view of Dalia's reaction taken from Ranzie's lapel cam, where it's easier to see she's not crying real tears.

On Tuesday, August 4, the day before Dalia was to be arrested, Ranzie was informed that *COPS* would be filming at the Dippolito crime scene. It is safe to say that he was less than enthusiastic about the plan.

> PARKER: How did you fit the *COPS* film crew into your operational plan?
>
> RANZIE: Well, unwillingly. I'd like to use that word. But I fit them in to just the staged crime scene portion, because we felt that at that point, as we mentioned earlier, the actual crime—the solicitation to murder—that's already happened. I didn't want *COPS* to be part of any of the case at all, but I don't have that authority, and so I fit them in to act like the press and stay behind a cordoned-off area at the staged crime scene.

At the end of direct, in quick succession, I asked him whether he was trying to become a celebrity ("Absolutely not"), launch an acting career ("No"), mount a publicity stunt on behalf of the Boynton Beach Police Department ("No"), or trying to help Mike, Dalia, or Mohamed get their own reality show (all "No"). On cross, Salnick tried to score a few familiar points—getting Ranzie to admit that releasing the crime scene video could have an impact on the trial (over my objections); questioning why Mohamed wasn't wired for audio (which would have precluded the dead air at the Chili's meet); digging into whether Ranzie fully explained Mohamed's obligations as a PI (or worse, lied to him); and, mainly, successfully underscoring his reservations about the *COPS* contamination, PR onslaught, and anything else that could lay the groundwork for believing manufactured reality had suddenly gained precedence over the quotidian.

> SALNICK: And the powers above you wanted this to be on *COPS*, didn't they?
>
> RANZIE: Yes.
>
> SALNICK: And you certainly weren't happy about that, were you?
>
> RANZIE: No, I actually spoke in that meeting and said I don't think it's a good idea.
>
> SALNICK: But you, I don't want to say nobody paid attention to you, but . . .
>
> RANZIE: You can say that.
>
> SALNICK: Did anyone pay attention to you?
>
> RANZIE: No.

Salnick spent extra time on the inherently theatrical nature of the crime scene, how Dalia's reaction to the word "killed" almost seemed to jump the gun, as if she were anticipating it, and Ranzie's prior assessment of her performance as "an Academy Award–winning act of grief."

> SALNICK: She was faking it, wasn't she?
>
> RANZIE: That's my belief.
>
> SALNICK: And the television show *COPS* is filming this.
>
> RANZIE: Yes.
>
> SALNICK: Through the equipment you have on.
>
> RANZIE: The audio is from the equipment I have on, but they are filming it from the van that was depicted.

And he paid special attention to the *COPS* waiver.

After he explained her Miranda rights to Dalia, and before he had her sign an affidavit to that effect, Sheridan had Dalia sign a release to allow footage of her to appear on *COPS*. As previously stated, *COPS* producer Jimmy Langley was livid when he found out, pronouncing the waiver useless, since it was easily argued Dalia didn't know what she was signing. (As far as she knew, her husband had just been murdered.) Cameraman Chris Flores later approached Dalia in a holding cell and persuaded her to sign a second waiver.

In his deposition, Sheridan stated that he had secured Dalia's signature on the form at Langley's behest, a claim that Langley took issue with in his own deposition. A proven supporter of law enforcement whose livelihood depended on it, Langley also took the additional step of complaining to Police Chief Matt Immler, presumably to protect his reputation and that of the series. Unbeknownst to him, at the behest of Chief Immler, BBPD Internal Affairs began an investigation into Sheridan's actions and subsequent statement, ultimately finding no fault with Sergeant Sheridan and attributing the discrepancy to miscommunication. On the basis of that, I successfully filed my motion to keep the IA investigation out of the trial, as well as any argument the defense might make that Flores obtained Dalia's second waiver improperly, arguing that whatever he did after Dalia was arrested had no bearing on the case.

"Their buttholes puckered over that whole brouhaha over who got her to sign the consent waiver," says Ranzie. "They were thinking they were losing their footage. They were scared to death about losing their fantastic story. And that's why they were concerned about following their rules even more so. Ratings. They didn't care about the case. They knew they were on the bubble because of that whole Sheridan thing. Again, I'm not picking on Paul. But the facts are there. The video is there and it shows what it is."

As a kind of grace note at the end of his cross-examination, Salnick said, "You said that you objected and made it very clear about the TV show *COPS* being involved. Tell us why."

"Because of what's happening right now," said Ranzie.

On redirect, I had Ranzie state for the record that the presence of the *COPS* crew had no effect on the crime scene or the way the case was investigated. Throughout his testimony, Ranzie was truthful in his answers, but I felt he largely kept his considerable opinions to himself.

Such is not the case if you talk to him outside the courtroom.

Internally, Ranzie was a vocal critic of almost every aspect of this investigation, beginning with the staged crime scene, which was predicated on a case Sheridan worked earlier in his career where they actually re-created a murder scene with fake blood and special effects, placed the daily newspaper by the victim's head, and took Polaroids as photographic proof. Sheridan also initially proposed himself to play the part of the undercover hit man.

"Basically, I love Paul Sheridan," says Ranzie. "He's a really good guy, but he started coming up with ideas on how to put this together based on something he did twenty years prior. I don't mean to say that in a bad way, but twenty years ago they had Polaroid cameras."

Ranzie's opinion did not change once the crime scene tape was uploaded to YouTube and the media took notice. "I was beside myself when the chief authorized the PIO to release that video," he says. "I was beside myself! It was almost like they put the cart in front of the horse, because I thought, Oh this is a slam dunk . . . I can guarantee you that no lawyer in the world wants the evidence out there before we've even filed the criminal charges."

These criticisms were largely procedural, and they tied the staged crime scene and the *COPS* presence together in a way that Salnick's vaunted defense largely did not, by measuring their impact on the people who were affected. As it was designed, the investigative plan would have unfolded in three parts: the meetings with undercover operatives to ensure the crime threat was credible; the fake crime scene to convince the suspect her efforts had been successful; and then a carefully choreographed interrogation, taking place over many hours, where the noose slowly tightens, cutting off her options. It was this last part that suffered in the final accounting.

"That plan didn't make it to its final end," says Ranzie. "Had it made it to its end, I believe we would have avoided even the prosecution's court case because I believe she would have pled out to something and took a serious hit. Here's the plan: You're the widow. We serve you up water or something and make you comfortable. Let her sell her soul with the lies about thugs and people that would want him dead. Then, after she's relaxed with her lies, we were gonna say, 'We got a guy we found in the area who matched the description. Come take a look.' She would have seen him [through a one-way mirror]. Who brings the suspect of a violent crime into the interview room? . . . Bring her back to the room. Corral her with some other nonsense. Twenty minutes later, the detective is going to come in with a cell phone. Do the whole thing, make sure she sees it. Step out for a minute, come back in: 'Dalia: You know that guy you said you don't know? Why is his phone number in your phone?' That was the plan. Then, she would have been like, 'I don't know.' And we already got her phone. That fell apart . . .

"Basically, we had all day. We could have talked to her for hours. And then got her to the point of possibly confessing. What I'm saying is, there was some overzealousness in that moment. Almost like a jump-up-and-high-five moment where 'we got this case locked and loaded.' And then guys start tripping over themselves and make mistakes."

In Ranzie's telling, the Boynton Beach Police Department was just learning something that Hollywood has been exploiting for well over a century: put a camera on somebody, and their behavior changes. Now they're watching themselves through someone else's eyes, and their behavior starts playing catch-up with everyone else's imagined expectations.

"I believe in the man, but for whatever reason, in that moment, Paul got frustrated that this was going to take time. You could tell . . . He's old school: 'Let's get this shit done.' So he basically kicked the other detectives out of the room and went in there and ended it. At the end of the day, did it harm the case? No, it didn't, but it did leave a lot of flexibility for the defense to run circles around a lot of things, including that waiver and a whole bunch of other stuff."

Ranzie voiced some of these concerns on day one, in a meeting with Jimmy Langley in attendance. Langley told him he appreciated his honesty, and promised his crew would never get in the way, which physically at least they did not. But it also didn't account for the things Ranzie witnessed that stayed with him—like how a potential victim had to learn his whole world was about to cave in on him with a big boom mic hanging in his face, or parading Widy Jean or her resurrected husband in front of Dalia for the cameras as a kind of visual "gotcha," the endless B-roll of walking, talking, and prefabricated interstitial moments, which under oath he called "an unpleasant experience."

"That's their show," he says, "but I didn't have to like it."

At the end of that first meeting, Sheridan overruled him and told him to make it work, and he said okay. It aired as a "special episode" on September 24, 2011.

After he testified in the Dippolito trial, Ranzie was severely dressed down by Chief Immler in a supervisor's meeting, essentially, he believes, for telling the truth. "Me and him have never been right since," he says. From where he sits, he can see his era ending.

"I don't know how else to phrase it, but this is not the decade of policing I signed up for," he says today. "It's not the political correctness and over-the-top liberalism that I signed up for. It's not what I've grown up to do, so I think it's time to turn over the reins and let a new generation that will be indoctrinated into this new way of policing handle it. Because, to be honest, I'm getting too frustrated with the way things have changed . . . I'm considered a dinosaur. I don't want to be that guy anymore. Let them take over and move forward."

After I was finished with Ranzie on the stand, I put up another five policemen in quick succession, beginning with Sergeant Craig Anthony, who helped set up the crime scene. My co-counsel Laura Burkhart Laurie conducted the examination. In between Anthony's accounts of securing the premises and the couple's pets, photographing interiors to maintain integrity (i.e., preserving their ability to restore everything to its original condition), stringing yellow tape, etc., Laura used him to tweak Salnick's imminent reality defense in rather pointed fashion: "Did you see any scripts lying around?" "Did you see any paperwork pertaining to a reality TV stunt?" On cross, Salnick tried to tweak Laura's tweak:

SALNICK: You didn't see any open file cabinets, did you?

ANTHONY: No.

SALNICK: Desk drawers?

ANTHONY: No.

SALNICK: . . . Okay, and I imagine you didn't find any notes saying, "I'm going to kill my husband," either, did you?

ANTHONY: I did not.

Detective Jason Llopis and Detective Brian McDeavitt drove Dalia to the station, which allowed me to enter the tape of their conversation into evidence. Llopis said it caught him off guard when Dalia asked how he got her number, and he improvised an answer on the spot that seemed to satisfy her. On cross, Salnick solicited Llopis's critique of Dalia's performance, and then tried to reverse-engineer that into proof of this reality TV gambit:

SALNICK: You weren't buying anything she was saying, were you?

LLOPIS: Not from what information I had been told.

SALNICK: Okay, you didn't believe anything she said. What she was saying? She was making things up. She was acting, wasn't she?

LLOPIS: I didn't believe everything she was saying . . .

When Llopis finally volunteered that he thought she was putting on a show, Salnick stopped fishing for a better quote.

Detective Brian Anderson talked about the search warrants, and about Dalia's interview at the station with Detective Sheridan, which he was present for. On cross, Salnick tried once again to solicit an admission from law enforcement that Dalia was acting—terminology crucial to his defense, but here elicited at a heavy price. In a lengthy back-and-forth with one of Dalia's inquisitors concerning her performance in the interrogation room, which should have been her finest hour, Salnick's own sense of the dramatic failed him, pitching over into farce, and leaving him clutching his empty moral outrage like a worthless prop.

SALNICK: How many times do you remember her saying that she wanted to talk to her husband?

ANDERSON: Once or twice.

SALNICK: She is pretty emphatic about it though: "Mike, Mike, come here!"

ANDERSON: Yes.

SALNICK: You indicated that when you met her, and when you were in the room with her, she had a total lack of emotion—is that correct?

ANDERSON: That's true.

SALNICK: As if she wasn't upset about her husband being dead.

ANDERSON: Correct.

SALNICK: As if she didn't care, in your opinion.

ANDERSON: Yes, that's my opinion.

SALNICK: What if she knew her husband wasn't really dead? Wouldn't you expect her to have a total lack of emotion?

ANDERSON: If she knew that.

SALNICK: And you said that there were no tears.

ANDERSON: I didn't see any tears.

SALNICK: In other words, it was sort of like acting, or a fake type of crying.

ANDERSON: A fake crying—yes.

SALNICK: How would she do that—can you explain to the jury?

ANDERSON: Like I said before: when someone goes through the motions and is making that crying noise and carrying on without tears.

Salnick asks him to demonstrate for the jury. In the courtroom, Dalia laughs at his attempt.

SALNICK: So she is sort of faking it, right?

ANDERSON: Yes.

SALNICK: Acting like she is crying.

ANDERSON: She was faking it.

SALNICK: Acting like she is crying.

ANDERSON: Faking it.

SALNICK: You don't want to say the word acting, do you?

ANDERSON: Why wouldn't I want to say that?

SALNICK: Well, was she acting like she was crying.

ANDERSON: She was faking like she was crying.

Salnick looks over at the jury dramatically.

SALNICK: I understand that, but I would like you to answer my question.

ANDERSON: I just did.

SALNICK: (emphatically raising his voice) Yes or no, sir: Was she acting like she was crying?

ANDERSON: Yes.

SALNICK: No further questions.

Crime Scene Technician Robin Eichorst testified next. I had asked him prior to trial to fingerprint the money Dalia gave to Mohamed, even though we both knew it was highly unlikely her prints would be found on it. In this CSI era, this is a question jurors want answered. Eichorst explained to the jury the procedure for fingerprinting evidence and why he was unable to retrieve any prints from the money. And Detective Brian McDeavitt had been located adjacent to Dalia when she collapsed into Sergeant Ranzie's arms, and had driven her to the station with Officer Llopis. He basically reiterated what Llopis said earlier.

I followed up with Sergeant Sheridan, who could remember only one other case like this in thirty-three years of law enforcement. For his part, Sheridan took responsibility for virtually every area of controversy raised by the defense. He owned the decision not to tape the conversation at Chili's, weighing the failure of the Unitel wire against the disruption of removing one from Widy Jean's vehicle, where it was already in place for the rendezvous at the CVS. None of his superiors oversaw his decisions in the case. It was his idea to bring the fake crime scene to *COPS'* attention, as it was to conduct the interview with Dalia himself. "I do that every once in a while," he claimed. He volunteered that he rarely tells suspects they are being taped in an interview room "because there is no expectation of privacy in a police station," making his argument for Dalia to sign the *COPS* waiver all the more specious. When I asked him why he didn't arrest Dalia after her meeting with the hit man, let alone the second she gave money to Mohamed, he said, "We still wanted to give her the benefit of the doubt, to see if she was going to continue with it and to see her reaction." When I raised the question why he didn't alert Mike any earlier, since there was ostensibly a murder contract out on him, Sheridan answered, "I didn't have a fear that he would be harmed by anyone else other than the person that she was planning on meeting with—that she thought was going to do the job."

And when I brought up the *COPS* waiver, he didn't shrink from the subject in the slightest:

PARKER: After she signed her Miranda rights, you put a piece of paper in front of her and ask her to sign it—do you remember that?

SHERIDAN: I sure do.

PARKER: What was that piece of paper for?

SHERIDAN: It was a waiver to appear on the television show *COPS*.

PARKER: Why did you put that card in front of her on that day and ask her to sign it?

SHERIDAN: It was given to me by a member of Langley Productions and they asked me to [have her] sign it so they could videotape her.

PARKER: Was this something that you have ever done in an interview before?

SHERIDAN: No.

PARKER: Would you ever do it again?

SHERIDAN: No.

PARKER: Did you tell her what the piece of paper was, that it was a waiver for the TV show *COPS*?

SHERIDAN: No.

PARKER: Why not?

SHERIDAN: I made a mistake.

On cross, Sheridan admitted that, by making it seem like standard police procedure, he was essentially lying to her. Salnick seemed most interested in belaboring Mohamed's instructions that they couldn't wire him in the standard way, since in a parked car, Dalia often went directly for his crotch.

SALNICK: If a CI were to tell you, with your thirty-three years of experience, I don't want to be wired in a certain way because every time I get near the suspect we have oral sex, would you have tolerated that?

SHERIDAN: Would I have tolerated that?

SALNICK: Would you say to the CI, "Okay, we will wire you a different way so that if you have oral sex, she won't find the wire"?

SHERIDAN: (laughs) That's an open-ended question. I would first tell him not to have oral sex and then second, I would wire him a different way.

SALNICK: So basically, if the informant is working for you, you're gonna say, "Look, pal, your personal life has to be dealt with later. You are working for the police."

SHERIDAN: Absolutely.

And over the course of ten questions, Sheridan repeatedly admitted that it was his decision not to record the conversation at Chili's, that his suspect and CI were essentially off the grid for thirty to forty-five minutes, that his subordinates (Ranzie, Moreno, and others) had expressed reservations, and that the evidentiary and exculpatory value of their conversation was now lost.

SALNICK: You made the decision, nevertheless, to go forward.

SHERIDAN: Yes.

SALNICK: It would have been good to have that recorded.

SHERIDAN: Correct.

After Sheridan, I put on John Yorganjian (with Laura doing the direct), the custodian of records for jail calls—now deceased—just to put Dalia's jailhouse calls into evidence. After Mike and Randa both identified Dalia's voice on her respective calls to them, Yorganjian fulfilled what we call the business records predicate, which documents how the calls were collected and stored, so that we were free to play them in court. Laura also questioned both Midian Diaz and Al Martinez, who followed Dalia to the gym and then back home to the waiting crime scene. This was designed to establish a time line and confirm Dalia's movements. Their testimony was brief and almost identical, and Salnick mounted no cross-examination.

Faux hit man Widy Jean took the stand next, now sporting a close-cropped haircut. A former member of the Community Action Team unit specializing in crimes related to narcotics, prostitution, and gambling, as well as of the BBPD SWAT team, Jean left the force briefly to start a business venture in Georgia, but was now back working as a regular patrol officer. I walked him through his involvement in the Dalia Dippolito case. He initially asked her to bring $3,000 and the keys to her house to their first meeting—the latter a last-minute strategic ploy to test the limits of her trust and credulity. He verified that the videotape of him was authentic and accurate, as were the brief recorded phone calls before and after. At first, he found Dalia nervous and somewhat flighty—cryptic when discussing the crime, loath to use the overt phrasings he did. But soon enough she settled down, and almost immediately began to press her advantage where money was concerned.

PARKER: Tell us about your conversation with her.

WIDY JEAN: We talked, initially, and I told her that I was a professional and about what I'd be doing. I told her about the amount of money I spent to get here, and I told her the amount of money I was gonna need, and I explained to her—at one point she told me that she didn't bring any money with her. She was going to pay me at the back end, meaning when it's all done. And we discussed different plans. She brought up the idea that her husband was going to go to the bank to take out $10,000, and I could kill her husband when he walks out of the bank. I can take that money. I told her I would check into it to see if that would work. If it didn't work, I'd call her the next day to tell her that the plan wouldn't work. And also, at the end, I gave her multiple opportunities to change her mind or get out of it. I asked her if she was sure about that, because I told her my experience as a hit man—I'd dealt with people who weren't sure and changed their mind. And I told her, if I leave here she wouldn't be able to get in contact with me, so this was the time to change her mind. And she told me she was 5,000 percent sure she wanted it done, and she wasn't going to change her mind.

Dalia gave him the address of Mike's bank in Boca Raton and the times he would be there. Since she failed to meet her financial obligation at their first meeting, she readily agreed to up his fee to $7,000 (plus the $1,200 she had advanced to purchase the weapon) if she could pay it on the back end. I walked him through the subsequent phone calls and his cameo appearance at the police station in handcuffs.

On cross, as he did with other key players in this case, Salnick got Widy Jean to admit he was essentially an actor asked to play a role in this drama. He never knew the identity of the Confidential Informant beforehand, nor realized who Mohamed was when he approached their car during the meeting with Dalia. (Dalia identified him only as her cousin.) He admitted this was his first time working undercover in the guise of a hit man. Through his questions, Salnick also emphasized that money was never exchanged between him and Dalia, nor between him and Mohamed except in the abstract (Dalia was told her $1,200 was spent on a gun with which to commit the crime). At one point, Salnick appeared to be closing in on a contradiction with Jean's earlier deposition, only to have it snatched from him at the last second.

> SALNICK: Do you ever remember that you told me that you had to get the guy a gun?
>
> WIDY JEAN: No.
>
> SALNICK: Okay, would it refresh your recollection to look at the deposition?
>
> WIDY JEAN: Yes.

Salnick approached the witness and read the sentence: "I said the reason why I need more money is I have to get the guy a gun."

> WIDY JEAN: No, it's mistranslated. I wanted to get it to buy a gun.
>
> SALNICK: You wanted to buy a gun. Okay, so the court reporter may have taken it down wrong.
>
> WIDY JEAN: Yes.

It's worth noting that according to Mike in his police statement, he planned to withdraw money from the Boca Raton Bank of America on the morning of August 5 to pay a business contact for the marketing leads that were the basis of his online business, just as he did every week. But certainly not the $10,000 Dalia promised the hit man—"hard, hard cash," as she put it, delivering her carny spiel. Mike couldn't have withdrawn $10,000 if he'd wanted to—it would have automatically triggered a notice to the IRS. It was "a few thousand dollars" at most, which he planned to drop off on his way to the orthodontist. This means that Dalia was actually scamming her hit man just like she scammed everybody else—even the hapless Sergio for a measly $500. The police had rejected Boca as outside the BBPD's jurisdiction. But what if they hadn't? What was Dalia's fallback when the savage killer she was convinced was going to murder her husband suddenly discovered she was seven grand short, and came looking for the balance?

Who cares?

No risk, no reward.

CHAPTER 12

Bane of Society

O ne phrase that I always emphasize when teaching new prosecutors is: "The physical evidence doesn't lie." Dalia's life was so compartmentalized, the selves she presented to the marks and victims that substituted for friends and colleagues so circumscribed, that it took tiny beads of provable fact to physically stitch them together. Entering the final phase of my case, I called to the stand Detective Pete McGovern, a forensic computer expert. Although he carries the rank of Detective, he is technically a digital forensics investigator with the Special Investigations Division of the Palm Beach County Sheriff's Office. His exploration of Dalia's HP Pavilion Slimline hard drive turned up a number of interesting items.

On March 23, 2009, someone using Dalia's password-protected computer ("BellaBella") did a Google search for Cayman National Bank and the current time in the Cayman Islands. This was in the thick of the confusion surrounding Dalia's wire transfer, and exactly halfway between the drug searches in Manalapan (March 16) and CityPlace (March 29). The counterfeit wire transfer receipt from a Cayman Islands bank discovered in her safety deposit box (filled out by hand, a violation of standard banking protocol and a dead giveaway) was dated March 3 and faxed to her friend Kerrian Brown from Cayman National Bank on March 23, after Dalia's phone records indicate she called the bank several times earlier that day. Had Dalia bothered to look at her bank statement, she would have seen that she deposited the last $47,000 from Mike on March 4, the day after she allegedly had the money wired.

On April 27, 2009, there was a Google search done on Dalia's computer for the Palm Beach Shooting Center, which offers a full-service indoor shooting range and basic handgun classes by appointment. That search lasted five minutes.

April 27 was less than a month after Dalia had approached Larry Coe and members of the Buck Wild gang as potential hired assassins, and the thirteen separate calls she placed to his number on April 2. It was also at the high point of tensions between Dalia and Mike, and around the same time she announced she was pregnant. As he was a convicted felon, the terms of Mike's probation clearly stated that he could not own or touch a firearm, and any trip to a commercial shooting range, which was tightly regulated, would mean an automatic revocation of his probation. Even if it were legal, he had no interest in having a gun in the house, and states he never heard Dalia express an interest in learning to shoot. A second search was conducted on June 5, 2009, this time lasting four minutes.

On August 3, 2009, at 3:46 p.m., two days before Dalia's arrest and Mike's intended demise, with Mike debilitated on the couch in the other room from his liposuction surgery and the aftereffects of what would turn out to be antifreeze poisoning, Dalia's computer shows a Google search for "funeral homes in Boynton Beach," lasting sixteen minutes. Included in these searches was a general Google search that contained several local funeral homes and crematoriums and included tips on how to have a meaningful memorial service. This comes an hour after Dalia spoke with Widy Jean, her presumed hit man, to set up a face-to-face meeting two hours later. The searches began five minutes after she hung up the phone with Mohamed and ended a minute before she called Michael Stanley. Seven minutes later, she called the hit man to check on his progress. Again, Mike denied conducting such a search on Dalia's computer.

On cross, Salnick sought to dampen what appeared to be irrefutable and damaging evidence by claiming that spouses often shared their computer passwords (although probably not spouses who intended to kill their significant other).

Finally, I put on Detective Alex Moreno. He was the lead investigator and a mainstay of the Major Case Squad, as well as my ticket to get all the remaining material into evidence so that it would be fresh in the jury's mind. During roughly two and a half days of testimony, he systematically walked the jury through the entire investigation, including the video and audio elements that had taken on a secondary life of their own on the Internet. In judicial parlance, this is known as "publishing the evidence." We worked on his testimony for hours in the days and weeks leading up to the trial. I depended on him to tell the story of the evidence—"evidence doesn't lie"—and so I wanted to fashion that into a seamless narrative, despite its complexity and potential confusion.

One part we wanted to handle carefully was the steamy texts between Dalia and Michael Stanley, which were strategic to the case and demonstrated Dalia's character, and her apparently limitless ability to manipulate the men around her to do her bidding, no matter how ill-considered her demands. Detective Moreno didn't want to read them into the record, and he didn't think he could get through it in court without seriously jeopardizing his composure. A line like "you are my unicorn" comes from some part of the spirit beyond the reach of self-consciousness; it would take an actor of considerable talents to sell it. I can't even tell you what it means with any real confidence—"you are rare, exotic, magical," probably. But in the context of unbridled sex and proximate death, Stanley's breathless sincerity and cloying desperation made the unintended listener more than a little queasy. Moreno opted for a flat monotone, sans inflection, but there was no way it wasn't going to be awkward. When he was on the stand, he even tried to substitute "Laugh Out Loud" for "LOL," and Salnick objected, forcing him to go back and read it verbatim—"L-O-L," excruciatingly slowly. I was unprepared for just how ridiculous the whole thing sounded; I repeatedly had to look away or down at my notebook on the podium to ask my questions. It probably seemed like I was embarrassed and regretted being brought into this intimate exchange—all true—but I was also trying my best not to laugh, because I knew I wouldn't be able to stop.

Moreno recounted how he became involved in the case when Sergeant Ranzie called him the morning of August 1 and he jumped on the moving train of Mohamed's murder-for-hire revelations. He told how he quickly got up to speed, taking over as Mohamed's handler after Detective Asim

Brown had signed him up as a Confidential Informant. This segued into the first phone call between Mohamed and Dalia setting up the strategy meeting between them, followed in quick succession by a second phone call and then surveillance video of the meeting at the Mobil station where Dalia gives him the $1,200. Her physical presence allowed police to run her plates, ascertaining the identity of both the suspect and the victim, and to obtain a photo of Dalia from the driver's license database with her address and identifying information. Next, we played a series of phone calls between Dalia and Mohamed made on the morning of August 3, setting up the meeting with the alleged hit man. In one call, Dalia pulled over on I-95 and exited her vehicle out of fear someone might have bugged the car. On instructions from Detective Moreno, Mohamed successfully dissuaded Dalia from coming to his house, which was not wired for audio surveillance. In another, she appeared angry with Mohamed over the fact that the hit man had asked for a key to her house, as she was afraid she would be robbed. We also played several calls between Dalia and Officer Widy Jean in the role of the hit man, as well as the surveillance video of their meeting in the CVS parking lot. Finally, we played a follow-up phone call from Officer Jean giving Dalia instructions for the morning of the hit.

Moreno recalled attending the operational planning meeting for the staging of the crime scene conducted by Sergeant Frank Ranzie (the same meeting where they learned that *COPS* would be filming). He notified the victim alongside Sergeant Sheridan, drove Mike to the station, debriefed him on the state of affairs (including playing him snippets of the surveillance tapes), and questioned Dalia along with Detective Anderson after Sheridan had exhausted his efforts to extract a confession. At that point, we played the videotape of the interview, as well as a brief video of Dalia being escorted from the police station on her way to County Jail.

Then began the portion of his testimony on the investigation proper—gathering the available evidence, securing search warrants and subpoenas, assembling bank and phone records, obtaining the contents of Dalia's safety deposit box, and executing a search warrant on her mother's house, all of which opened up new avenues of exploration. Once a clearer pattern had emerged, Moreno conducted more detailed interviews with both

Mohamed and Mike Dippolito. He confirmed their stories with the Land Rover dealership, Mike's probation officer, investigating officers from the various jurisdictions, Officer Wilson as an early observer of Dalia's intentions, etc. Dalia's phone records revealed the presence of spoof calls, multiple cell phones, Michael Stanley, and his calls to the IRS, the U.S. Treasury Department, the Department of Corrections, and the rest. Her real estate license gave a clearer picture of her employment history. Her text history colored in Michael Stanley, the sexting established his motive, and Dalia's moonlighting as an escort (even though we didn't mention it at trial) left little doubt she was the one pulling the strings. Moreno's testimony ended with playing Dalia's jailhouse calls to her mother and to Mike for the jury. These included an especially damning incidental comment made when Randa mistook "Mike" for Mike Dippolito instead of Mike Stanley:

DALIA: He doesn't want to come here? Mike?

RANDA: Mike who? Which Mike?

DALIA: He's not going to come here?

RANDA: Why would he go, Dalia? Why would he go? You were trying to kill him.

On cross, Salnick emphasized the number of times Mohamed was in contact with Dalia after July 31 outside of police control—there were an astounding seventy-five calls within the span of six days, Mohamed's entire career undercover. Then, while arguing for the inclusion of Mike's bank records before 2009, which I opposed as irrelevant, Salnick inadvertently led the discussion into a cul-de-sac that articulated what many of us had been wondering since the trial began:

JUDGE COLBATH: How is it that this evidence [Mike's 2008 bank records] falls into that category [evidence that might "impeach him, which goes to the heart of the case"]?

SALNICK: Because the jury has to decide as part of their fact-finding process here if they want to believe Mr. Dippolito or not. If they don't believe Mr. Dippolito, and they think that—yeah, he could have put his wife up to this, and this was partly his idea—they have the right to look at everything that he's been cross-examined on.

JUDGE COLBATH: That's what's been mysterious to me: Where is there any evidence thus far . . . Let's say the State didn't put Mr. Dippolito on, or let's say that everything that came out of his mouth is a lie: Where is *he* pointing the finger at your client? What testimony? I mean, he was kept in the dark about this whole thing until . . . Where is there evidence [he] orchestrated any of this?

SALNICK: That's for the jury to decide, Judge.

JUDGE COLBATH: No, no, no—I'm asking *you*: What evidence do you have that Mr. Dippolito had anything to do with her arrest?

SALNICK: He doesn't have to say the magic words "We're involved in a reality television program."

JUDGE COLBATH: You've got to tell me the evidence upon which you want to offer this in. It's wishful thinking.

SALNICK: It's not wishful thinking. The evidence deals with his credibility.

JUDGE COLBATH: Let's say he's the most incredible person in the world!

SALNICK: I think that the defense has the right to argue to the jury that he is as *in*-credible as he is, and therefore we can't believe what he says. And one of the things that he clearly said was, he didn't know anything about a reality TV plot. He didn't know anything about reality TV. And I use that term "reality" generically—whether it's viral YouTube or reality TV, he told the jury he had nothing to do with that.

JUDGE COLBATH: Well, where is the evidence right now? Now, maybe something is going to come out in your [cross] that will change the complexion of this, but where is the evidence right now that he did have some knowledge of reality TV?

SALNICK: Judge, that evidence is going to come out in the defense's case.

JUDGE COLBATH: Well, that may be true, but right now I don't see it.

At this point, I tried to jump in, which the Judge addressed with his typical wit:

PARKER: Judge, may I put something on the record?

JUDGE COLBATH: If you'd like to snatch defeat from the jaws of victory, go ahead.

PARKER: No, I just wanted to point out one other thing: Mr. Salnick said the reason he wants to put these records in is so that he can basically backdoor that Mike Dippolito was money laundering. And that's exactly why these records are inadmissible—to prove that Mike Dippolito is committing another bad act, or something like that. That is not admissible.

Salnick continued to try to chip away at both Mike's and Mohamed's credibility, as my two key witnesses. He cited instances from the phone records where Dalia spoke with Mike either before or after she spoke with Mohamed, to insinuate the men knew each other. He hammered home Mohamed's preventive measures regarding Dalia discovering the wire—the one they wanted to hide in his pants—a subject Salnick couldn't seem to get enough of. And he focused on the *COPS* cameraman hovering outside the interview-room door once Dalia had effectively been taken into custody—like a gunman on the grassy knoll, this random figure that redefined the actions of everyone around him.

On the subject of Dalia and Michael Stanley's infamous electronic flirting—"sexting," as he couldn't stop reminding the court—Salnick tried to defuse the topic with humor.

SALNICK: What's sexting? Did you ever hear of sexting? Do you know what that is?

MORENO: Yes.

SALNICK: What is that, Detective?

MORENO: Um, pretty much what I read yesterday.

Salnick laughs.

SALNICK: Okay, sexual conversation between two people, is that right?

MORENO: Yes.

SALNICK: All right, if it's sexual conversation between two people and they're adults, there's nothing wrong with that, is there?

MORENO: No.

SALNICK: It's not a crime, is it?

MORENO: No.

SALNICK: Those things were steamy, weren't they? Are they steamy to you?

MORENO: I wouldn't say that, no.

Dalia laughed at this, a deferred tension-breaker from earlier, when Moreno earned hazard pay for reading these things in the first place.

SALNICK: All right, so when a comment is made between the two of them about sex, that's normal if that's what two people want to do.

MORENO: Yes.

SALNICK: Have you ever sexted?

The courtroom dissolves into laughter, Dalia included.

PARKER: Objection, your honor—irrelevant.

SALNICK: I'll withdraw it. I'm sorry. Don't answer that.

JUDGE: And it was going so well there for a while.

On redirect, I returned to the issue of the seventy-five phone calls between Mohamed and Dalia.

PARKER: Did you tell Mohamed to act normal in his actions with Dalia?

MORENO: Yes.

PARKER: Why was that important?

MORENO: We didn't want her to get suspicious in any way. They were friends; they talked on a daily basis. I directed him that if she calls you at any time and she starts talking about the case to contact me—which he did numerous times, and I was able to record some of those conversations.

Detective Moreno noted that some of the calls Mr. Salnick had asked him about dated back to March 2009, although he became involved with the case on August 1, the day after Mohamed walked into BBPD with a story to tell. Using their phone records as a guide, he confirmed there were seventy-four phone calls between Mohamed and Dalia in the period from July 31 to August 5. On further questioning, he revealed that forty-five of them—about three-fifths—were a minute or less.

PARKER: Tell the jury how many of the calls are over 180 seconds, or three minutes in duration.

MORENO: Seven calls.

PARKER: Now, of those calls, and you may need to refer to your report, how many of those did you record?

MORENO: Three calls were recorded that we heard in court.

I had to make one final point about the text messages.

PARKER: In all of the text messages that you reviewed in this case, including the ones that you read out loud in court, did you ever read anything about the defendant being involved in a reality show stunt?

MORENO: No.

PARKER: Why did you never have a conversation with Michael Dippolito about this being a reality show stunt?

MORENO: Throughout my investigation, that wasn't brought up—not when I spoke to Mike Dippolito or the defendant. I didn't even find out about that until just recently.

Detective Moreno stepped down from the witness stand and I rested my case. At last, it was time for Salnick to present this audacious defense he had been threatening for months. First to the stand he called Dalia's mother, Randa Mohamed.

Randa has three children, of which Dalia is the oldest. She has been divorced for ten years, and has worked in the health care industry for twenty. She first met Mike in October 2008 when Dalia brought him by the house.

SALNICK: What do you remember about him when you first met him?

RANDA: (laughs) Not a good impression. I didn't like him as soon as I saw him. As a mom, I felt something—I don't know, I just felt something. He wouldn't look in my eyes. Every time he would talk, he had a nervous tic, a nervous smile, and he would laugh when there was nothing funny.

She began crying while recounting the happy times she had spent with Dalia before the marriage, which abruptly came to an end once Dalia met Mike. As if on cue, Dalia cried along with her. According to Randa, Mike and Dalia were always together, always rushing off somewhere to do something. She was taken aback when they announced they had gotten married without telling her, which flew in the face of all the plans they had made as mother and daughter. She remembers Mike's celebrated outing to the Marlins-Phillies game as a burden on her father, who was very sick and had to be encouraged to go. (Outside of court, Mike was surprised to learn of Randa's comments on the stand, recalling how he had teased her about her paramours, their frequent outings to Ruth's Chris steakhouse and the Cheesecake Factory—always as his treat. He thought she was "fun" and that their relationship had been "casual and friendly.")

Randa's father passed away from prostate cancer the same week Dalia was arrested, having briefly lapsed into a coma. This was Randa's explanation for why Dalia had been searching for funeral homes and crematoriums.

> RANDA: While I was going through that, I was taking care of every-
> thing for my Dad, so I asked my daughter for help to go online
> and do some researches to get everything prepared, because that
> is what hospice advised us to do.
>
> SALNICK: What did Dalia do to help you?

Randa Mohamed being sworn in to testify during the trial.

RANDA: She looked for different places according to the budget—he wanted to be cremated, and she needed to look at different places, and from there she needed to decide which one we were going to go with.

She testified that she ultimately picked one of the places that Dalia had researched and given her information on.

On cross-examination, as gently as I could, I tried to establish a time line and context in which to better understand this computer search for which Dalia had taken time out from planning her husband's murder. It was a balancing act, since the witness had just lost her father, and stood to lose her daughter. I wanted to respect that, and I also didn't want to appear aggressive or uncaring in the eyes of the jury.

PARKER: I'm sorry that I have to ask you questions about your father—I know this is a very uncomfortable and upsetting situation to talk about him in.

RANDA: It is.

PARKER: . . . Now, do you know what day she did that funeral search on her computer?

RANDA: I don't remember exactly—the week before. I would say a week or two. I don't know exactly when.

PARKER: And when she was on the computer, did she call you right then and tell you what she found?

RANDA: I don't remember. Obviously, at one point we discussed the prices, but I don't know if it was right then—I was going through a lot.

Her voice started to rise.

PARKER: Can you tell me if it was the same day?

SALNICK: Objection—she has already said she doesn't remember.

PARKER: Can you tell me if it was before or after she was arrested?

SALNICK: Objection! She has stated she doesn't know.

PARKER: Judge, I'm trying to get a time frame.

RANDA: (yelling) I don't have a time frame! This is about my Dad! You should have a little respect for this—you are talking about somebody who passed away who has nothing to do with this! [She's yelling and crying now.] This is about him being cremated, and you want me to go back through all that!

PARKER: Ma'am, I apologize. I did not mean to upset you.

RANDA: (screaming) You are, because you are asking me so many times and I already told you!

PARKER: I'm just trying to find out—

RANDA: Find out what? When she called me, and when she did this? I already told you that she did research a lot of places. I was here by myself taking care of my Dad.

Forget for a moment that Randa had agreed to return as a defense witness explicitly to discuss the details of her father's cremation, as they pertained to the assistance Dalia allegedly rendered her. Many in the courtroom doubted the sincerity of her outburst, and a number of them sought me out afterward to tell me they thought it helped my case—especially the fact that I didn't take the bait and push back. In fact, the crematorium Randa settled on for the disposal of her father's remains, A Cremation Service of the Palm Beaches, briefly appears on a long list of options brought up by a Google search on Dalia's computer on August 3, but neither the website itself, services offered, nor pricing information was ever accessed. In addition, Dalia's phone records, which were in evidence, indicate that she did not speak to her mother either that day or on the day before (when she might have received a request for help). They did speak the day after, August 4, but for no longer than one minute and twenty seconds—hardly long enough to present a credible list of choices with prices and variety of services, as Randa testified. Dalia's grandfather died on August 9, and the arrangements were made on August 10. I knew that I would point all of these inconsistencies out in my closing argument.

Next up, the defense called Dr. Sarah Coyne to the stand. Dr. Coyne—still in her twenties, attractive, relentlessly positive—is a Professor of Human Development at Brigham Young University in Salt Lake City, with a PhD in psychology. When her name turned up as an expert witness a few weeks before the trial, I researched her pretty thoroughly. I also took her deposition—by phone, since there was no time to fly to Utah and depose her in person—to get a sense of her particular approach to the material. That first exposure was entirely a fishing expedition on my part, and my first real confirmation of where Salnick might try to take the defense, which at that point still seemed kind of mind-boggling. They had a mouthpiece for some of the trial balloons they were floating in Michael Stanley, but at this point it was pretty clear they wouldn't be calling him to the stand. Coyne had published thirty-eight peer-reviewed articles on the subjects of reality TV and violence, its effects on children, and other social implications of popular entertainment. Under Florida law, an expert witness can testify on any subject, but it must be outside the general knowledge of the jury, as well as something in which the witness has specialized knowledge, training, or experience. What I learned in the deposition is that since she was strictly an academic, she would not express an opinion on this particular case—whether it was a reality show stunt or whatever they might allege. She would merely talk in general terms about reality television, the function of fame and celebrity in society, and the lengths that people have gone to historically to gain access to what is still a new and evolving medium. So that's what I concentrated on in my research.

Salnick spent the first part of his questions managing our expectations by having her designate what she would not address: She would not speak about any of the personalities in the case, discuss their psychological development, or offer clinical evaluations of their behavior. Nor would she discuss the television production process from anything more than a layman's understanding. Her testimony would remain solely theoretical.

SALNICK: How do you define reality TV?

COYNE: In the academic world, we think of it as "unscripted drama," and anything goes in reality television. You have reality shows about [everything] from baking cupcakes to catching fish to building a home to falling in love, falling out of love and breaking up and eating bugs . . . A lot of boundaries are tested there. They kind of push the limits on what is accepted behavior on reality TV and what's normal, and so pretty much anything goes on reality TV.

She identified six categories under the heading of Reality TV: Reality Dramatic (documenting a group of individuals, like *Big Brother* or *Jersey Shore*), Crime Shows (following law enforcement, like *COPS* or *America's Most Wanted*), Romance Shows (*The Bachelor*), Game Shows or Competitions (*Survivor* or *Fear Factor*), Talent Shows, where people try to become famous (*Dancing with the Stars* or *American Idol*), and Information (anything focusing on a single topic and ostensibly educational or anything else). She defined YouTube as a distant cousin—unscripted, but with no production elements—and "going viral" as something possibly for just friends and family that gets passed on by word of mouth or e-mail.

SALNICK: From your studies and your work, why do people watch reality TV?

COYNE: There's a theory out there, it's called "Uses and Gratifications Theory," and it answers that question. It talks about why we watch anything on TV: we watch things to fulfill a certain need that we have. So for reality television, we've done quite a bit of research on this, and there are a few characteristics of people who really turn to reality television. The first is "voyeurism," and that's just kind of getting a sneaky peek into other people's lives. It's our curiosity to find out what happens to other people—what goes on in other families. Another one is "status," and people who are highly motivated by status want other people to pay attention to them; they have a desire that they'd like to become famous—fame is important to them. Things like having a lot of money is important to them, having the right look, the right clothes, driving the right cars, status.

Salnick asked her how people get on reality shows, and she listed three avenues: The extensive and somewhat grueling audition process, which amounts to an open casting call. Pitching your own series to a producer or production company. Or doing something crazy enough that people take notice.

> COYNE: A good example of this—if you remember the "Balloon Boy" hoax: he told the media that his son was in the balloon, and there was this big chase on television, and it came out later that the guy was on *Wife Swap* before, and he'd done this whole thing as a kind of way to get back into reality TV. And so, not a very successful way to get on it, but people certainly do it.

> SALNICK: Do people gain fame or celebrity status from doing this type of thing?

> COYNE: Yeah, sure. The thing about reality TV is anyone can do it; anyone can become famous. When you're watching it, that's kind of the message . . . They say, "Oh, well, he's just an ordinary guy. If he can do it, if he can behave like that, so can I. I can become famous." And some of these people go on and make millions. They get endorsement deals and spin-off shows, and so, you know, there's a lot riding on it.

I started out my cross-examination of her by clarifying some of her bona fides. I established that her PhD thesis consisted of five separate studies of the effects on children ages eleven to fourteen of viewing "indirect aggression" (manipulation, gossip, verbal cruelty) on television, and that she had never done a study on the effect of reality TV on individuals—presumably her highlighted area of expertise. That expertise came exclusively from reading journal articles and researching on the Internet. Although she had testified on the reality casting process in direct, she admitted that she had never been to an audition, never interviewed anyone about the audition process, or even so much as looked at a reality show application.

Expanding on her earlier testimony, I keyed in on those examples of public behavior designed to establish notoriety that Salnick cited in his opening statement, presumably Mike's inspiration in whatever scheme he had concocted.

PARKER: Let's talk about the Balloon Boy Incident. That was a couple trying to gain notoriety to land a reality show.

COYNE: Yes.

PARKER: The son who was thought to be in the balloon actually said that the couple told him they were doing this for the show.

COYNE: Both of the parents were actors. They had been on *Wife Swap*.

PARKER: Did you know they were actors, though?

COYNE: No.

PARKER: Did you know they had a production company?

COYNE: No.

PARKER: That they had been on a reality show two times previously?

COYNE: The father had been on *Wife Swap* twice.

PARKER: That the husband had pitched a reality show idea to TLC?

COYNE: No.

PARKER: That they actually had a show in development with the producer of *Wife Swap* at the time of the Balloon Boy incident?

COYNE: No.

PARKER: Did you know that the Balloon Boy incident actually occurred on October 15, 2009?

COYNE: No.

PARKER: And that was after the defendant in this case was arrested?

COYNE: Yes.

PARKER: *Jersey Shore*. Are you familiar?

COYNE: A little bit. I watched twenty minutes.

PARKER: A little silly . . .

COYNE: Yes, a little over the top.

PARKER: And isn't it true that *Jersey Shore* didn't actually air until December 3, 2009, after the defendant was arrested?

COYNE: Sure, I'll believe you. Yeah.

Although I didn't bother to point it out at the time, Salnick's third example of a successful reality show stunt—the so-called White House Crashers, Tareq and Michele Salahi—made their first unauthorized appearance at a state dinner in November 2009, also long after Dalia was taken into custody. At the time, they were already filming *The Real Housewives of D.C.*, which aired in 2010.

As she readily admitted, Coyne had never interviewed a producer or any crew member working on a reality show, had never been on the set of one, and had never talked to a single reality show contestant, either actual or aspirational. On the material she reviewed from the Dalia Dippolito case (the surveillance tapes of Dalia and Mohamed and Dalia and the hit man; the crime scene video; Dalia's police interview), she admitted she had heard no references to reality TV, and she had never talked to any of the principals, including the defendant. Like all expert witnesses, she was being paid for her time—in this case, $175 an hour. By the time I was finished with her, I felt like there was very little left.

Salnick did come back on redirect and try to undo some of the damage, but in a way that I thought further undercut his witness:

SALNICK: This is the first time you've ever done this, is that correct?

COYNE: Yes.

SALNICK: It's not like you testify for the government or for the defense or the plaintiff or the defendant—this is the first time you've been in a forensic setting, is that right?

COYNE: That's right . . .

SALNICK: The prosecutor asked you about how much you're getting paid. Do you wanna hang out here in South Florida?

COYNE: Not so much.

SALNICK: Do you have children?

COYNE: I have three little kids.

My objection as to relevance was sustained, but the gist of it was that she was ready to get back home. To salvage the Balloon Boy reference, Salnick asked if Balloon Boy's father went to jail for falsely reporting a crime. She said she thought he did. Neither of them really seemed sure.

Once Salnick finished his questions, the Judge unexpectedly inserted himself into the proceedings, asking Coyne from the bench what the most popular reality shows were. She told him *Dancing with the Stars* and *America's Got Talent*.

COLBATH: Reality TV: bane of society or benign entertainment?

COYNE: (laughs) I'm still thinking about it. Let me research it for the next five years and then I'll let you know.

Salnick also called his own computer forensic expert. It's not uncommon for opposing sides to engage their own expert witnesses in a criminal trial, since especially with the advent of new technology, so much of the evidence is open to interpretation. But in this instance, exactly why the defendant couldn't have simply volunteered her own search history remains unclear.

Carol Peden is a Senior Computer Forensics Analyst with Global CompuSearch in Spokane, Washington. Unlike Dr. Sarah Coyne, Peden *does* testify in jury trials for a living—"consultation and litigation support," in her words. Analyzing the same cloned hard drive from Dalia's PC that Pete McGovern had, she found the same funeral home searches on August 3, as well as searches that revealed a tip sheet on how to beat anabolic steroid tests and companies that train and sell attack dogs. She also testified she found web searches on May 13 for "VH1 Castings," "Castings Reality TV," and "Castings Reality TV in Florida," as well as related websites accessed on May 26, June 2, and June 17 with names like AffinityModelsTalentBlogger .com and WelcomeToRealityTVCasting.com.

On cross, I focused in on the funeral home searches. I would save the reality TV searches for my closing argument.

> PARKER: And did you find a specific part of the website for A Cremation Service of the Palm Beaches?
>
> PEDEN: I know I saw a website for South Florida Cremation. I don't remember it specifically.
>
> PARKER: My question to you is, did you find a specific visit to the website A Cremation Service of the Palm Beaches? And I can give you the defense exhibit if it will help you look at the name . . .
>
> PEDEN: I do not recall seeing that particular service.
>
> PARKER: Do you not recall, or it's not on the computer so you couldn't see it?
>
> PEDEN: I can't say it's not there, but I didn't see it.

She also denied seeing any specific information related to the business in question or its pieces. On redirect, Salnick had Ms. Peden identify A Cremation Service on a fragment of a web page, but failed to disclose that it appeared in a list of companies and was never singled out for further viewing.

And then—nothing.

This was where Dalia would have taken the stand, and where all this loose-flying debris of a ramshackle construction site could have been nailed down once and for all. There were promises Salnick had made in his opening statement—"The evidence will show . . ."—that there was no other way to prove than if Dalia testified. And I was ready for her; my cross-examination questions alone ran to thirty-two pages. I would have forced her to admit that if we were to believe her reality show defense, her plan involved lying to the police, wasting their resources, reporting a nonexistent crime, and obstructing an investigation. I would have confronted her with every piece of evidence in the case that makes no mention of this alleged reality show plot, including the phone records, her calls from jail, and her statements. I would have walked her through every single lie she told the police—just as Sergeant Sheridan and Detectives Moreno and Anderson did before, but with everything we know now—and watched her wriggle, pinned there by her own treachery. That way, in the closing statement, I could refer to her as an admitted liar.

As a member of the Florida Bar, Salnick was ethically prohibited from putting on perjured testimony, and yet the defense he had been insinuating—which we only had in flickering images at this point—required a suspension of disbelief, one that would prove short-lived if I got the chance to dismantle the defendant under oath. The defense he had built, a castle in the air, needed Dalia to document its provenance, yet we had all seen her acting skills on conspicuous display. If he called her as a witness, it would turn the entire courtroom into a bunch of drama critics, comparing this latest appearance to her signature role. And so the defense rested.

Suddenly, my side was up.

CHAPTER 13

Chasing Chickens

In closing arguments, the State has what we refer to as "The Sandwich": we get to make the first statement, but also to offer a rebuttal after the defense has presented its closing argument. This allows the prosecution to put things back on the rails if the defense wanders too far afield in its allegations or conjecture. I wanted to give my co-counsel Laura Burkhart Laurie an opportunity to participate on a larger scale as we neared the end of the trial, since she did a stellar job handling some of the direct examination of witnesses. So we decided that she would get up first and address the basic facts of the crime itself, the law that applies, and how we had met the burden of proof. Then after Salnick had his final say, I would rebut his reality show defense and whatever dark-hearted tributaries his argument led him into, and then try to reshape the evidence in the image of Dalia, and the considerable lengths she went to in order to commit the crime she did.

Laura first addressed the jury by restating the crime Dalia was accused of: Solicitation to Commit First-Degree Murder with a Firearm. In order to find the defendant guilty, the State had to prove two related facts, which we call elements of the crime: that Dalia solicited Widy Jean, in his role as the contract killer, to commit first-degree murder with a firearm. And that during the solicitation, Dalia "commanded, encouraged, hired, or requested Widy Jean to engage in specific conduct, which would constitute the commission of first-degree murder with a firearm or an attempt to commit first-degree murder with a firearm." As Laura explained to the two men and four women of the jury, to solicit means to ask earnestly or to try to induce the person solicited to do the things solicited. Dalia herself need take no other action in furtherance of the crime in order to be convicted of it.

This solicitation began on July 31 when she asked for Mohamed's help in killing her husband, the inciting incident that set her arrest and prosecution in motion. It continued on August 1 when Dalia and Mohamed met in the parking lot of a Mobil gas station and discussed the terms of engaging a professional assassin to realize her plan. In this conversation, Dalia argued the logistics of how such a plan might be carried out, proposed an alibi (demonstrating intent), provided photos of the intended victim, instructed Mohamed to wipe her fingerprints off the pictures, and made it easy on the jury by telling him to smile, in callous disregard of the circumstances.

Two days later, she met the hit man in the parking lot of a CVS, where at first she appeared nervous (indicating she understood the consequences of her actions), and discussed the setting, time frame, and murder weapon. She didn't flinch when he described the victim's fate in graphic detail. She conspired with him to approach her husband when she knew he would be carrying a large amount of money, in effect having him finance his own murder. When the hit man asked her for a key to her house, she later complained to Mohamed, fearing she would be robbed. And when the hit man allowed her an out, she assured him she was tougher than she looked, nailing it shut with a million-dollar tag line: "I'm 5,000 percent sure."

"During what should have been the honeymoon phase of her marriage, she was sleeping with three different men, blowing through her husband's money, and planning Mike Dippolito's murder. She got herself in too deep, and the only way out was murder. Without a second thought, she planned her husband's murder as though it was as simple as making a dinner reservation." At every stage of this presentation, Laura augmented her statement with video clips of Dalia, which put the jury directly into her mind-set.

Salnick began the defense's closing statement with his signature gesture: staring at the ceiling for a long moment, as if to collect his composure. He opened with some larger observations on the still-evolving role of reality TV in society.

"Our culture is so dominated in today's world by film and by television's reality that sometimes people are not even aware of how blurred those lines become. You might remember a few weeks ago, there was a horrible series of storms in St. Louis, and they blew the windows out at the airport—it was on the news. It was terrible, it was devastating, and the person who was there described the event this way: 'It was very real; it was like being in a movie.' We've reached a point in our society when people evaluate real experiences against the constructed realities of the movies and TV."

He quickly moved from the general to the specific.

"Mike Dippolito thought he lived in a movie. He had a beautiful wife. He didn't have to work very much at his company—MAD Media kept the money rolling in. He went to the fitness center every day. He was a regular at the tanning salon, and he talks about going to Starbucks as if it was his private club." Salnick lavished special attention on the tanning salon as a custom-built metaphor—here in South Florida, where unfiltered sunlight is both a marketing hook and our natural bounty. "The fake tan of the salon is more in keeping with the celebrity status that Mike Dippolito likes," in keeping with "his appearance, his vanity, his bulking up, his braces, his liposuction."

"Mike's dream is money," says Salnick: "Money without working for it, and status with no skill or talent to earn it. His obsession with his status, and his constant pursuit of get-rich-quick money schemes, certainly makes him the exact profile of the type of person that would be drawn into reality TV, to YouTube, into some sort of concocted event . . . that ultimately goes—what was the term—'viral.'" He attributes this to "the lure of the media spotlight and how it can cause anyone to make a bad judgment or overlook things of critical importance that impact somebody's life. The notoriety that a police department can gain from its moment in the spotlight, the opportunities that individuals can avail themselves of from their moments in the spotlight of the media is something that we have to talk about. The seduction of the media as a means to the end." And not just Mike Dippolito, but Mohamed Shihadeh, Sergeant Paul Sheridan, and the Boynton Beach Police Department as a whole. "I believe that this case proceeds along two different lines," he says, "that are *inextricably intertwined*" (there's that phrase again): "the desire to create a media event that would result in notoriety, and Mike Dippolito's constant, calculated efforts to avoid paying the restitution that was required as a condition of his felony probation." In his estimation, the money trail was confusing for a reason; the "best proof" that Dalia wasn't stealing from Mike was that her bank account was overdrawn at the end of every month. The money he gave her in $6,000–$7,000 increments was what financed their lavish lifestyle. He used her to front for him—implying that she was laundering his cash, filling out police reports for him, holding his house in her name—which would allow him to shield his assets from creditors and allow him to keep a low profile. "The prosecution has attempted to portray Mike Dippolito as somebody who is deaf, dumb, and blind," he says, reminding the jury that he lied to his probation officer, wrote checks he can't explain, and has been through five sets of lawyers and still can't manage to pay off his debts. And, Salnick adds, he called me a parrot.

"There's an old saying: You can't scam a scammer. And Mike Dippolito is a convicted felon and scam artist. That's his talent . . . [But] what Mr. Dippolito told us with his words, and showed us with his body language and through his demeanor, is a message that he said he learned from one of his treatment programs: Nothing changes. Nothing changes. If an individual doesn't make a change in their lives, then their lives don't change. Mike Dippolito hasn't changed one bit since he got arrested and sent to prison."

When he asked Stephanie Slater why she released the videos to YouTube, "She said that it had all of the moments of a great media event; it was a great story. But she attempts to justify her action by saying, 'Well, those records were going to be public anyway.' But we also know that she wasted no time making sure that her chief was on the *Nancy Grace* show a very short time after Ms. Dippolito was arrested. Now, the investigation in this case was compromised the moment that these tapes were released to the entire country . . . Releasing that video resulted in the investigation going in one direction that justified first impressions."

He moves on from Slater to discredit Sergeant Paul Sheridan. "Sergeant Sheridan was in charge of the investigation, and he did an unbelievable job of trying to cover up the lack of judgment that he showed when he kind of got sucked into the *COPS* whirlwind." Sheridan admitted "he lied to Ms. Dippolito with respect to the *COPS* waiver," and then makes it worse when he writes in the report, "'I also asked if she would mind if the *COPS*

TV show could record her. And she agreed and signed a release card that had been supplied to me.' [But] that's not what he did. So the State says, 'He's a good guy. He owned up to it. He made a mistake.'" Salnick raises his voice for emphasis. "In a case of this nature, *shame on him!* He botched the investigation, and he tells you that, too. Does that make it okay? Does that make it any fairer, or better for Dalia Dippolito?"

"And according to Miss Slater, it was Paul Sheridan's idea to feature this case on *COPS*. And he said that it was his idea to stage the fake crime scene. And he tells us that, when he was at Mike's front door, and he broke the news to Mike that his wife tried to have him killed, he goes on, 'Mike fell backward. He was in shock!' Now that's as sensational as anything else. Sheridan takes over this investigation so he can be the one on camera, and in the footage that makes it to national television. He stages a face-to-face meeting with Ms. Dippolito when she is in the police department with what? With the so-called hit man. Well, we also know at some point that a camera from *COPS* peers into the room."

According to Salnick, "Frank Ranzie told you that's not real life . . . This is a twenty-five-year veteran. He disagrees obviously with people in his agency, and he tells you that essentially the Boynton Beach Police Department was doing things that are just not normal procedure . . . You heard what he said, and you heard what he talked about, and you saw how upset he was at the idea that the media had entered the realm of law enforcement. And he was honest enough to tell you that he balked about the idea of *COPS*, and he said because of what's happening now. I think that's how he ended his testimony. But what's happening now"—he walks over to stand in front of Dalia and points at her—"is that this lady is on trial for an offense that, number one, didn't happen the way it's alleged, and number two, is fraught with so much inconsistency and so many things that don't make sense . . ."

And then there is Mohamed—Salnick calls him "an opportunist," "a liar," and "the uncontrolled informant" who "was lying from the moment that he met Detective Brown," and spends a great deal of time highlighting the contradictions in his testimony: The police kept him waiting two hours, or was it three? He knew Mike or else he didn't. He had been lovers with

Dalia for a decade, but he couldn't remember her last name—even though
it was Mohammed. The incident with the gun occurred in early March or
late July or both, at the Mobil station or a clothing store in Riviera Beach,
in the Range Rover or the Lexus, while he was buying an energy drink or
smoking a cigarette with his cousin. Or maybe "there's no evidence that
Ms. Dippolito ever touched a gun, other than his word . . . I don't know if
Mohamed really owns guns like he says he does." He's just "going with the
flow . . . saying what he has to say."

Salnick questions his motives: "'I want to get my friend help, so I'm
going to get her turned in to police on a major felony charge.' That makes
no sense. What Mohamed really wanted was a sensational story to tell the
police, and to get them to react." He "couldn't wear a wire" on account of
the "disgusting . . . episodes of oral sex" he was used to receiving from the
defendant. "Of course Mohamed didn't want to wear a wire—that certainly reduces a lot of his opportunity to communicate." He points out the
seventy-five calls and texts with Dalia during Mohamed's one-week stint as
an undercover operative, the vast majority of them not monitored by police.
Showing a text on July 28, 2009, at 8:37 p.m., in which Dalia says, "Stop by
when you get out," he peddles it to the jury as a clear invitation to come by
the house, as well as incontrovertible proof that Mohamed and Mike were
acquainted, even co-conspirators. And he reminds them that Mohamed was
once a "part-time/very slight-time actor." And he notes that "there isn't one
question that the prosecutor ever asks Mohamed Shihadeh about reality TV,
about any plot, about any scheme, about any ruse. Ask yourselves why. Did
the prosecutor forget? Well, if the prosecutor forgot, we've got that citizen
over there who's on trial. If the prosecutor didn't ask, that's something you
have to factor in. Ms. Parker and I had ample opportunity to talk to him.
The defense doesn't have the burden of proof."

(Forget that we took Mohamed's testimony months before the trial,
when Salnick's vaunted reality defense was even more opaque than it was
now. I have always found it an act of desperation when defense attorneys
attack me during the trial, and apparently juries often agree with me. But
since he's attacking me personally: I had a burden of proof to prove Dalia

Dippolito's guilt, not to disprove whatever crazy idea the defense attorney gets in his head. If it was the other way around, we might still be there today.)

"The believability of the State's case is tied to the character, behavior, and truthfulness of Mohamed Shihadeh," states Mr. Salnick. "And I would submit to you that, from the evidence, he fails miserably on all three points."

And Salnick questions the evidence against Dalia. "She didn't give Widy Jean any money, and she knows that there's a camera—she's looking at the camera . . . Widy Jean says that a number of things he did weren't real, and she knew that. He says she can pay him later. That's absurd. You're dealing with a hit man. Says he's got to make a phone call to the police to see how long it takes for the police to respond. He says he's got to get other people involved." Salnick claims that Dalia did nothing illegal as revealed in her texts with Michael Stanley: "[T]here's no text about her planting the drugs. Their discussing them in the context that they did isn't a crime . . . There's no talk about killing Mike. There's no talk about hiring a hit man . . . They texted, they sexted—does that mean a crime was committed?" Even their alleged extramarital affair may have been a put-on, if you read all the way to the end: "There's that one little line in the evidence where it says, 'Hey thanks for the service, my confidence is so much better, and I think I may start seeing somebody very serious. I talk to girls so much better now.' So what is it? Is she manipulating him with sex and sexting and all these things, or are they just talking?

"Let's talk about Dalia Dippolito. You've seen her in the video, you saw her in the police station, and what's most telling are the things that Dalia says when she's in police custody. She wants to go home. She doesn't understand what's happened here. She didn't have any idea that she had done something criminally wrong. She wants to talk to her husband. She wants to talk to her mother . . . What does she say to her mother—remember those jail phone calls? 'They did this to me.' She wants to tell the police what really happened: 'Is it gonna change the outcome?' She even tells Mike he was never going to be a dead victim." And then there's her phone call with Mike from jail. "When she first calls, it's like nothing's wrong: 'Hey! What's up?'" He tells her he called her mom: "Why is he going to do that if she's really trying to kill him?" It's simple: "[H]e knows the phone calls are recorded . . . He's been in prison. So he's being careful, but he's trying to tell his wife what's going on here . . . And on the phone, he says, 'I'll fix it.' He'll fix it. He's the only one who does what he says he's gonna do. Keep your mouth shut. Say nothing . . . We know how cunning he is, but he's certainly trying to get a message to his wife."

Which brings Salnick to the concept of reasonable doubt. "We believe that you'll look carefully at that evidence, and where there's a lack of evidence and unanswered questions, you're going to have a reasonable doubt . . . We're confident when you look at Mohamed and Mike and the police tape and what the police did, that you'll look at it and you'll understand there are a lot of questions here." (This said as Dalia wipes away a carefully orchestrated, nonexistent tear.) "You don't even have to articulate or explain your doubt to anybody.

"Dalia Dippolito is now appealing to your better judgment," Salnick says in closing, "and asking you to let her wake up from this nightmare and finally move on with her life. We're asking you to return the only verdict possible based on the evidence that's presented to you. And that's 'not guilty.'"

This is, to be charitable about it, chock-full of what we in the legal world refer to as red herrings, although I prefer the term of art "chasing chickens." Take as many disparate notions as you can carry at one time, target those parts of the prosecution's case that are the most complicated or confusing, and then toss an armful of them into the proceedings, where they'll run every which way at once. None of them will fly—they're far too bulky and misshapen—but with all the squawking and flapping of wings, they can easily pitch the proceedings over into chaos. A prosecutor must stay focused on proving the crime as charged; even if you spend the entire trial chasing those chickens down, one by one, you merely confirm the defense's core belief that by acknowledging them, you grant them power, which is more than half the battle.

To be fair, Salnick was saddled with a client who was caught dead to rights on videotape—repeatedly. There was very little conjecture in the story I had to sell to the jury. On the other hand, he's got *COPS* lurking about and the Boynton Beach Police Department arguably playing to the cameras, doing B-roll while they're setting up a fake crime scene. He has Mohamed somehow involved, who not only looks shady—owns and carries guns, half the time he's on the nod—but he actually can act, at least well enough to play a terrorist on television. He's got Mike—image-conscious, a bit of a dandy, a weakness for the fast lane, and a convicted criminal and ex-con. And he's got incidental evidence in computer searches and the like that he can use as filigree for his story. He couldn't say she didn't do it, and he couldn't argue mistaken identity. So it was either "they made her do it" or "she did it, and here's why." He used a variation on both. What other choice did he have, really?

But anyone who has ever bothered to watch a reality show rather than pontificating about them would know that there is only one possible role that Dalia ever could have fit into comfortably:

The Villain.

Her pillowy lips, luxuriant lashes, saucer eyes, and Barbie doll physique, not to mention her terror-baby persona, make her a shoo-in for the part of the home wrecker, hussy, or hell on heels: the devious, put-upon Tierra LiCausi or bad girl Vienna Giardi on *The Bachelor*; shit-stirrers like cutthroat Danielle Staub or table-flipping Teresa Giudice on *The Real Housewives of New Jersey*; quick-tempered Angelina Pivarnick, whose dustups with Snooki and JWoww fueled the first season of *Jersey Shore*; or Omarosa Manigault-Stallworth from *The Apprentice*, whose relentless ambition and no-holds-barred methods were anathema to viewers. In the reality TV universe, to those obsessed with being famous, cancellation is the punitive equivalent of a long prison sentence, proving that behavioral standards still do exist, even if it takes some digging to reach them. If a career as a reality star really was Dalia's goal, or even Mike's goal for her, then the virtues and skill set that could have cinched one for her are the same ones that would seal her fate as a defendant. Either way, she was living on borrowed time. Some monsters are too scary, even when you're just playing one on TV.

CHAPTER 14

. . . .

A Tangled Web

I had two hours to complete my closing statement, minus the time that Laura had taken to present hers. In it, I set out two goals: to prove the crimes that Dalia was accused of by demonstrating how the evidence created a seamless pattern of guilt, and to disprove the alternative history the defense had attempted to erect in its place. That theory, balanced on the precarious fulcrum of reasonable doubt, urged us in shadows and insinuation and specious logic, over and over again, to ignore one simple organic truth: Connection does not imply causality. Saying so doesn't make it so. I walked to the podium and addressed the jury.

"Oh, what a tangled web we weave

When first we practice to deceive."

This is the famous summation from the epic Scottish poem *Marmion* by Sir Walter Scott, published in 1808. The aphorism has survived the play, but Lord Marmion himself didn't fare so well either: Working with his corrupt mistress (a fallen nun), he framed a rich woman's fiancé for acts of treason, forcing him into exile. When he ruthlessly cast the mistress aside, she went to the local authorities (the abbess of her convent), who informed the victim of the plot against him, which he had been totally oblivious to. Before the wheels of justice could sufficiently turn, Lord Marmion died at the Battle of Flodden Field in 1513. Then as now, their tangled web encompassed lies and manipulation, sex as a weapon, greed, lust, and most of all, the unhinged certainty that all of the above was somehow justified. Having just listened to an elaborate justification from Mr. Salnick of similar events that seemed to explain themselves, I asked the jury, "Were we sitting through the same trial over the past two weeks?"

A simple but effective metaphor I often use when first instructing a jury, which I reprised here, was to think of the trial as an Oreo cookie: The opening statement and the closing statement, those are the chocolate wafers; they screw the contents into place. The white stuff in the middle, the good stuff, that's the evidence. And the evidence in this case, I assured them, was overwhelming. The defendant solicited Officer Widy Jean to commit first-degree murder with a firearm. She was caught on phone calls to confidential informant Mohamed Shihadeh. She was caught crying (or not crying) to Sergeant Frank Ranzie. She was caught by the detectives in the interviews she did in police custody. And she was caught on those final, desperate phone calls she made from the Palm Beach County Jail. The evidence is in photographs and documents and bank records and safety deposit boxes and electronic texts, and in the money that changed hands. The defense claims this was all a hoax, a reality show stunt. Mr. Salnick's suggestions tell a great story but they are nothing but innuendos. Where is the evidence? Not one document, not one phone call, not one video, not one statement, not one word—not one word was uttered during this investigation, not one word was uttered to the detectives, not one word was captured on the phone calls about this being a reality stunt, not by the defendant or anyone else.

Dr. Sarah Coyne, the so-called reality TV expert, conceded that every reference Mr. Salnick could cite in his opening statement that might have enticed Mike Dippolito into this reality TV circus—the Balloon Boy, *Jersey Shore*, the White House crashers, and their stint on *The Real Housewives of D.C.*—all occurred sometime after the defendant's arrest on August 5, 2009. Ms. Coyne testified that after reviewing the evidence in this case, she found not one single mention of reality television in any of the material she reviewed. Carol Peden, the defense's computer expert, found evidence of Internet searches on the defendant's computer outlining how to get on a reality TV show. What those instructions conveyed is that participants are chosen almost exclusively through casting calls and the audition process. So the defendant would be the very last one to pull some crazy publicity stunt if that were her actual intention. Stunts are, well, for amateurs.

What the defense presented was the hoax. The evidence shows the exact opposite. This was a plan, a plot, a calculated procedure for murder.

At one point, I address the topic of reasonable doubt; I made the following statement:

PARKER: The defense wants you to speculate, to think, could it have been possible, maybe—could it have been true that this was a stunt for reality television? But again, where is the evidence? Where is the testimony? Where is it?

Salnick objected and asked to approach the bench. In a sidebar, he took exception with what he took to be my veiled suggestions regarding his client.

SALNICK: Judge, I read the case law that's presented and that comment, zealously said, when you look right at Ms. Dippolito— 'Where's the testimony?'—could not be any more clear a comment that she didn't testify than I have ever seen. I am going to move for a mistrial. That has clearly vitiated the fairness. If the words were "Where is the testimony?"—that is not like she said she didn't tell the police this or didn't tell the police that. That was an absolute direct comment on her failure to testify.

In my mind, he had his motions for mistrial spring-loaded in his arsenal and was merely looking for a pretext to use them. I took this as an encouraging sign. Judge Colbath denied the motion, and I finished my thought.

PARKER: Where is the evidence, ladies and gentlemen? That's what they want, they want you to speculate, because there is no evidence. We talked in jury selection, and the Judge instructed you that it is not a possible doubt, it is not a speculative doubt, it's not an imaginary doubt. Your doubt has to have a reason. It can't be forced. And if you are sitting in your chair right now after listening to Mr. Salnick talk, when he was speaking and you're thinking to yourself, *"Maybe it happened, maybe what he's saying is possible.*" Based on the law, what is your verdict? Your verdict is guilty because your doubt can't be a possible doubt, speculative doubt, a forced or imaginary doubt. Mike Dippolito loved his wife. In his case, love wasn't just blind, it was blind, deaf, dumb, and sensory-challenged. He trusted her so much that it was inconceivable she had manipulated him. What the defendant loved was the lifestyle: how Mike showered her with gifts, spent money on her he didn't have, treated her family like royalty; bought her a quarter-million-dollar house, nice furniture, expensive jewelry; financed her endless shopping sprees, a New Year's trip to Vegas while he was still on probation—every little thing her heart commanded. His friends, his first wife, his father who died, and a mother who eventually had a breakdown—everyone else got washed over the side in the wake of this new and terrible force in his life, and still his feelings remained resolute. A week after his divorce was finalized, on February 2, 2009, they were married.

Dalia kept two cell phones on her at all times, allegedly for her real estate business (not to mention the escort work she met Mike through and continued to broker for others, although I was prohibited from telling the jury that). She seemed successful, and had her own money. Yet she only ever sold one house and collected a commission—Mike's. Although it wouldn't have occurred to him at the time, this was also the perfect cover under which to mount an orchestrated campaign against him. So when, mere weeks after they were married, and three months after she met him, the defendant suggested a plan that would pull Mike clear once and for all of his debilitating twenty-eight-year probation—one for each year she had been alive—and the prohibitive restitution demands crushing down on him, it seemed like she had been heaven-sent. On February 18, he began depositing what would eventually total $100,000 in Dalia's bank account, six or seven thousand dollars at a time, so as not to attract attention. She would add $91,000 of her own and convert the total to a cashier's check for $191,000, his final restitution tally, and he would be home free.

The defendant had known Mohamed since she was eighteen, when she picked him up at the convenience store he was managing. They had continued to see each other off and on, even after he met the woman he would marry (and divorce, and marry again, and then divorce again). At some point before her marriage (he's hazy on the details), the defendant ran into him after a several-year hiatus and they renewed their friendship. She had a fiancé, she seemed happy; everything was looking up. Sometime in probably early March, she called again, wanting to meet. Her new husband (not the same fiancé) was abusive, threatening; she was afraid for her life. Maybe he could help. The next morning, she swung by his house to seal the deal, bearing gifts.

March 6 marked the last of the payments for Mike's restitution money, which the defendant dutifully deposited in her bank account. Also in early March, at her behest, he added her name to the title of his townhouse, listing her as co-owner. Both of these transactions were completed by March 11, when an anonymous call was placed to David Banks, Mike's probation officer, alleging that he was dealing steroids out of his home. A second call a day later expanded his alleged product line to include ecstasy. Late that night, Officer Banks showed up at their townhouse for the first of many unannounced searches. Any illegal drugs would have automatically violated Mike's terms of probation and returned him to prison. According to his log notes, Banks received approximately twenty such calls over the ensuing months.

On March 15, the defendant called and made a last-minute reservation for a night at the Ritz-Carlton in Manalapan, paying for it out of the checking account that held Mike's hundred grand and the ticket to his future. The next morning, as they were checking out of the hotel, they were stopped by local police who searched Mike's vehicle based on an anonymous tip that he was selling cocaine and Xanax—a drug that Mohamed held a prescription for and was frequently under the influence of. On March 17, Mike discovered a plastic bag full of pills and powder taped inside the well of his gas tank, which he disposed of immediately. That same day, Mohamed brokered an introduction between the defendant and Palm Beach Gardens Police Officer Robert Wilson, whom she told that her husband would be carrying drugs if he was pulled over within the city limits. They spoke three more times between March 19 and 23; each time, the defendant offered Officer Wilson money if he would arrest her husband and violate his probation. Wilson ultimately terminated the relationship.

As March dragged on, it became apparent that what should have been a simple clerical task had failed spectacularly, and the defendant's $191,000 cashier's check to pay off Mike's restitution to his fraud victims would not be forthcoming. Unbeknownst to Mike, a fifth of it, nearly $40,000, had gone to purchase Mohamed a brand-new Range Rover on March 18 in exchange for his unspecified help. In his later testimony, Mohamed claimed that the defendant told him she wanted the title to Mike's house in her name and was getting it switched over, that she needed to borrow $200,000, that she'd taken Mike's money and couldn't pay it back. She asked Mohamed to help her create a fake wire transaction. On March 23, according to her phone records, the defendant had a blank wire transfer form faxed from a bank in the Cayman Islands, which she forged as proof that the money had been wired to a third party—even though the date she used on the form, March 3, was several days before Mike had paid her all the money.

On March 29, with the defendant present, Mike's vehicle was searched a second time by local police at CityPlace mall in West Palm Beach, based on another anonymous tip. This time, a drug dog discovered a small bag of cocaine improbably wedged beneath the spare tire. Police who responded remained unconvinced that Mike was responsible and released him. The next day, another anonymous call was placed to Mike's probation officer, this time by a female caller citing the event at CityPlace, claiming that Mike was selling steroids. Ask yourself this: Who else would know about that except for the officers and the defendant? In both the Manalapan incident and the incident at CityPlace, as well as when the defendant approached Officer Wilson in Palm Beach Gardens, special care was taken to contact the police department in whose jurisdiction the alleged crime took place.

The evening of March 30, the defendant finally produced a cashier's check in the amount of $191,000, drawn on the account of Erik Tal, the husband of a friend, and plans were made to meet with Michael Entin, the attorney handling Mike's restitution in Fort Lauderdale, the following morning. At that meeting, on March 31, the defendant demanded that Mike replace her $91,000 contribution with his own money, and he was forced to drive an hour each way to his safety deposit box to acquire that much cash. When he returned, gave her the money, and completed the transaction, the cashier's check he received in return was now mysteriously in the amount of $191, causing his attorney to throw them out of his office and Mike to seize the money from Erik Tal, who he discovered waiting at the car with his wife. On the drive home, with the defendant driving, there was a moment when he thought she was going to kill them both.

Following the debacle at Entin's office, and now facing another meeting with his probation officer a month after he believed the matter resolved, Mike gave the defendant an ultimatum to produce his money or else he would leave her. The next morning, April 1, Erik Tal called and offered Mike a deal to get his money back—a loan for $50,000, the amount he still needed to make restitution, for a 10 percent fee. They drove to Tal's bank, where he withdrew a cashier's check in the full amount of Mike's restitution in exchange for $141,000 in cash. Mike took that check immediately to his attorney, only to find that the deal was now complicated by a lien document on Mike's house that Tal's attorney had faxed moments before. Entin refused to have anything more to do with any of them and severed all remaining ties. By the time Mike had secured a new attorney on April 2, Tal claimed his funds had been frozen, the check was now worthless (made out to Entin, who refused to accept it), and Mike was out almost a quarter of a million dollars.

Most probably at the same time Mike was meeting with Erik Tal (the dates are unclear), the defendant went with Mohamed to his cousin's clothing store in Riviera Beach. There, through a chance encounter, she attempted to engage Larry Coe and members of the Buck Wild gang to kill her husband—disappearing with them to go case her house, and at one point, suggesting they could have Mohamed's Range Rover in the bargain. Mohamed later testified that the only regret she ever seemed to feel was over showing these known thugs where she lived. The next day, the defendant placed thirteen calls to Coe's cell phone, most of which went unanswered. Mohamed discouraged Coe from pursuing her offer, claiming a police officer was already looking into her allegations. He also returned the Range Rover to the dealership for cash shortly afterward, fearing Coe might make some claim on the vehicle. That evening, April 2, an anonymous call reported a domestic disturbance at Mike's townhouse, and again, that he was dealing drugs out of the house. Police responded and determined there was no cause for further action.

And then—things seemed to settle down for a while. Although I was prevented from telling the jury, I believe this was when Dalia told Mike she was pregnant. Whatever problem she represented, now she was his problem. They entered counseling together, and she begged him to take out a life insurance policy for him in her name, for the baby.

On May 1, a "Detective Hurley" called them from the Boynton Beach Police Station claiming he knew what the defendant was up to, and demanding she confess to her husband. When she reported this to the police, they determined it had been a "spoof call" made by a third party from another number. From May 11 to June 20, Mohamed was visiting his family in the Middle East and out of the picture. On May 14, as part of the terms of his probation, Mike testified at the trial of some of his former associates in the boiler-room operation—the same people who, Dalia suggested, might now be behind some of the recent craziness. On May 27, Mike discovered a note on his windshield at the gym demanding $40,000 in exchange for information about his wife. The defendant called the number and spoke with the blackmailer in Mike's presence, claiming he threatened both of their lives, and they later reported this information to the police.

Beginning July 9, according to the text record, the defendant rekindled her relationship with Michael Stanley and began conspiring with him to once again try to have her husband's probation violated—alerting his probation officer, the IRS, the Treasury Department, and anyone else they could think of to Mike's imagined indiscretions. (She also suggested planting cocaine, ecstasy, and Xanax on his vehicle.) On July 19, after Mike spent $3,000 to rent a private box at the Marlins-Phillies baseball game in Miami, inviting Dalia's whole family as his guests, including her dying grandfather, Stanley anonymously reported the incident as a violation to Mike's probation officer, since he had traveled outside the county unannounced. On July 22, the defendant told Mike a lawyer friend could help him get "administrative probation," whereby he could be free of the constraints posed by his current legal status. Posing as an attorney, Stanley instructed Mike to bring signed documents to the Miami courthouse steps and give them to his paralegal—in reality, a friend of Dalia's mother's from her church. On July 30, Dalia successfully had the deed to their house placed solely in her name. The lawyer who oversaw that transaction, Todd Suber—like Officer Wilson and Michael Entin before him—testified that the defendant seemed to be the one in charge. He also informed them that, despite documents to the contrary, the house was a marital asset and, under Florida law, shared equally between them. (In late July, Dalia attempted to poison Mike's Starbucks iced tea with antifreeze, although again, I was legally prohibited from telling the jury.)

The next day, the defendant tried to steal Mohamed's gun from his parked vehicle, and, after some soul-searching, he brought the matter to the police, agreeing to work as a Confidential Informant. On August 1, he met with Dalia at the Mobil station—on camera, it turns out—to arrange for a prospective hit man and receive $1,200 payment for the murder weapon (technically, the crime she was charged with). She called Mike Stanley both on her way to and leaving that meeting. On August 3, the day she met with the hit man to seal Mike's fate, again on video, she had an especially busy day:

- 7:36 a.m.: A forty-one-minute phone call with Mike Stanley.
- 8:32 a.m.: Three more calls with Stanley, totaling seventeen minutes, during which she also fields a text from her husband and tells him she loves him.
- 9:55 a.m.: Several business texts concerning upcoming meetings, which she pushes until after Wednesday the 5th, the day she anticipates the contract hit on her husband. (Although I couldn't spell it out for the jury, these were escort clients looking to arrange private sessions.)
- 11:31 a.m.: She calls Mohamed, followed by a three-minute call to Stanley.
- 2:47 p.m.: She receives a call from "hit man" Widy Jean informing her that he is on his way.
- 2:48 p.m.: She calls Mohamed in a panic that the hit man has requested she bring a key to her house.
- 3:08 p.m.: She immediately calls Stanley and speaks to him for nearly half an hour. Overlapping with this call, she takes a seven-minute call from Mohamed on her second phone.
- 3:46 p.m.: She searches for local funeral homes and cremation services.
- 4:07 p.m.: Over the next two hours, she calls Mohamed four times, Stanley three times, the hit man three times, and Mike once; she receives two calls from Mohamed, one from

Mike Stanley (for thirty-six minutes), and five from the hit man, at which point she meets him in the CVS parking lot at 5:55 p.m.

Two days later, she was arrested.

In his closing statement, Mr. Salnick claimed that I intentionally failed to ask Mohamed about reality TV, implying that I had something to hide. But in the trial interview, I asked him of the defendant, "Did you ever tell her that you could make her famous or that you could make you famous with all of this?" to which he replied, "No." Since that testimony was taken on March 7, 2009, seven weeks before the start of the trial, the defense's case was not quite so clear then (if in fact it is even now). But leaving that aside, consider Mohamed in the context of the reality-TV plot the defense is suggesting. Look at his testimony as he's sitting across the table from her, staring at her, discussing their sex life, and betraying their shared intimacy. He looks down, away. He laughs at inappropriate times. He doesn't want to say anything bad about her—he even tries to minimize her role at times, almost to protect her. He said he just wanted to stop her from doing something crazy; he thought he could talk to the police once and that would be the end of it. In private, he urged her to divorce her husband, go to the police, and report his crimes or abuse, walk away even. He tried to talk her out of hiring a hit man—the very one he allegedly had just procured for her. He never spoke to the media, never made a dime off of his privileged vantage, even though the offers were substantial and he was in bankruptcy. He just didn't want to see someone get killed. But he clearly didn't want to have to testify; his body language screams it.

The defense wants you to believe that Mohamed went to the police because the defendant asked him to, because her husband wanted his own reality television show. To believe that, you would have to believe that Mohamed was willing to lie to the police for Mike Dippolito, a man whom he'd never met and whose wife he was sleeping with. If so, wouldn't he have been a little better prepared—by knowing the defendant's last name, for instance, or where she lived, or anything about her? If it was a publicity stunt, why go ballistic once it was posted to YouTube and garnered publicity—even calling the Boynton Beach Police Department and getting into a heated and protracted argument with one of the detectives he felt had misled him? This was his moment to shine; his audition tape had just gone viral. He'd won the lottery, the one most actors only dream of, and instead he claims he didn't know he was being filmed at all. And then, why bring Larry Coe into it, a man he claimed to fear, and whose violent exploits later earned him a lengthy prison sentence in the next courtroom over—or if he did, then why regret it so vocally afterward, unless the Buck Wild gang had shown up at his convenience store and branded him a snitch?

If this were all a reality stunt, wouldn't Mohamed the failed actor have been a little more on his game? If he wanted his big break for reality television, wouldn't he have been here live to testify? On some of those phone calls, you can barely understand what he's saying: he's zonked on Xanax, asleep on his feet. If this was all acting on his part, don't you think he would have put a little more effort into it, planned it out a little bit better, played it up, maybe have not slurred his speech so much, or tried to enunciate just a little more? It doesn't make any sense.

For the second time during my Closing Statement, Salnick asked to approach the bench. In a sidebar, he called attention to my reference to Mohamed's presence in court.

SALNICK: I don't know if the State misspoke or not, but I was told that I couldn't mention any of that in terms of why he wasn't here. For the State to make the comment, "Wouldn't he have been here live to testify?" is certainly not within the spirit of perpetuated deposition testimony.

JUDGE COLBATH: Is there an objection?

Salnick asked that the comment be stricken and for the court to reread the instructions on perpetuated testimony.

> SALNICK: And I am going to move for a mistrial because had I stood up and said, "Where is Mohamed?" I would have invited error, and I would have breached an agreement. Again, things are said in zeal during closing argument. I'm not mad at Ms. Parker; it's just not what we agreed to.

I tried to explain my meaning, which to me was obvious: if this were really his big break, he would have shown up, regardless of the reasons he didn't. The first rule of show business: the show must go on. The fact that it didn't meant that in his mind, it couldn't have been a performance. Judge Colbath overruled the objection and again, we continued as we were.

> PARKER: Why did the defendant overreact when her hit man asked for a key to her house, other than because it was a spontaneous request on the part of Officer Widy Jean, and Mohamed hadn't warned the defendant it was coming? She is on her way to Mohamed's house to discuss the matter in person when Mohamed tells her not to come, since his house was not wired to record their conversation. Rather than talk in the car, she pulls over on I-95 and paces on the shoulder of the freeway while she debates the hit man's motives. After telling him to make sure he's not near anyone while they discuss this, she informs him that Mike will be carrying a large sum of money when he leaves the bank on Wednesday morning—money that Mohamed and the hit man could dispose of as they see fit. She does this because she is driving Mike's Tahoe, which already has been stopped several times by police for suspicion of drug dealing. Why would that matter if this were all pretend? It seems like she would welcome the attention, and certainly the drama. Let them record everything. On that call,

she tells Mohamed that in the future if she can't talk, she will use the code phrase "I pulled up some listings for you"—ostensibly a common phrase associated with her real estate career. But the likely reason she gives for not being able to talk is if her husband is nearby—the one who, under the defense's working theory, is actually calling the shots. In frustration, she even tells Mohamed to give her the gun she paid for and she'll do it herself. That does not sound like an elaborate joke.

The defense would have you believe that after seventeen calls and countless texts taking up pretty much the previous eight hours arranging for a murder two days hence (or, in the defense's version, orchestrating a faux hit and elaborate cover story), the defendant suddenly takes time out of her busy schedule to help her mother make funeral arrangements for her grandfather who has not yet died. A far better explanation is that she is planning for a death in the family even closer to home. This is the real reason Randa didn't want to answer my questions under oath and

©The Palm Beach Post/ZUMAPress.com

Elizabeth Parker delivering her closing statements.

expressed momentary moral outrage: she didn't want to have to commit perjury.

Before the meeting with Officer Widy Jean in the CVS parking lot, Mohamed and the defendant went across the street to Chili's—a setting that, as the defense would not let us forget, was not conducive to surveillance. In theory, this meant that they could have talked about literally anything, including the strategy they would employ manipulating the would-be hit man within the contours of their elaborate ruse. But in reality, Mohamed always believed he was wired for sound. If he wasn't being taped, he was certainly prospectively being listened to, even if the added element of video came as something of an unwelcome surprise when he discovered it several months later. During the meeting with the hit man, if this were all an elaborate ruse, why would the defendant lie about Mohamed being her cousin, if not to reassure a stranger with a rarefied service skill? She lies because blood is thicker than water, especially in matters of the blood. Why would she reiterate what she told Mohamed about Mike carrying money on the morning of the August 5, even if Mike's Boca Raton bank branch was far outside the Boynton Beach Police Department's jurisdiction, were it not for the fact that this way, Mike could unknowingly finance his own assassination? On the day she made that argument, she was overdrawn on her bank account—the same bank account that five months before had held a six-figure balance.

During the meeting with Widy Jean, she is cautious, evasive—overt language unsettles her, the naked acts of her aggression somehow offend her delicate sensibility. When she has her preliminary meeting with Mohamed the day before, she is careful to instruct him to wipe her fingerprints off the photo she gives him—the one from the baseball game in Miami that she orders him without a wisp of sentimentality to cut her dying grandfather out of. She can't leave town to float an alibi like he suggests because she never leaves town; it will look too obvious. She'll go to the gym instead. She takes special care to point out the security cameras and motion detectors to the hit man so he can plan around them. These aren't the actions of a budding reality star imagining how she'll look on camera. They're the self-conscious actions of a criminal who is building an alibi and doesn't want to get caught.

And Mike Stanley, her hapless accomplice and bumbling suitor: Why does she text him at key moments in this run-up to the coming atrocity, but not Mike Dippolito, the supposed architect of their plan and puppet master of their collective fates? And why do the text messages between her and Stanley—callous, brazen, sexually unbridled—suddenly change after she meets with Mohamed and removes the brakes from this runaway train? Suddenly they no longer talk about violating her husband's probation; suddenly she is no longer his "unicorn," his rare and cherished object of devotion, but someone who is giving him lessons in how to talk to women. The simplest explanation is that this isn't a stunt for reality television. It is cold-blooded, calculated, premeditated murder with a firearm, two shots to the head, in the home that her husband bought her, filled with the artifacts and trophies of their lavish lifestyle, but strangely few photographs of them enjoying it. It's what Mohamed said it was: she wanted the house, and she wanted his money, and she didn't want to be married anymore.

When the defendant arrived at the crime scene, her reactions were mostly ad-libbed. She thought she was coming home to a dead body and she'd have time to plan her action. Instead she found police tape and a media circus and cameras in her face. She responded with hysterics and crocodile tears because it was the best she could come up with. Nobody who could have warned her—Mohamed, Widy Jean, Mike—was in on the prank, because there was no prank. If this was a reality stunt gone awry, that's the moment when she should have pulled the plug—like someone who's expecting a surprise party that never comes. Eventually, she'd have to ask someone what's going on, what just happened, where's Mike? He can't be dead, so where is he? At no time in the well-documented record does she allow herself a moment of victory for having pulled this off—even when her partner in crime and future reality series costar walks through the door. Instead, she plays the grieving widow, and then the grateful spouse.

But more than the defendant's dubious reaction, look at how their alleged caper is designed. If you believe what the defense has said about this being a reality show setup with Mike the mastermind, does it make any sense that the defendant is the one in all the videos? Look at what his wife is doing to him. He has no role. He's not even in the spotlight. It's all about her. He says it himself in their one jailhouse phone call: he looks like a dumbass. Not only is she two-timing him, taunting him like the spider does the fly, blinding him with rocket sex, and targeting him for destruction— he doesn't even get his moment in the sun. If he knew this was going to happen, doesn't it make sense that he might have been awake, dressed, ready for his close-up? He still has his braces on, his liposuction has left him bandaged and debilitated, the *COPS* cameras are buzzing around, and he looks like a deer caught in headlights. He's in shock; he thought *he* was about to be arrested.

If it's a stunt, why does Dalia take every piece of expensive jewelry with her when she goes to the gym? Because she's been told the house is about to be robbed. In the defense's Bizarro World, wouldn't the safest place for the valuables have been home with Mike, watched over by his surveillance cameras, motion detectors, and alarm system? On the ride to the police station, she's less concerned about her dead husband than she is about her $3,000 Prada bag with its $33,000 worth of jewelry and the key to her safety deposit box, with its field guide to her life in crime (none of it related to a reality stunt). She zeroes in on the black guy somebody saw running: Did they get a good look at him? There have been lots of suspicious black people in their neighborhood; one even told Mike he liked his Porsche. Why ask how they got her number if they had planned out together that Mohamed would give it to the cops?

Safely ensconced in the interview room at the police station, she tells Sergeant Sheridan they've been married going on a year, which sounds less suspicious than six months. She has to be talked into signing a waiver to be videotaped, unlike any reality star ever. And before she knows what evidence they have against her (or even that they're looking), and therefore what her options are, she makes it her stealth agenda to portray Mike as someone whose bad decisions and shady associates have finally caught up with him. She volunteers the Cliff's Notes version of his life on the mean streets. She says he owes his business partner $40,000—the same amount in the mysterious note left on his car. He's an alcoholic, a crack addict, an ex-con with Mob ties. Her husband's body is still lukewarm, and she can't wait to roll him under the bus. If this singular moment is the apex of their plan, their star turn as actors and producers, and their red carpet to coming stardom, why trash him so severely?

And then there's the jailhouse call with Mike—the last-act confrontation between conspirators and lovers, the dramatic crest where the fire meets the fireworks. Except that it fails a basic rule of drama: it doesn't advance the narrative. They don't take a victory lap, finally home free. They don't even speak in code (all defense claims to the contrary notwithstanding) and set the stage for their next unbelievable high-stakes act. The defendant alternately tries to convince the victim that she still loves him and excoriates him for not doing enough for her. She is distraught and delusional. You can see the gears inside her head spinning furiously, running on adrenaline and panic. It's high drama, all right, just not for the story the defense is telling; only for the consensus one that really happened, sanctioned by the police, the prosecution, the principals, and your own common sense.

To go with the defendant's version of events, you'd have to believe she took the fall for Mike, the man she had just spent the last five months stripping of his possessions and trying to return to prison. She's going to cover for a man she cheated on with not one person but two, the man she told Mike Stanley she hated, whom she told Mohamed she didn't want to be married to anymore—she just wanted his house. Who thought she was off selling real estate in Aventura; whose money she used to buy Mohamed a Range Rover, money she conned him out of after offering to help him with the most protracted problem in his life. She had a radar for human weakness: she did what she wanted, when she wanted, with whomever she wanted, at whatever cost.

And she told no one.

The simplest answer is the right answer: Dalia is deceitful, scheming, lying, and manipulative. She's not concerned with who gets caught in the swirling vortex surrounding her, or the carnage she wreaks on innocent bystanders or her unwitting, often all-too-willing victims. She is shameless in the way she uses her sexual powers to bend the will of others. She shows no guilt, no remorse, and no concern for the safety of others. She will play the victim when it suits her, invent acts of abuse against her, and prey on others' sympathy or emotions. She sees herself as invincible, never thought anyone would suspect her, and believes she can lie her way out of any situation, even murder. She merely has to bat her eyes, like she did with Widy Jean (or Michael Stanley, or Mohamed, or Mike), and obstacles will dissolve before her. Her only emotion was outrage that she was being treated like a criminal.

The last thing she told Detective Anderson in the interrogation room is the way she wants to be remembered, and the whole of her defense: "I didn't do anything." Denial and arrogance. That's what she leaves you with. The evidence against the defendant is overwhelming. She is shameless about the way she uses her sexual power to get what she wants. She shows no guilt, no remorse, no concern for the safety of others. She faked being a victim to manipulate Mohamed. She doesn't care who she lies to or who she manipulates. She intentionally creates acts of harassment against herself. She is scheming, devious, deceptive, and manipulative. You haven't heard anything different in this trial, not even once. There is no denying the evidence in this case. It is overwhelming.

And here I slowly took a step back from the podium and pointed at Dalia, who looked tiny seated between her two lawyers.

She did it.

Then I swung around and pointed at the jury.

And you know it.

CHAPTER 15

Nothing of Nothing Is Nothing

F ollowing minimal instructions from Judge Colbath, the six-person jury was dispatched to begin deliberation. They broke for lunch and then asked to watch both the Dalia-Mohamed video and the Dalia–Hit Man video—I suspect they were looking for specific references to a firearm, since they were asked to determine whether one was involved in the commission of the crime. In less than three hours they were back—far sooner than anyone expected—and the principals were summoned to hear the verdict. Mike was in the courthouse, but I had asked him not to attend the closing arguments, because I knew Salnick would make it a point to search him out in the crowd and point at him as much as he could. Dalia appeared, dressed conservatively, visibly nervous for the first time during the trial (as was Mike), with two beefy deputy sheriffs stationed behind her at all times, and several more stationed throughout the gallery. (This is common in high-profile trials.) Judge Colbath cheerfully invited the attendees to take their seats and asked them to please hold their reactions in check.

After silently reading the verdict, he asked that it be published, and the clerk read it in its entirety:

"In the circuit court of the Fifteenth Judicial Circuit, Criminal Division, in and for Palm Beach County, Florida, the State of Florida vs.

Dalia Dippolito, the verdict, we the jury find as follows: As to Count One, we find the defendant guilty of solicitation to commit murder."

In addition, they found that there was a firearm used. Dalia sat stone-faced throughout.

The Judge thanked the jury for their service and released them from their order not to talk about the case. The State asked that the defendant be remanded into custody, which the court granted over Salnick's objections. The Sentencing Hearing, including any post-trial motions, was set for June 16. As the deputies escorted Dalia out, Salnick addressed me directly.

> SALNICK: Ms. Parker, would you be kind enough to agree to let her give her mother a hug before she leaves?

I told him that was fine—I didn't want to be seen as totally heartless—but the truth was that no one was getting through that sea of green. Deputies appeared out of thin air and escorted Dalia out of the courtroom without further incident. One of the alternate jurors, Sandra Clutter, was quoted in the *Palm Beach Post* later that day saying of Salnick's defense: "He can take a steel girder and bend it into a pretzel. Dalia is certainly getting her money's worth."

On May 20, Salnick filed his first Motion for a New Trial, which he couldn't do until after the verdict had been reached on May 13. Many legal issues can't be raised on appeal unless you object at the time they occur, which explains his motions for mistrial during my closing statement. Salnick's motion was based on six alleged legal errors that occurred during the trial that he claimed collectively denied Dalia her right to a fair trial:

- My use of the rhetorical "Where's the testimony?" as I supposedly walked from the podium to the defense table and leveled an accusing finger at Dalia—in his estimation, an unfair challenge to his client's right to remain silent and refusal to take the stand. This is different from Salnick's own description in "the cold record"—i.e., the unembellished court transcript—where I merely glanced in her direction. He is particularly adept at "laying the record," or describing the nonverbal actions that transpire during trial—e.g.: "Let the record reflect that the witness has pointed to the defendant." And lest we forget, in his opening statement, Salnick did promise to provide evidence that this was "a stunt, a hoax, a ruse—a plan that Mike Dippolito, whether he'll admit it or not, hoped [would] capture the attention of someone in reality TV"—a claim that, barring a last-minute revelation from the victim, could only come from Dalia.

(I did point at the defendant several times during my closing, just not right then.)

- Judge Colbath should have allowed for the individual questioning of potential jurors, due to the national publicity surrounding the trial.
- As a consequence, when one juror said they heard that the defendant had tried to poison her husband with antifreeze, thus tainting the entire panel in open court, the judge should have declared a mistrial.
- Judge Colbath also made an improper comment when, welcoming witness Dawn Hurley, who testified on behalf of Bank of America, he noted the similarity of her name to the mythical Detective Hurley who allegedly contacted Dalia and Mike from the Boynton Beach Police Department. Wrote Salnick: "The Trial Court's comments, in the form of 'levity,' clearly were a comment on the weight of the evidence and the Defendant's guilt."
- Rearguing one of his motions, Salnick argued that Judge Colbath had erred in allowing into evidence such "prior bad acts, inextricably intertwined" as the texts, phone calls, planting of drugs, extortion note, and Dalia's alleged theft of Mike's restitution money, all of which he suggested were irrelevant to the charges filed.
- Finally, Salnick took exception to the form of the verdict, in which jurors determined that Dalia had "possessed, used, or carried a firearm."

After the verdict, I took a much-needed vacation. While I was away, on May 25, Judge Colbath denied the motion before I even had a chance to respond. The next day, Salnick sent a letter to Judge Colbath claiming he had understood time would be set aside at the Sentencing Hearing on June 16 for an evidentiary hearing on his motion. On June 2, he filed a second Motion for New Trial based on additional grounds, reiterating the circumstances of Mohamed's perpetuated testimony, and claiming his client had been deprived of her legal right to confront her accuser in court due to the revelation (from unconfirmed sources) that the witness had returned to the United States on April 22, three days before the start of the trial, meaning Mohamed was available to testify on April 29, the day his videotaped testimony was played in court. The motion also impugned my integrity, I felt, by suggesting that I must have known Mohamed was back in the country. "If Mohamed Shihadeh was present and the State had knowledge of this or that he was willing to return to testify and the State turned a blind eye to the fact, the Defendant was denied her right to confront the witness live and before the jury and the State used perpetuated testimony contrary to the rule."

In my written response, I revisited the circumstances surrounding Mohamed's perpetuated testimony, taken over an eight-hour day on March 7, 2011, after Mohamed informed the court he would be out of the country for an indefinite period including the trial dates. He contacted me on April 15 asking if we would fly him back for the trial, but I declined, citing the cost, and dutifully notified the defense. Although Salnick was willing to pay to change his ticket, Mohamed declined, citing family obligations. A contact in ICE confirmed on April 19 that Mohamed had indeed boarded a plane to Jordan and was outside the United States, with no information regarding a return flight in their system. Mohamed's attorney, Ian Goldstein, also confirmed this on April 26 after the trial had begun. When I was informed of Mohamed's DUI arrest on May 4, I called Mr. Salnick, and together we informed the court of his unanticipated return as soon as the trial resumed on Monday, May 9. As is clearly reflected in the court record, Salnick very clearly rejected my offer to have Mohamed testify live in court if his client so desired, and Dalia concurred. In fact, in Salnick's own closing statement, he had twice argued for the authenticity of Mohamed's perpetuated testimony—once referring to Mohamed's "video testimony, which is exactly the same as if he was sitting here," and later reminding the jury it was "like the State calling a witness and me cross-examining a witness, as you've seen during the course of this trial . . ."

At the Sentencing Hearing on June 16, Dalia was led in wearing prison blues and handcuffs with her ankles shackled. As his first order of business, Salnick continued his one-sided debate on the Motions for New Trial, claiming that he had never waived his right to have Mohamed testify in court.

> SALNICK: When the issue came up about Mohamed Shihadeh's DUI arrest and being back in the United States, we obviously did not know at that time that Mr. Shihadeh might have been back in the United States before the date of his perpetuated testimony.

Meaning that although Mohamed clearly was back on May 5 when he was arrested, and the defense turned down the offer to have him testify again on May 9 when court was back in session, it now made a difference if Mohamed had been back on April 29—six days earlier—when his testimony was played in court. Salnick claims he never would have stipulated to the introduction of Mohamed's testimony coming in if he knew Mohamed was here.

> JUDGE COLBATH: My recollection was that up front, you would have preferred to have him live. It was an accommodation to present his video testimony. That was before the trial started. Then, midway through the trial, at some point we all became aware that he was present, and I think I offered to have him forcibly brought here at your request, and I think at that time you were, "Nah, I better not," and you were not content in having him here live.

Salnick went on at some length, "so that it's in the record for the appellate court," why the distinction is relevant. Judge Colbath next thanked the defense for submitting its Sentencing Memorandum. In it, Salnick noted that Dalia was a first-time offender and model prisoner (while lounging around her mom's house) and launched into a detailed history of the plea-bargaining process in this case, and the State's steadfast position from the outset that there would be "no plea offers" due to the seriousness of the crime. In response, he quoted Mike Dippolito from his deposition as saying, "[I]f she fixed my mess, they could let her go . . . I don't care if they send Dalia on a trip to Vegas . . . All that does nothing for me. I wouldn't gain nothing by it." While acknowledging "the parties will never agree as to the reason for this occurring," Salnick insinuated that Dalia purchased the couple's home in her name with Mike's money to aid him in shielding his assets, and referenced having sent Mike's divorce attorney an e-mail within the past week offering to return it, claiming he "made it very clear . . . that the Defendant was not asking for anything in exchange but simply wanted to give the property back." He appended to his memo correspondence between him and me, as well as a quitclaim deed for the house dated June 10.

In my remarks, I moved that all references to plea negotiations and any supportive material be stricken from the court file and this hearing, since I didn't want the court taking them into consideration in its decision. They were inadmissible, hence irrelevant, and Salnick was attempting to admit them as evidence through the back door at the Sentencing Hearing. Judge Colbath sustained the objection, adding that such communications between us carried no weight, and he gave them no value.

Salnick's Sentencing Memo also went into Dalia's domestic history— particularly the actions of her father, who left the family in Dalia's early adolescence following an extramarital affair. According to Dalia, her father experienced "anger and emotional problems." She watched him kick her maternal grandmother and physically throw her grandparents out of the family's home. He beat Dalia's mother until she bled and cut her hair with scissors against her wishes, once forcing Dalia to call the police in his presence, which he never let her forget. He had a gambling problem and often left his children in the car outside of casinos. He was also overly strict with his children, particularly on issues of dating: Dalia was not allowed to receive phone calls or visits from boys, wear makeup or fashionable clothing, or go out on dates. According to the memo, "After the divorce was finalized, the Defendant rarely communicated with her father. In the Defendant's eyes her father always had a habit of 'walking out' on the defendant and her family.

The Defendant's father had an uncontrollable temper at times and was abusive both physically and emotionally to the Defendant and her mother."

The memo also quoted liberally from testimonial letters written in support of Dalia, including at least one from an old boyfriend, Julian Santana, who served as a Marine in Iraq, dated Dalia for six years, and remained friends with her, claiming she took care of him while he recovered from combat-related injuries. In closing, Salnick once again admonished Chief Immler of the Boynton Beach Police Department for releasing evidence ("shame on him"), and referenced the prosecutor's "improper comment" regarding Dalia's failure to testify and lamented the circumstances underpinning Mohamed's testimony. He also took what I felt was one last gratuitous jab at me: "Following sentencing, it is likely this case will be publicized in the national media. Some of the participants in this case may even appear extolling their virtues of obtaining a conviction. That benefits no one in this case except those seeking attention."

Salnick called five character witnesses to speak on behalf of Dalia, including her sister Samira, her brother Amir, Randa Mohamed in her now third appearance at the trial, and two longtime friends of her mother's who had watched Dalia grow up. He also presented sworn affidavits from another roughly twenty family friends and community members familiar with Dalia's circumstances, as well as a petition purportedly signed by roughly a hundred Palm Beach County residents requesting mercy and leniency from the court. All were generally effective at accomplishing what character witnesses are designed to do: focus attention away from the defendant's crimes and the victim's suffering, and instead appeal to the jury's shared humanity. Randa cried openly during her testimony, as did Dalia along with her. "I have no words to explain why this unfortunate event happened," Randa said, "and I am sorry that it did."

The only witness I chose to present prior to sentencing was Mike Dippolito. I asked him a single question and then I let him have the floor.

PARKER: Mr. Dippilito, would you like to tell the Judge how your life
has been affected by the defendant's actions?

In a long, rambling, somewhat jumbled soliloquy, Mike presented a heartfelt and, for all its disjointedness, really quite eloquent dissertation on where this experience had left him, and what he hoped to salvage from it for the remaining future.

> MIKE: How my life is affected? I don't have my freedom. You know, for two years [now], I should be a free man. The difference between me and what's going on here: I went to prison. You know how I got there? I said I did it. Yeah—I did it; let's get this over with and handle it. That hasn't happened here . . . And believe me, I don't want to get up here and be nasty, but the reality is, I sit up here and listen: Even today, we're talking about a retrial? Retrial for what? What is it we're doing? Who doesn't understand what happened here? I still don't hear her admitting anything happened. "It's all good, let's get out of here, it's fine." I'm not okay. You know, my father died. I was supposed to be able to travel to see him. I didn't get to see my Dad. You know, my Dad's dead, and that was part of my plan: get off probation, go see my family, spend time with my father. That didn't happen; it's not gonna happen now . . . These people [the victims in his case] didn't get paid. I'm a nervous wreck. I'm not working, practically. My business has failed. My life is ruined. I walk out of here today, Judge, what is it—2032 I get released, if I pay the money? I didn't commit a violent crime, and I got thirty years. That's not a joke.

Mike summarizes the remaining consequences of meeting Dalia: His mother had a nervous breakdown. He was under the impression he was starting a family, even if he wasn't allowed to talk about it in court, and that was ripped from him in the same moment he lost his wife, lover, only remaining friend, public reputation, and future. Yet here he is again, a short two years later—pilloried, pitied, and forced into the public eye.

> MIKE: If she would have owned it like a normal person, and would have owned up to something—I would have respected that. But

when I get to court, I hear that I want a reality television show? Not only is she saying that, but her lawyers allow it? It's ridiculous. You should have just said space aliens landed and they did it. That would have been a better defense . . . If she wanted to steal my money and leave me, she should have got a divorce. What was I gonna do—cry? You know. Who does this? This isn't a wholesome person. This isn't a person that has any regret, any remorse. As soon as we walk out of here, they're filing for an appeal. You know why? Because they think everybody in this room is stupid, that's why. They think we're all stupid, and they're smarter than us, and nobody did anything . . . I'm just a fool, I guess.

When he was finished, Salnick got to take one last crack at Mike on the stand, a fraught dynamic that had dominated a large portion of this trial. Salnick started out by trying to make a joke, but all it did was fall flat—coming as it did immediately after the soul-baring moment preceding it—and reignite the tinderbox.

SALNICK: You're not gonna call me a parrot today, are you?

Mike tells him no, clearly not amused.

SALNICK: Did anybody along the way, Mr. Dippolito, advise you that through me, Dalia Dippolito was willing to pay you back the money that she owed you?

MIKE: No deal is in front of me.

SALNICK: No deal. But did anyone—your lawyer, Ms. Parker, anyone involved in the case—tell you that we made that offer?

MIKE: No.

SALNICK: Did anyone tell you that we wrote a letter agreeing to do that?

MIKE: No, I never saw a letter. Do you know that I'm still on probation today? You understand that, right? And I still don't have my house. Do you get that? Do you understand what's going on here?

SALNICK: I get that.

MIKE: I just want to make sure *we're* clear.

SALNICK: I get that.

MIKE: Nothing in my life is good. It's all bad. Trust me.

SALNICK: All right. Tell me when you're ready.

MIKE: I'm ready.

Salnick continued hammering away at the same point—picking at the same scab—until I finally had to object.

SALNICK: Was it communicated to you that Ms. Dippolito was willing to give you back your house?

MIKE: Uh, it was communicated to me, but I said that wasn't acceptable because I still needed to pay my victims back. And then it was communicated to me that any money she has is going to go toward her appeal. Because, God forbid she pays any of my victims. Because this is all nonsense here! This doesn't count, right?

By now, Mike was furious. Salnick tried to steer the argument around to the deed for the house, and by extension, what such a concession might still be worth in this much-diminished market.

SALNICK: Okay. Did you become aware that I wrote a letter to your personal lawyer offering to give you back your house, no strings attached?

MIKE: You're gonna give me back something that I already own? That's mine? [incredulous] You're gonna give me back something that's mine?

SALNICK: You need it back legally, right, Mr. Dippolito?

MIKE: I'll get it back legally. In the other court—trust me.

SALNICK: I appreciate that, but you've got to answer my question: Did anyone—was it communicated to you that Miss Dippolito signed a quitclaim deed and, no strings attached, was willing to give you back the deed to your home?

Mike recounted how before his eyes the deal had changed, curdled, until once again it was all just game playing. As he spoke, Salnick left the lectern and approached the witness without asking permission—a violation of courtroom etiquette and a slight to both the witness and the court—before tossing the quitclaim deed into Mike's lap.

SALNICK: This is the deed to your home. We want nothing in exchange. This was offered to you last week [as] it was months ago. If you want it, there it is. I don't want anything in exchange.

MIKE: Wow! Thanks for giving me back my own house! You did me a solid. I already own this house. I paid for it.

SALNICK: It's now in your hands.

On redirect, I talked Mike down off the ledge a little bit—he looked like a man who had been put through the wringer for longer than he could remember.

PARKER: Mr. Dippolito: The conversation of that deed to your house—do you remember when that issue even came up?

MIKE: Friday.

PARKER: Last Friday? Right before this sentencing?

MIKE: A little convenient, yes.

I also made the point that regardless of what the defense maintained or seemed willing to do in these last few moments before judgment was rendered, they had never placed Mike's money or property in a trust account, where its power as a bargaining tool would have been beyond debate. When we were done, Mike addressed the bench directly.

> MIKE: I'm sorry. I'm a little upset, Judge. I just, like I said, I meant it when I said it. If this had gone a different way, I would have had a completely different attitude. It just hasn't—and I'm a liar, and I'm a reality show guy, and all these things that, you know what? I'm not. That's the only reason why I'm upset, and I apologize—even to everybody here. Like I said, I don't want to be here. I wish this didn't even happen.

> JUDGE COLBATH: There's no need to apologize. It's an emotional time, it's an emotional place, and for visitors here, it's a strange land with strange rules. So anyway, thank you very much.

In my closing comments to the court, I called Dalia "an unsuccessful murderer." Had she been successful, then she would not only have been charged with murder, but would have been eligible for the death penalty for such aggravating factors as the Florida Supreme Court has upheld are relevant: if the crime was committed "for pecuniary or financial gain" (Dalia wanted the house free and clear without a mortgage, and Mike's restitution money to spend at will); "while an accomplice in the commission of a robbery" (she enticed Widy Jean to target Mike when he was leaving his Boca Raton bank with a promised bounty of $10,000); or "in a cold, calculated and premeditated manner" (she is seen on video laughing as she plots her husband's murder, tries to hire thugs and mercenaries to carry it out, and plots her alibi days ahead of time). She was married to a man who adored her and gave her everything she wanted. And the proposed restitution that Mr. Salnick repeatedly alluded to was irrelevant from a legal standpoint, in that Dalia was never charged with grand theft, since Mike gave her his money willingly, if extremely unwisely.

"She blamed the Boynton Beach Police Department for what happened to her. She blamed Mohamed Shihadeh. She blamed Mike Dippolito. And now she's coming into court and shifting the blame onto everyone else, including her father. We request the court to hold the defendant accountable for her actions and sentence her to thirty years in the Department of Corrections. Unsuccessful isn't a reason to mitigate a sentence, or to be lenient. The defendant is an unsuccessful murderer, and should be treated as such."

Salnick led his closing statement with a rebuttal of this idea of aggravating factors, which he felt should be restricted to first-degree murder cases. Putting her in prison until she's fifty-eight years old, he went on, serves neither justice nor the principals in this case. If his life changed dramatically after he met Dalia, as Mike Dippolito attests, the opposite could also be argued: Dalia had no criminal record until she met Mike and was seized by his seductive lifestyle. If she doesn't appear remorseful here today, that's merely to protect her appellate standing.

As for his defense strategy and the willing suspension of disbelief it never quite achieved: "Notwithstanding what's been suggested by the State, I still submit that it's no coincidence that, on a computer seized that Mike Dippolito told the police to take, there are numerous things that deal with reality TV, casting calls, and a way to gain fame and fortune . . . When this case is over, and the lights go out, and the media moves on, and *20/20* has aired their story, and *48 Hours* has profiled the trial, and Nancy Grace has criticized the defendant for the umpteenth time, and the TV show *COPS* is finally giving the Boynton Beach Police Chief the attention he was seeking, what we finally have left is a young girl with no criminal history convicted of a crime that carries with it a maximum sentence that is as good as a life sentence for Dalia Dippolito." Whether the irony was intentional or not, he asked the court to sentence Dalia to something consistent with the guidelines (the minimum sentence was four years) in home confinement, "followed by twenty-eight years probation."

Judge Colbath thanked him for his statement and addressed the defendant:

JUDGE COLBATH: And, Ms. Dippolito, do you want to make any statement? You don't have to, but I feel it's incumbent on me in the circumstances to ask you.

The courtroom drew a collective breath, me included—even Salnick seemed to want her to say something on her own behalf. He leaned in, entreatingly, his hands open and apart. But she shook her head no.

Before announcing his sentence, Judge Colbath conducted a leisurely tour of both the range of sentences available to him—no more than thirty years and no less than forty-eight months—and the factors he took into consideration in arriving at his decision. These included deterrence ("to say 'don't do that again,' and they won't do that again because they have been punished"), as well as general deterrence ("everyone else watching a sentence imposed"). There was rehabilitation: "How do I rehabilitate you for what you have done? And I think that's a function of spinning your moral compass. I think your moral compass is askew. I think it's something that—it's not like getting an addict off drugs or an alcoholic off alcohol—but rehabilitation, I hope that occurs as part of this sentence." Most conspicuously, there was the act of punishment ("to punish bad behavior, criminal behavior") shading into retribution ("giving society the vent, the outlet, the sense of 'that person got what he or she had coming'").

> JUDGE COLBATH: So I consider those factors and try to figure out what weighs most in tailoring a sentence for you. And it has to do with the facts of the case, and it has to do with who you are and what you were thinking. And here's the way I see it. I think a lot of it is: What were your motivations? What were you doing? What were you thinking? What was going on? And I've just come to the most obvious conclusion that you were motivated by greed, by avarice; that you were motivated by lust for another person; that you were motivated by your desire to be free of your husband, and it all started manifesting itself after two or three months after y'all were married. And the sad thing for me is, there is absolutely no moral justification for your conduct. There is no evidence that you were being beaten and you were defending yourself, that you were a battered wife, that you were an alcoholic, that you were a victim of child abuse, that you were somehow acting in defense of yourself, even under a misguided notion. There's none of that

here. All of your conduct was just for self-indulgence, and taking just every bit of money that you could get ahold of so you could go on with this fast life.

Now, Mr. Salnick tries to allude that you had this lifestyle before you met Mr. Dippolito that was pristine and moral, and maybe so. I don't know about your behavior before you met Mr. Dippolito, but I think it's a folly to suggest that you somehow were pure of heart on the day that you met Mr. Dippolito back in October 2008, and then somehow being exposed to him for two months caused you to plunge into some moral decay that caused you to become a would-be murderess. I just don't buy that. I think that was—notwithstanding everything your mom and your family tried to give you—that was who you became, who you were, and it manifested itself within these horrible acts. You met and married a man, and shortly after the honeymoon, you set him up, trying to get him arrested for violating probation. Trumping up charges, planting drugs on his car, having others call the police, trying to get his probation officer involved in it. In as early as March, you began this relentless campaign to get rid of your husband. First, you're thinking, "Well, I'll just get him sent off to prison, and that will be good enough." You used guile and sophistry to dupe others into your web of deception. You were the puppet master that was pulling all the strings. You weren't acting at the direction of somebody else. You weren't under the influence of somebody else. You were the one calling the shots, and you were engaged in a course of conduct, not over some momentary lapse of good judgment—this wasn't like, "I ran a red light, I shouldn't have done that," or "I had the gun in my hand and I shot him because I was angry." It was weeks and months that you continued with these different schemes to try to rid yourself of your husband; that was something out of a novel, and it was horrible to watch it unfold as the trial testimony came out. It was pure evil. You were taking advantage of a guy that was gullible and that was in love with you, and you contrived these elaborate plans and cajoled others to assist you in these efforts that were unwitting participants in your plan, and they didn't work.

When the Manalapan Police Department failed to find the drugs you planted, you tried again, and you planted them again. And the West Palm Beach Police Department found it so preposterous that law enforcement—not known to give drug dealers who are on probation a break—*they* didn't buy it. It was so ludicrous what was going on that they let your husband go at that point. Still, it goes on. And Mr. Dippolito looking for a guard dog: I don't know how Mr. Salnick is trying to make that seem offensive. Mr. Dippolito during the trial was going, "I don't know what's going on. I don't know who is trying to get me. I don't know who is planting drugs on my car." I don't know that he suspected you at that time, but that seemed kind of reasonable. You put the alarms on, and he was trying to protect himself any way that he could. After those attempts to have your husband taken out of the picture by having him sent back to prison for a long time, and when you learned that it wasn't good enough to have the house in your name—if you wanted to sell the house, you still needed his signature—that's when it started to turn to more sinister behavior. That's when it was that the plot to have him killed started to take form.

During this time was when your husband was trying to make restitution, and I don't think he was motivated because he was pure of heart—he wanted some quid pro quo, he wanted to get assurance that "if I give this money up, I'm gonna get off probation." Not completely unreasonable, but for self-interest and not some altruistic desire to help the victims. But I think that's when you saw nearly $200,000 of assets close to leaving your clutches. That's when things started heating up, and that's when Mohamed Shihadeh entered, trying to help you get someone to kill your husband initially, and that's when things started getting out of hand and Mr. Shihadeh realized that he'd be on the hook for being part of this murder, and that's when he contacted Boynton

Beach Police. And so, fortunately, through no help of your own, the Boynton Beach Police Department came in and collected the evidence of your true intent, and that was to have your husband murdered. And the State is right—Ms. Parker is right: if it had been successful, this certainly would have been a case where the death penalty would have been a *real* possibility. And so to that extent, the fact that you were caught and Mr. Dippolito was not murdered, one, and two, you're not facing life in prison or the death penalty. So those are some of the factors that I've considered.

A couple of other things: I find it disingenuous that it was always your desire to give the house back. The videotape when you got caught, the telephone calls where you were saying, "Get him out of *my* house," and turning over the quitclaim deed here in court is grandstanding. If you wanted to give him the house back, then give him the house back—long, long ago. You didn't need anything other than someone helping you to understand how to fill out a quitclaim deed, like you had participated in before. But if it was truly in your heart, all you had to do was give him the house back. Your attorney giving it back seems appropriate, and maybe Mr. Dippolito was right that he was going to get it back no matter what happened.

Mr. Salnick indicates that saying you're sorry or being remorseful really doesn't mean anything. I disagree. I think that Mr. Dippolito—still your husband—I think that "I'm sorry," "it's my fault," "I did it" would have gone a long way—not only with his healing, but it perhaps would have suited your own purpose. I haven't heard an ounce of remorse when confronted with the obvious facts, the testimony, as to who you are. When you were in the police station and your husband walked by, you said, "Tell them this is all wrong." And then later when you were on the telephone and he was confronting you with the evidence—"I saw you tried to have me killed"—and you just cold-bloodedly said to him, "I saw what you saw, and I'm telling you that's not true." It was astonishing. [He gazes down at her sternly.] Come on!

A cold-blooded denial you were willing to go [to] to avoid the obvious.

And so, you are different people to different people. You have a facet of who you are to your mom, sister, and brother, and they see the good in you—as siblings and parents should. But who you are when no one is looking, other than a camera in a police car, is quite different, and I think that peers deeply into your soul and speaks volumes in the way that you were presenting this, and it was quite chilling to witness that. Based on those factors, I will accept the verdict of the jury. Miss Dippolito, I adjudicate you guilty, and I'm sentencing you to twenty years in the Department of Corrections, including the time you've been on house arrest, from the day of your arrest. And I wish you well, and I hope things turn around for you, and hopefully you will take the time to make the most of what lies ahead of you. I don't think restitution is appropriate. There is enough of a nexus between the crime and Mr. Dippolito. My heart goes out to him. I think he was fleeced, but I'll also impose the mandatory court costs.

©The Palm Beach Post/ZUMAPress.com

Dalia Dippolito waits for the jury's verdict.

There is no change in Dalia's demeanor as she is led from the courtroom.

When he was asked by a reporter as he was exiting the courthouse if he was satisfied with the verdict, Mike replied, using Dalia's own infamous words, "I'm 5,000 percent satisfied."

What I never said during the entirety of the trial, but what I fervently believe, is that Dalia is a sociopath. I truly believe she has no soul. She doesn't care whom she hurts, and she'll use anyone and anything to save herself. That allows her to stop at nothing to accomplish the goals she has put forth. "When I say I'm gonna do something, I'm gonna do it." And Mike was the perfect victim. As a woman, it pains me to say this, but Dalia was the kind of woman who gives women a bad name. She takes the tricks and feminine wiles we all use, the flirtation and sex appeal, the stroking and massaging of the male ego, and she field-strips and armor-plates them for open warfare. The ruthlessness with which she juggled these men, ordering them into battle and sometimes certain death—it takes someone a breed apart. Some of the law-enforcement witnesses told me they thought she was flirting with them in the courtroom during their testimony or on breaks during the trial. What could she hope to gain at that point? Was it for practice? Or was she still cataloging her assets and playing the percentages? She's poison candy—something found in a fairy tale, the province of witches or ogres or evil wizards. She's our greatest childhood fear—a predatory adult, that dark presence waiting for us beyond the protective vale of youth.

The criminal justice system is predicated on the notion that justice must be served: that good should ultimately win out and evil must be vanquished—both as a deterrent, as Judge Colbath noted, and simply to maintain the cosmic balance. But maybe there's another reason. Maybe jurisprudence is a permanent quest to identify the face of evil, to show it free of shadow, so that we can recognize it when we see it in the supermarket or in the tabloids or across the breakfast table. If so, then Dalia Dippolito is a pretty good candidate to be its poster child.

Dr. Stephen Alexander, a Palm Beach–based clinical and forensic psychologist, discussed Dalia's case with me when I was trying to learn what made her tick. Many of his observations were echoed by others throughout the trial.

"Let's assume Dalia has a sociopathic personality disorder with strong narcissistic features," says Dr. Alexander. "The antisocial sociopath—we all recognize them: they lie, cheat, steal, and everyone wants to stay away from them. Prisons are full of these guys. Politics is full of these guys. Captains of industry are these guys. They are particularly ruthless. No particular remorse. Dalia has primary narcissism: just like a child—'Mine! Mine!'—a temper tantrum–throwing three-year-old. Dalia never matured past that point. She did amass a wealth of experience and a sense of exquisite entitlement. She had vengeful thinking and fantastic planning. Her fragrant lies run the risk of charming people on the stand. She could have made the jury afraid of her. There are two basic categories of the above—bullies and victims—and she is not going to be the latter because of her sense of entitlement. She's been socialized, she's attractive, and she has learned to manipulate through her guile and access to sex. 'Guys are going to get you anyway, so I might as well make money off it.' There is no shame in it—strippers, or in Dalia's case, the escort business. And it was that enterprising part of her nature that impressed Mike."

Like shapes in a jigsaw puzzle or the symbiosis found in nature, Dalia and Mike were character types who needed each other to thrive—at least until their resources were depleted. If Dalia had no friends, only interchangeable "plug-ins," ranked by expediency, then Mike was a necessary host for her to feed on. So for her to function, his dominant character profile was as important as hers—what Dr. Alexander terms "a rare form of gullibility."

"He's a hustler," says Alexander. "There was an affinity for Dalia, in that she was just like him—only if he's a five, she's a ten-point-ten. He thought he was pretty good at spotting people, being the huckster, the pitchman—you know, you can't con a con man. Well, yeah you can; all you need is a better con man. He had what I call 'the strip club mentality': they always want to go to the strip bar in the nice Mercedes, rain money, and be the big shot. Being able to get a limo to take us down to the Marlins-Phillies game. The boring he can tolerate for a little while, but he needs a little flash, a little panache. *The Big Book of AA* says, 'Children of chaos, we have defiantly played with every brand of fire.' Here's a guy who is always pulled to things that are injurious to him. So he's attracted to women that are flashy as well. He's used to meeting girls who are looking for a guy who's basically a vibrator with a wallet, or their umbilical cord is looking for a place to plug in. He understands that and is perfectly capable of dealing with that type of situation. But he was completely defenseless against Dalia Dippolito because he doesn't have the capacity to perform a fully accurate self-appraisal. He thinks he's a little smarter, shrewder, more capable than he actually is, and those are the people that Dalia can spot in a bar and control him like you cannot imagine.

"She is impervious to shame and guilt, and prone to rage and retribution. Dalia knows that everyone works on stereotypes. She studied other women, and she thought one thing about other people: *idiots*. Dalia's life was a perfection of her art of manipulation and deception, so by the time she met Mike, she was skilled—a master. There is no core to Dalia, just layers. She transitioned from being the unpleasant emotional three-year-old to being extraordinarily dangerous. When she can make people trust her, she can get everything from them—and the freedom to go elsewhere for more. She knows how to lead him on and then be coy enough. Is she letting him in on her little secrets? No, she's reeling his ass in like a bass. About taking his townhouse, she thinks, 'I'm your wife—I'll take from you what can otherwise be attached for restitution.' Mike wants to do the right thing, but not at extreme sacrifice to himself. He has that all-in personality. He's given up the wife, broken the vow of loyalty, and Dalia is asking him to go all in. She is seductive, angry, petulant . . . and '*pregnant!*' And he wants to be a white-picket-fence guy now, so she will exploit that desire with her lies.

"Dalia was masterful on that videotape [of her interrogation]: she lies, and then lies some more. If you're in trouble, stop the conversation, redirect and deflect. You never stop talking. The greatest defense you have is the smoke screen. This is an art that Dalia has practiced and mastered her entire life. From men, she steals integrity, honor, and a sense of decency—every time. She's never too tired to have uproarious sex. She is an absolute animal in bed. She's just playing roles. To Dalia, objects and people are the exact same thing. Whatever she gives you, she is always getting far more. Mike gets depleted. When that occurs, she ceases to be adoring. She becomes critical and hateful. Eventually she hates him; she has no use for him. She despises him now. He's run out of gas and she must destroy him. This is the narcissistic rage of a parasite: incapable of generating anything from themselves, they are now capable of doing anything because you have failed to supply their needs. And they will continue to wreak a path of destruction of this type and intensity. Dalia is incurable. She has no moral compass."

"She can't admit that she's guilty," says Mike today. "In her mind, she's still not guilty."

Mike still has prospective groupies who recognize him at Starbucks. He has "8-5-09" tattooed underneath his bicep, as a memento mori to remind him of his journey on the road of excess—and that point at which, if he'd traveled any further, he couldn't have realistically made it back. He's had about as near a near-death experience as one could have and still discuss it calmly. He remains fairly even-keeled about the sentence Dalia drew, even if the friends who have made their way back to him in the new post-Dalia part of his life are far less forgiving.

"I'm not violent," he says. "If we had to go in shotguns blazing, I'm no good. I don't think I could do it. People always say, 'Why didn't you kill your wife?' If I was my friends, I would have killed that bitch, but I'm not them. I'm not that person."

He recalls the last time he spoke to her: at their final divorce proceedings a few months after the trial, which was supposed to be a pro forma proceeding but quickly devolved into another walk of shame, public spectacle, and press field day.

"They didn't tell me that she was going to be there—which was another mistake, because they all assume I'm cool as a cucumber," he says. "How do they know I'm not going to snap out at the divorce hearing? And they're all there chuckling and giggling like it was funny. I should have said something to the judge. What part of this is funny? I have to stand next to this broad. But when I was walking out, I looked at her and said, 'Good luck.' And she was like an airhead, she goes [in a sing-songy voice], 'Oh, you, too!' I was thinking, 'What the fuck did they do to this girl, because she is not in reality right now.' I was saying fuck you to her without really saying it: Good luck to you, good luck in prison. And she was all happy and giggly." (As of October 2011, Mike and Dalia are officially divorced.)

He remembers the moment, many months into their marriage, when he was sitting there looking at her, listening to her run her incessant game, and it suddenly became clear to him: I can see you now. You're not a smart businesswoman. You don't finish anything you start. You're just full of nonsense. She could not have invented a more perfect fall guy. And yet, when he allows his mind to roam back over their ten months together, that completely derailed any momentum of the forty years leading up to them, he still can't help but think about the sex.

"Dalia, right at the end—I'd be in my office and she'd come in and say, 'You want a blow job?' I'd be like, 'No . . .' Looking back Mike recalls in the last couple of weeks, near the end, she was offering him new and kinky sexual experiences that she had previously forbidden. "Toward the end, when I called her out a few times, it was the whole smoke-and-mirrors thing. She'd say, 'You don't even want to have sex with me anymore?' and I'd be, 'No, I'm good.' I got bigger things than that. I don't need to fuck you right now. You *already* fucked me. But still . . . I hate to say it, but I'd go another round out of principle."

He suggests, only half-jokingly, that they do a reality show together.

"*Me and Dalia: The Reconciliation* . . . You put a little money in front of her, she'd do it," he says. She's been sentenced to twenty years in a spotlight trial. She has her own Facebook page. The Son of Sam laws dictate she can't directly profit off the case, only her notoriety, and she has already announced plans to write a cookbook. Except very quickly, he imagines, they would come up against the same dramatic deficit that scuttles most outsiders' forays into the easy money of show business, including even the imaginary one in Dalia's defense team's dreamworld.

"What would they do?" he asks. "Follow us to the mall? Follow us to Bal Harbour? What's that going to be about? . . . She wanted to be on TV doing something. But she doesn't understand—it would have been different if she was really selling real estate and had something going on. The reality show could have been me doing my thing and her running the whores around.

What would it be otherwise? Her watching me work? There's no premise. There's no crazy kid. There's nothing there."

Once during the period leading up to the trial, when we were e-mailing about some court documents, Mike wrote to me: "Know what's funny? I could have landed with any girl in the world and had a decent future with them, and I landed with one who has no appreciation for anything or anyone in the world. I told my mom I won the reverse lottery." In retrospect, for the money he spent, he could have gotten a new escort every night since and still come out ahead.

"Look, if she was real, it would have been perfect," he says. "But she wasn't real. My therapist spoke to me about 'duality': I know what I want to think, but you also have to look at what the reality is. When it first happened and I was alone at my house for the first couple of weeks, I'm expecting to see her come down the steps and walk around the corner. This happened so fast that I didn't have time to process it. It was just so . . . different. It's hard to explain. I went from having, I thought, a really exciting, fast future to almost being broke now, divorced, and by myself. With a snap of a finger, I find myself in the complete opposite world from where I thought I was heading. So in the beginning, my normal reaction was to look around and think, 'Where's she at?' And then I'd go, 'Oh, that's right. She tried to kill me. She's not here.'"

Epilogue

B ut, of course, that wasn't the end of it.
Because, as we've seen, there was still room under the bus for more bodies.

On July 13, 2011, three weeks after sentencing, Salnick filed a notice of appeal, and on September 13, 2011, Dalia was released on a $500,000 bond and house arrest, pending appeal. In August 2012, Dalia discharged Michael Salnick as her attorney.

On September 24, 2011, *COPS* finally aired their long-awaited Dalia Dippolito episode, titled "Smooth Criminal," as the third episode of their twenty-fourth season. To commemorate the event, Sergeant Ranzie appeared as a guest on a live Internet broadcast called "Boynton Beach Police Live Chat" with Public Information Officer Stephanie Slater, in which she noted from the Internet chatter, "Lots of you are saying this was your favorite *COPS* episode ever." In answer to the question, "What's the most exciting part of your career?" Ranzie gave the following answer: "I don't know, but I've got to say, this has got to be on the top of the list, right here. Being part of this case was awesome, and being part of the *COPS* TV show was unbelievable. So to finish out the end of my career like this, I'm ecstatic." Those familiar with his testimony in the Dippolito trial, particularly his honest opinions on actions taken by the Boynton Beach Police Department to promote the case, may have had reason to doubt his enthusiasm.

A year later, on October 1, 2012, an article in the *Palm Beach Post* reported that Sergeant Frank Ranzie, who had set up the Dalia Dippolito fake crime scene, informed her of her husband's fake death, and was there to catch her when she fake-collapsed into his arms, was reported to be under investigation for "images that might be child pornography," which were discovered on his department-issued laptop computer. According to the article, during a routine service check, he told the police computer tech he thought his teenage son might have downloaded porn onto the hard drive. The tech in turn informed department higher-ups, triggering an automatic investigation. As the attendant media commotion once again played out in the public sphere, it was quickly determined that it wasn't "kiddie porn" (a staple of the early headlines), just normal garden-variety porn. Once Internal Affairs determined there was no criminal activity, it became a departmental matter due to the computer being official police property. Ranzie was not so lucky in clearing his name of the inaccurate kiddie-porn allegations: he was removed as a coach from his son's soccer team, restricted from visiting his son's school, and called a pedophile, child molester, child pornographer, and good candidate for lynching on the Internet.

On October 29, 2012, citing the *Palm Beach Post* article, Dalia filed a handwritten, notarized affidavit stating that she was "shocked" by these revelations and a number of others that had been dredged up by zealous reporters from Ranzie's colorful career: a brief 2003 suspension when he visited a strip club while on duty, a second suspension after he counseled two undercover female officers posing as prostitutes to have a couple of drinks to steady their nerves, and a 2001 accusation of sexually molesting a teenage girl and witness tampering—charges that were dropped when prosecutors determined the girl was lying, and the case was expunged from the official record. The fact that Michael Salnick had represented Sergeant Ranzie in the 2001 incident that had been brought up in light of the new allegation compelled Dalia to report these allegations to the court.

"Right away," she writes in a breathless prose, "I got in contact with my attorney because I couldn't believe that Mr. Salnick had represented Sgt. Frank Ranzie prior to taking my case and did not inform me or the Court . . . I never would have let Michael Salnick represent me if I had known he had previously represented Sgt. Ranzie because of the conflict of interest."

Salnick had dutifully informed me within days of representing Dalia of his involvement in the Ranzie matter of a decade prior, and he maintains that he informed his client soon after her arrest, before signing on as her attorney. A memo dated August 27, 2009, from Salnick's file says that Dalia understood that any arrests or accusations from Ranzie's past would not be admissible in court, and that she had no issue with it and still wished him to represent her. The memo also states that Salnick told Sergeant Ranzie the same thing, and that he would share nothing with Dalia that was covered by attorney-client privilege. Prior to taking Ranzie's deposition, the three of us discussed the issue once again so that there could be no appearance of impropriety. It makes no sense that Salnick would openly and candidly discuss with me his prior representation of Sergeant Ranzie, yet fail to notify his client.

In November 2012, Julian Santana, the ex-boyfriend and combat veteran who wrote a letter to the court claiming Dalia had nursed him back to health after being wounded in battle—*Officer* Julian Santana, it turns out—was dismissed from the West Palm Beach Police Department. Among his investigations he was found to have been visiting Dalia, a convicted felon, while she was in custody in the Palm Beach County Jail. An arbitrator ruled against his reinstatement on September 4, 2013.

On January 16, 2013, Dalia's new attorneys filed a Motion for Stay to suspend the appellate proceedings and to relinquish jurisdiction to the trial court. Concurrent with this, they filed a Renewed Motion for New Trial in which they claimed that Salnick's refusal to inform his client of his previous representation of Sergeant Ranzie—and failure to secure a written waiver from her regarding this conflict—violated her Sixth Amendment right to counsel unencumbered by conflict of interest, which they held out as tantamount to "fraud on the court." Their reasoning is that any such allegations concerning Ranzie (which were inadmissible, as the Salnick memo patiently explains) would certainly damage his credibility on the witness stand, thus increasing the defendant's advantage. The only reason Mr. Salnick would not have done so, they suggested, was out of misplaced loyalty and residual obligation to his former client, to the detriment of Dalia Dippolito.

"Any capable defense attorney would have tried to introduce evidence of Sergeant Ranzie's misconduct by whatever creative theory he or she might muster," their motion reads. The Stay and Motion to Relinquish Jurisdiction was denied by the Fourth District Court of Appeal.

On April 12, 2013, Dalia's attorneys finally filed an appeal on Dalia's behalf, citing four issues that Salnick had flagged earlier: the court's refusal to conduct individual, sequestered voir dire, resulting in a tainted jury; the perpetuation of Mohamed's testimony, even though he was secretly back in the country; evidence of prior bad acts, inextricably intertwined, which should not have appeared at trial; and improper comments by the State, particularly in closing arguments.

Sergeant Ranzie was fired by the Boynton Beach Police Department on May 15, 2013, based on the allegations of having accessed Internet pornography on his department-issued laptop computer. (There was never any proof in the internal affairs investigation that Ranzie was the one behind his computer and responsible for the pornographic images that were accessed on his computer or that they occurred while he was on duty.) Ranzie is currently fighting to get his job back with the help of the Police Benevolent Association.

Before he was fired, Ranzie had this to say about Salnick and this latest appellate strategy:

> I understand that it's a dog-and-pony show for these lawyers to try and suggest that, because I had a past relationship with Mike Salnick, that I would somehow work *with* him. But I wouldn't try to help his clients—at all. I'm trying to put them in jail. I'm working with the prosecution. And I did nothing or said nothing to allude to giving her an out on anything, because she didn't have an out. She was guilty. We had her dead to rights. So I think it's a bunch of nonsense, these type of appeals processes. Knock yourself out.

On July 31, 2011, I ended my thirteen-year career as a prosecutor at the Palm Beach County State Attorney's Office. I opened my own law practice on September 1, 2011, in West Palm Beach, representing individuals who have been accused of a crime, and passionately advocating for the rights of victims of crime. I currently teach on behalf of the Florida Coalition Against Domestic Violence to law enforcement officers in the State of Florida on domestic violence investigations. Ironically, my first client was referred to me by Michael Salnick.

Mike Dippolito is trying to move on with his life. He is still on probation until the year 2032. His divorce was finalized in October 2011; he got his house back, but not his money. I currently represent him, and we are working toward trying to get the victims in his original case paid their restitution in full, and hopefully to lessen the length of his probation. He still has days where he can't believe the extent to which his life has been turned upside down.

Mohamed moved to Ohio for a while and then returned to the Middle East, where he currently resides. Michael Stanley probably dodged a bullet, and seems to be lying low.

And Dalia is still out there, free from institutional incarceration—plotting her next move, playing the percentages, awaiting appeal. Alone in the darkness. Eyes wide open. Missing nothing.

This case and its repercussions will no doubt continue for some time.

Acknowledgments

For his part in this collaboration, **Mark Ebner** would like to thank Elizabeth Parker for trying the case her way (despite admonishment from above), and the exhaustive amount of gold standard research material resulting from her thorough investigation. Thanks also to Michael Wright for matching him up with Parker; Joel Gotler for always standing his clients' ground; partner-in-crime Paul Cullum; the BenBella Books crew; and the great state of Florida for being a wellspring of fantastic crime stories.

I would like to acknowledge those special people in my life without whom my career, this case, and this book would not have been possible. First and foremost, my mother Donna and father Edwin who instilled in me a tremendous work ethic and have supported my every endeavor in life. My brother, Jeff, for always being there to help and encouraging me when times were tough. My grandmother Doris, thank you for being my number one fan! Michael Kenyon, your friendship means the world to me. Larry Wood, my friend and talented photographer.

To the prosecutors I worked for at the New Orleans District Attorney's Office, Glen Woods, Margaret Hay, Roger Jordan, and Tim McElroy, for mentoring me and instilling a desire to always fight for what is just.

To Barry Krischer, thank you for hiring me as a rookie prosecutor in 1998, but most important, without your support and belief in my abilities I would not be where I am today. You have always encouraged me to reach for the stars and to never look back.

To Ted Booras, thank you for your friendship, for picking me as your Deputy Chief in 2003, and then running for office, winning, leaving, and letting me take your spot.

To Douglas Duncan, thank you for mentoring me, but above all for being such a terrific and supportive friend.

To Pat McKenna, you are the best! Thank you for calling in your favors for my endorsements.

To all the prosecutors, defense attorneys, judges, and law enforcement officers that I have had the privilege to work with over the years. Through teaching, training, challenges, trials, and investigations, you have all been instrumental in shaping my career and contributing to my successes.

To all of those people that contributed to this case in so many different ways: Terri Skiles for letting me use your tag line, "She did it and you know it"; Jill Richstone for helping me find Larry Coe; Greg Kridos and Cheryl Caracuzzo for your intel on Buck Wild; Pete Zampini for your help in researching the reality show information; Dr. Stephen Alexander for your unique insight into Dalia's personality; Pete McGovern for teaching me everything I ever wanted to know about computer forensics. To the State Attorney Investigators, Glenn Wescott, Mike Waites, Eric Hutchinson, and Theresa Wyatt, thank you for responding to my endless requests.

To Michael McAuliffe, for giving me the case and opportunity of a lifetime.

To the prosecution team: Terri Bramhall, there isn't a day that goes by where I don't miss you as my assistant. Lindsey Marcus, thank you for all of your hard work and dedication to this case. Your investigative skills and ability to follow your intuition will serve you well in your career. I am so very proud of the lawyer you have become. Laura Burkhart Laurie, my co-counsel and friend. You are an unbelievably talented prosecutor. I was so honored to have you by my side in trial.

To Alex Moreno, Brian Anderson, Paul Sheridan, Frank Ranzie, Ace Brown, Widy Jean, and the entire investigative team from the Boynton Beach Police Department. Thank you for your dedication to seeking justice in this case, for spending hours with me preparing for trial, and for always having my back.

To Michael Dippolito, thank you for your support on this project. I hope this book helps give you the closure that you deserve.

A special thanks to Donna Tolmas for encouraging me to tell my story and for pitching it to Michael Wright for me. To Michael Wright, my publicist and friend, thank you for believing in me, arranging this deal, and guiding me along this journey. To Glenn Yeffeth, my editor Erin Kelley, and the terrific team at BenBella, for allowing me the opportunity to tell my story and expertly steering this project.

Last but not least, to Mark Ebner, thank you for your genius story telling ability and for being my partner on this endeavor.

About the Author

Elizabeth Parker began as a prosecutor in the Palm Beach County State Attorney's Office in 1998 where she quickly rose through the ranks and achieved the position of Chief Assistant State Attorney in which she litigated high-profile cases.

She has appeared on *Dateline, Snapped, Sins and Secrets, Nothing Personal,* and *In Session* for her role as the lead prosecutor in the Dalia Dippolito case. In 2011, Parker opened her own victim advocacy and criminal defense firm in Palm Beach County, Florida.

As a criminal defense attorney and former prosecutor, Elizabeth has appeared on *Nancy Grace, In Session,* and in *USA TODAY* as a legal analyst on high-profile cases such as Jerry Sandusky, George Zimmerman, John Goodman, Adam Kauffman, and Tammy Smith.

2/₁₄